Waiting for Hope

WAITING
for HOPE

Jewish Displaced Persons
in Post–World War II Germany

ANGELIKA KÖNIGSEDER
AND JULIANE WETZEL

Translated from the German by John A. Broadwin

NORTHWESTERN UNIVERSITY PRESS

Evanston, Illinois

Northwestern University Press
Evanston, Illinois 60208-4210

Originally published in German under the title *Lebensmut im Wartesaal: Die jüdischen DPs (Displaced Persons) im Nachkriegsdeutschland.* Copyright © 1994 by Fischer Taschenbuch Verlag GmbH, Frankfurt am Main. English translation copyright © 2001 by Northwestern University Press. Published 2001. All rights reserved.

Printed in the United States of America

10   9   8   7   6   5   4   3   2   1

ISBN 0-8101-1476-3 (cloth)
ISBN 0-8101-1477-1 (paper)

Library of Congress Cataloging-in-Publication Data

Königseder, Angelika, 1966–
    [Lebensmut im Wartesaal. English]
    Waiting for hope : Jewish displaced persons in post World War II Germany / Angelika Königseder and Juliane Wetzel ; translated from the German by John A. Broadwin.
        p. cm.
    Includes bibliographical references.
    ISBN 0-8101-1476-3 (cloth) — ISBN 0-8101-1477-1 (pbk.)
    1. Holocaust survivors—Germany. 2. Jews—Germany—History—1945– . 3. World War, 1939–1945—Refugees. I. Wetzel, Juliane. II. Title.
DS135.G332 K65513 2001
943'.004924—dc21

                                                                    2001001063

❀

Contents

❖

Translator's Note

Wherever possible I have indicated variant geographical names. In the case of Kowno, for example, I have written Kowno (Kaunas). For Yiddish and Hebrew words, I have generally given the spelling as it appears in the original German edition of the text, occasionally followed by a phonetic transcription in Roman letters, usually following the YIVO transcription and "secondary Romanization" system for Yiddish terms. In the case of Hebrew words, I have usually followed the Library of Congress system. For words or names that have gained acceptance in English, I have retained popular spellings even if they do not always conform to the transcription conventions developed by YIVO and other organizations. For example, I use "kibbutz" instead of "kibbuts" to designate a collective settlement and Beth Jacob instead of Bet Ya'akov for the religious school for girls referred to in the text.

There is an additional problem. Displaced persons often transcribed Hebrew and Yiddish words (and names) into Roman characters as if they were part of the phonetic system of other non-Hebraic, non-Germanic languages, especially Polish. In some instances, they were forced to do so by circumstances. After the end of the war, for instance, displaced persons did not have access to Hebrew type and were obliged to print their newspapers and other materials using Roman letters. The title of the first issue of the Belsen Yiddish newspaper, for example, was written *Unzer Sztyme* (*Our Voice*), the Polish letter combination *sz* being the equivalent of the English *sh*. Based on the English phonetic system, the Yiddish title would be transcribed as *Unzer Shtime*. Hebrew words rewritten in Yiddish are a further problem because the "Yiddish pronunciation of the vowels is usually not the same as their pronunciation in modern Sephardic or Israeli Hebrew (and in fact not exactly the same in Yiddish as in Ashkenazic Hebrew either)."[1] It should be noted that there are also numerous inconsistencies in the way in which names are spelled: Zalman Grinberg versus Zalman Gruenberg; Berl Friedler versus Berl Fridler; Zvi Azaria versus Zwi Asaria; Joseph Rosensaft versus Yossele or Josef Rozensaft; and so forth. In these cases I have tried to determine the most frequently used variant and then adhere to it throughout.

To the extent possible, I have translated Hebrew and Yiddish terms into English.

There are a number of instances in which the German authors translated quotations from English- language documents into German. In many cases I managed to locate the original English-language materials. I also ordered documents from the Archives and Records Department of the American Jewish Joint Distribution Committee.

I would like to thank Hanna Berman, a lecturer in the Division of Literatures, Cultures and Languages at Stanford University, for aiding me in the translation and transliteration of Hebrew and Yiddish terms and Nick Szegda of the Menlo Park Public Library for his persistence in acquiring material on interlibrary loan. Thanks are also due to the staff of the Archives and Records Department of the American Jewish Joint Distribution Committee for obtaining documents for me both from their own archives and those of YIVO. As always, Barbara Bernhardt of the Goethe Institute Library in San Francisco made herself available to help me resolve various questions of translation. A final debt of gratitude is owed to my mother for listening to me read major portions of the text and offering numerous suggestions for improvement. Any shortcomings that remain in the finished product are, of course, my own responsibility.

Waiting for Hope

❁

Introduction

When the Allied armies occupied Germany in 1945, they found some 6.5[1] to 7[2] million displaced persons (DPs) in the areas that were to become the three Western zones of occupation. They applied the abbreviation DP to individuals who had fled or been driven or deported from their countries of origin as a result of the war and its aftermath.[3] In practice, it included forced laborers who had been employed in German factories during the war, prisoners of war, former concentration camp inmates, and Eastern Europeans who had either voluntarily sought work in Germany at the beginning of the war or had fled from their homelands to escape the advancing Soviet Army in 1944. Not included in this category were the many millions of German refugees and expellees who, like the Silesians and Sudeten Germans, had also been forced to leave their countries of origin as a result of World War II.

Jewish survivors constituted a relatively small minority among the multitude of DPs. However, because of their experience during the Nazi period and the persecution to which they had been subjected, they were more dependent on external aid than other displaced persons. The Jewish survivors called themselves *She'erit Hapletah*—the "spared remnant"—a term that can be traced back to a reference in the Book of Ezra 9:14–15: "After all that we have suffered . . . shall we again disobey your commands and join in marriage with peoples who indulge in such abominable practices? Would not your anger against us be unrelenting, until no remnant, no survivor was left? O Lord God of Israel, you are righteous; now as before, we are only a remnant that has survived." A similar reference can be found in 2 Kings 19:30–31: "The survivors of the house of Judah shall strike fresh root under ground and yield fruit above ground, for a remnant shall come out of Jerusalem and out of Mount Zion a band of survivors." The motif of resilience and vitality and the theme of the Jewish state as the central object of Jewish longing are reflected in the symbolism used to depict *She'erit Hapletah*. In many publications we find a picture of a felled tree with its stump still rooted firmly in the soil. The underside of the trunk lies on the ground, desolate and lifeless, while the stump sprouts fresh shoots that twine around an outline map of Palestine. With each passing year the DPs spent in the camps, the picture of the tree changed—the shoots, bursting with life, increased in number.

It was this courage to face life under the pressure of extreme uncertainty, as it were, that characterized the situation of the Jewish DPs in Germany. Zalman Grinberg, the first chairman of the Central Committee of Liberated Jews for the U.S. Zone of Occupation in Germany, referred to their plight in an address he delivered in Munich in October 1945: "The remnant of Jewry is gathered here. This is its waiting room. It is a shabby room, so we hope the day will come when the Jews will be taken to a place they can call their own."[4] An article in a 1953 issue of the *Süddeutsche Zeitung* entitled "Föhrenwald—Waiting Room for Unhappy People" noted that there were still 1,500 Jews living in Jewish DP camps, waiting to leave Germany.[5] The majority had departed after the state of Israel had been proclaimed in 1948 and after the United States had liberalized its immigration laws that same year. Meanwhile, given the continued precariousness of their situation, a number of the Jews who remained in Germany opted to move out of the DP camps to various German cities, where they settled after a fashion and began to build new lives for themselves—in spite of their initial and understandable aversion to becoming involved in the rebuilding of the German economy. They were subsequently integrated into the newly established Jewish communities, the majority of whose members even now are the children and grandchildren of former Jewish DPs. Other Jews, mainly the sick and the elderly, remained undecided where they should immigrate to or—because many suffered from tuberculosis—simply could not find a country that would admit them. Although most of the DP camps had been shut down after the establishment of the state of Israel, this group of the "spared remnant" again found itself in what was to be the last operational Jewish DP camp in Germany: Föhrenwald. It was not until Föhrenwald was closed in February 1957 that the long years of camp life came to an end for *She'erit Hapletah*, concluding a dismal chapter of Jewish life in Germany that had been played out in the "ghettos" of the DP camps, in isolation from the German people.

Paradoxically, while the Germans were working to overcome the devastation of the war as quickly as possible and, in the course of rebuilding their economy, trying to repress or even forget the crimes the Nazis had committed, centers of Eastern European Jewish life, chiefly in the U.S. Zone but in the British Zone as well, were emerging in the very country responsible for the death of millions of Jews. Contributing to this development was the fact that the residents of these centers were often Orthodox Jews from Eastern Europe who were insulated from the surrounding German population. Their attitudes stood in stark contrast to those of the highly intellectual, assimilated Jews who had constituted the majority of German Jewry before Hitler's accession to power in 1933.

National Socialist policies had led to the eradication of Jewish culture in Germany. The Nazis had murdered between 165,000 and 180,000 German Jews and had forced some 230,000 others to emigrate. In the spring of 1945, there were only a handful of German Jews left in Germany to liberate. After the war, a small number returned to Germany from the concentration camps and even from exile. However, many of them had moved away from the Jewish faith and Jewish traditions even before the Nazis came to power. This was especially true of those whose lives had been saved because they had Christian or "Aryan" spouses. It was largely Eastern European Jewish immigrants who sustained Jewish life in postwar Germany. For this reason, the German Jewish survivors and their reconstituted religious communities are not the subject of this book.

The largest number of Jewish refugees fleeing from Eastern Europe reached the Western zones of occupation during the summer and fall of 1946 following a pogrom in Kielce, Poland. Over 100,000 Jews, mainly from Poland but from other Eastern European countries as well, illegally crossed the Czech and Austrian borders, making their way to already existing or new, hastily built DP camps, where they cultivated their ancient traditions, spoke Yiddish, and turned the camps—as well as a number of so-called assembly centers[6] of various sizes—into cultural centers where religious life flourished. The camps were located at Föhrenwald, Belsen-Hohne, Landsberg, Feldafing, Deggendorf, Lechfeld, Zeilsheim, Eschwege, Pocking, and many other places. Jewish relief organizations, headquartered in the United States, Britain, France, and Palestine, furnished the survivors not only with financial support, medical aid, and food but with urgently needed psychotherapy as well. The Allied soldiers who had liberated the survivors of the Holocaust were not prepared to deal with the unique problems confronting the Jews. Their first responsibility was to bring some order to everyday life amid the chaos of postwar Germany and quickly find accommodations for both the Jewish DPs and the millions of other non-Jewish displaced persons. It was virtually impossible for them to give Jews the special help they needed.

Gradually, however, the military authorities of the three Western Allies began to understand the unique problems facing the Jewish DPs. Beginning in the summer of 1945, the United States government and military leaders in particular began to rethink their approach to the problem. This resulted in a series of positive steps with regard to the situation of the Jews in the U.S. Zone. The British military administration and His Majesty's government in London, on the other hand, refused to follow the liberal practice of the Americans in deciding who would be granted DP status. In addition, the British rejected the idea that the Jewish survivors should be housed separately from other DPs. Conditions in the Middle East largely determined British policy toward the Jewish displaced persons. Because of their mandate in Palestine, the British feared that any relaxation of their restrictions on Jewish immigration to Erets Yisrael (the land of Israel) ran the risk of provoking the Arabs.

The British had placed some 15,000 Jews in DP camps by 1946, whereas the American military administration had to provide for more than 140,000 Jewish DPs housed in camps in the U.S. Zone, principally in Bavaria, following the influx of Jewish refugees from Poland. In the French Zone, there were only about 1,000 Jews living in DP camps and smaller agricultural training centers with associated collectives (kibbutzim) by the end of 1945; by November 1946, that number had fallen to around 700.

The Soviets did not recognize the Jewish DPs as a separate problem and therefore did not accord them special status. The Soviet attitude can be attributed largely to the radically different way in which the Soviets perceived themselves as an occupying power. Their primary aim was to restructure all society and fill the most important government posts with communists, some of whom had themselves spent the Nazi period in concentration camps. The persecuted assumed positions of political leadership and were therefore considered fully rehabilitated and no longer in need of any special or preferential treatment. Those who adapted to the classless society became part of the system. What counted was one's attitude toward communism; the "antifascist democratic" revolution had rendered National Socialism a dead issue. Consequently, the Soviets saw no reason to set up DP camps in their zone or to provide for thousands of displaced persons. Any major gathering of DPs was quickly broken up, and Holocaust survivors were given the choice of being repatriated or forgoing any public assistance. Thus, survivors from Eastern Europe arriving in the Soviet Zone, who (unlike most other Jewish refugees) had not proceeded via Czechoslovakia and Austria, quickly set off again in hopes of reaching the Western zones, in particular the U.S. Zone in Germany.

The story of the Jewish DPs is still largely unknown. Most histories of Nazi persecution of the Jews end in May 1945, that is, when Germany surrendered. The aim of this study is to show that the suffering of the Jewish survivors did not end when the war was over. In researching our topic, we found little in the published literature. The only historian to have written several studies of the subject is the Israeli scholar Yehuda Bauer. Hence, we have based our work in large measure on the displaced persons records housed in the YIVO Institute (Yidisher Visnshaftlekher Institut) in New York, microfilm copies of which have been part of the collection of the Zentrum für Antisemitismusforschung (Center for the Study of Anti-Semitism) of the Technische Universität in Berlin since 1991. Aside from its library holdings, the center provided us with whatever facilities we needed in order thoroughly to research our topic. We wish to express our gratitude to the center's staff and in particular to its director, Dr. Wolfgang Benz, and to our editor, Dr. Walter H. Pehle, who helped us make this topic accessible to a wide readership.

❖

Liberation

Did liberation in fact signal an end to the torments and terror of the Nazi death camps? Majdanek near Lublin in eastern Poland was liberated on 24 July 1944, Auschwitz on 27 January 1945, Buchenwald on 11 April 1945, Bergen-Belsen on 15 April 1945, Dachau on 29 April 1945, and Mauthausen on 3 May 1945. What did this word "liberation" fail to convey? Leslie Hardman, a Jewish chaplain in the British Army, who reached Bergen-Belsen on 16 April 1945, described the horrors that awaited the liberators:

I shall always remember the first person I met. It was a girl, and I thought she was a negress. Her face was dark brown, and I afterwards learnt that this was because her skin was in the process of healing, after being burnt. When she saw me she made as though to throw her arms around me; but with the instinct of self-preservation, I jumped back. Instantly I felt ashamed; but she understood, and stood away from me.

I looked at her; fear, compassion, and shame were struggling for mastery within me; but she was the more composed of the two. We walked into the compound, keeping our voluntary "no-man's-land" between us. Suddenly my body stiffened, and I stood still in my tracks. Before and around me were lying dozens of emaciated bodies, naked, semi-naked, huddled together.

"Are they all asleep?" I asked.

"No, they're dead; they've been there for days," the girl replied unemotionally, stating the simple fact.

I tried to look at them again. I had to look in order to know, to learn, and if possible to help; but these were beyond help: these, my people. The foul stench which polluted the air sickened me, and only the girl's presence enabled me to overcome my nausea.

As we walked on, towards us came what seemed to me to be the remnants of a holocaust—a tottering mass of blackened skin and bones, held together somehow with filthy rags.

"My God, the dead are walking!" I cried aloud, but I did not recognise my voice.

"They are not dead," said the girl. "But they soon will be."[1]

The British Army freed an estimated 60,000 prisoners in Bergen-Belsen, but, despite their best efforts, British forces were unable to prevent the death of further thousands during the first weeks following liberation. The Nazis originally designed the camp, built in 1943, to house so-called exchange prisoners. However, conditions deteriorated markedly during 1944, and the camp lost its status as a center for the "privileged" when it became a receptacle for survivors of the death marches from camps evacuated in the East. The camp administration had made no preparations to accommodate the tens of thousands of prisoners coming from Dora-Mittelbau, Buchenwald, Groß-Rosen, Sachsenhausen, Natzweiler, Flossenbürg, and Auschwitz-Birkenau. The chaotic conditions in the camp led to a typhus epidemic that raged from January 1945 until liberation in mid-April 1945, taking the lives of some 35,000 people; in March 1945 alone 18,168 prisoners died of hunger and disease.[2] Most of the roughly 60,000 survivors were in such poor health that another 9,000 died in the first two weeks after being liberated.[3]

There are still no satisfactory data on the number of Jews liberated from the concentration camps. The so-called death marches claimed countless victims among the horribly debilitated Jewish prisoners, as SS guards, with utmost brutality, drove stunned evacuees away from the Red Army's advancing front and into the Reich's heartland. The historian Yehuda Bauer assumes that over half a million Jews were still alive in the concentration camps before the death marches began. Approximately 60 percent of them perished during the evacuations or in the final weeks before liberation as a result of epidemics or the effects of dietary deficiencies in the overcrowded camps in Germany. Bauer estimates that the Allies actually liberated a total of some 200,000 Jews.[4] This figure includes between 50,000 and 75,000 survivors on the territory of the future Western occupation zones.[5] These figures, however, are merely surmises, since there are no exact statistics for this early period and the few surveys conducted by the Allies did not distinguish between Jews and non-Jews but only between nationalities. In addition, one has to take into account the enormously high mortality rate during the first days and weeks after liberation, which invalidated the reliability of statistics almost as fast as they could be collected.

The situation was extremely difficult for the soldiers of the liberating army. They were aghast at the gruesome sight that greeted them, a horror so enormous in scale that it was beyond imagining. A GI who experienced the liberation of Buchenwald noted that as his eyes became accustomed to the darkness in the barracks, he could see a tangle of men "emaciated beyond all recognition or description." Their legs and arms were sticks with "huge bulging joints. . . . Their eyes were sunk so deep that they looked blind," he remembered. "If they moved at all, it was with a crawling slowness that made them look like huge, lethargic spiders. Many just lay in their bunks as if dead."[6]

Another American soldier described conditions in Mauthausen: "When you see them, there is nothing to distinguish them. . . . Shaved heads and sunken cheeks . . . it is hard to even see them as human. Under the circumstances you try to avoid seeing them too much. It is hard to do. It is too hard to handle."[7] The horrifying scenes of thousands of dead and dying human beings in unimaginably unsanitary conditions completely unsettled the soldiers and crept into their dreams at night.

Victims reacted in different ways to the liberation for which they had yearned so long. Those who had the strength could barely believe that the day they had dreamed of but thought would never materialize had actually arrived. They were filled with a deep sense of gratitude and openly exhibited their enthusiasm. Ernest Landau, a Viennese Jew who was liberated between Feldafing and Tutzing on the shores of the Starnbergersee in Bavaria, put into words the feelings of concentration camp inmates who were being transferred in railway freight cars to the Nazis' Tyrolean redoubts for use as slave laborers:

Then all of a sudden American officers and soldiers appeared. Forgotten were hunger, exhaustion and despair, forgotten the deprivations and strain of the transport, because now we were free, truly free. Everyone poured out of the boxcars. The American soldiers were thronged, embraced, kissed, and hoisted on people's shoulders. We, the former inmates, welcomed our liberators with tears in our eyes, with joy verging on hysteria, and occasionally with heartrending bewilderment, but always with unparalleled enthusiasm and the deepest emotion. Even officers and soldiers hardened by war were profoundly impressed and moved. Time and again they would gaze at liberated prisoners who had been reduced to mere skin and bones, practically to skeletons, and hand out chocolate bars, canned food, and cigarettes.[8]

Other liberated inmates remained silent, unable to express their joy after what they had experienced. A Jew from Vienna who was liberated in Mauthausen described his reactions: "I was lying wrapped in my blanket in the *Block*. Someone else was looking out of the window, and I heard him say in Yiddish, 'An American soldier.' I didn't get up. I didn't move. I lay there. The feeling cannot be described, you would have to make up a new word. 'I've done it. I've made it.' But then I thought: who has survived? I. I alone. My father had just died. My sister and my mother were gone. I covered my head and wept. That was the moment of my liberation."[9]

The survivors' initial encounters with their rescuers proved tremendously important. A positive memory of liberation would not, of course, heal all the wounds inflicted by time spent in the concentration camps, but a negative experience at that moment might produce a complete psychological breakdown. To treat the survivors as though they were lepers was clearly unacceptable. Otherwise they would be robbed of the last ounce of their faith in humanity.

Each of these former concentration camp inmates had his or her own tale of suffering and had experienced years of humiliation. In contrast to most non-Jewish concentration camp inmates, they had lost many of their relatives, all their earthly possessions, and their homes. After liberation, their pain and suffering were far from over. Living with the past proved to be extremely difficult and in some cases impossible. Many freed prisoners became depressed and had nightmares. Uncertainty during the weeks following liberation was an additional burden. How were they to go on with their lives? Would they, like some non-Jewish displaced persons, be forcibly repatriated and sent back to countries that were no longer home to them? What was the fastest way for them to obtain information about their families? Where would they live and where would they get food and clothing in the midst of this chaos, inside a hostile country destroyed by war?

❖

Conditions in the Summer of 1945

Taking the First Steps in the Chaotic World
of Postwar Germany

The number of displaced persons liberated by the Allied armies—
6.5 to 7 million—suggests the dimensions of the problems faced
by the liberating troops. Yet, in spite of all the difficulties involved in
transporting and providing for this mass of humanity in war-ravaged
Europe, the military managed to repatriate 4.2 million DPs[1] by the
end of July 1945 and nearly 6 million by September 1945.[2] There
were around a million DPs who for one reason or another were nonrepatriatable. These people may be roughly divided into three categories: (1) non-Jews from Poland and the USSR whom the Nazis had
forcibly brought to Germany to be used as slave laborers in Germany
but who did not wish to be repatriated because of their political differences with the new regimes in their home countries; (2) Poles,
Ukrainians, Russians, and Balts who had willingly come to work for
the Germans during the war and were for the most part sympathetic
to the Nazi regime, often volunteering to join the SS. These individuals feared being prosecuted for treason or war crimes in their countries
of origin and felt more secure living in the chaotic conditions of postwar Germany than in their homelands. (3) Then there were the Jewish
DPs.[3] Totally debilitated, they had survived the horrors of the concentration camps or, more rarely, lived out the war in hiding.

However terrible the fate of the non-Jewish displaced persons may
have been, it does not compare to the tragedy of the Jews. Millions
of non-Jewish slave laborers and POWs at least had the option of

returning to their homes and families, whereas the Jewish DPs were completely cut off from their roots and had nowhere to go. One survivor described the experience: "The Jews suddenly faced themselves. Where now? Where to? For them things were not so simple. To go back to Poland? To Hungary? To streets empty of Jews, towns empty of Jews, a world without Jews. To wander in those lands, lonely, homeless, always with the tragedy before one's eyes . . . and to meet, again, a former Gentile neighbor who would open his eyes wide and smile, remarking with double meaning, 'What! Yankel! You're still alive!'"[4]

Accommodations had to be found for the nonrepatriatable DPs who remained in Germany, Austria, and Italy. The U.S. Army set up camps that were technically known as assembly centers. They varied in size from sites with fifty people to camps housing over 7,000 persons. They comprised barracks, former POW and slave labor camps, industrial workers' housing, tent cities, hotels, apartment buildings, garages, stables, monasteries, hospitals, sanitariums, schools, and so forth. Some, like the exclusively Jewish camps at Landsberg, Feldafing, Föhrenwald, Belsen-Hohne, and Eschwege, for instance, were former German military barracks. For the camps at Lampertheim and Zeilsheim, the U.S. Army evacuated German houses and moved in Jewish DPs. In Stuttgart West, the DP camp was a group of apartment buildings on Reinsburgstraße, while in Stuttgart-Degerloch it was a former sanitarium beautifully situated on top of a hill. In some instances the military authorities even turned hotels into camps, for example, the Karwendel Hotel in Mittenwald and the Elisabeth Hotel on the shores of the Starnbergersee, which served as a Jewish DP hospital. Jewish DPs were housed in a former hospital for tuberculosis patients in Gauting and in part of a monastery in St. Ottilien.[5]

In the first weeks after liberation, the Allies did not recognize the Jews as a separate group. Nor did they consider them a nationality. This had far-reaching consequences, because it meant that camps that housed only Jewish DPs were the exception and that Jews who had suffered persecution were often forced to live in camps alongside their former tormentors, for instance, concentration camp guards. It is difficult to gauge the psychological effects this new form of humiliation had on them. During the long years of persecution, Jews had come to believe that after liberation the world would welcome them with open arms and seek to make amends for the injuries that had been inflicted on them. Instead, they were once again compelled to live in camps. Although these could not be compared to Nazi concentration camps, they nevertheless kept alive the negative feelings associated with the Nazi period. Jacob Biber described his initial experiences in the DP camp at Föhrenwald:

> I had thought this might be a place of quick transit, a chance briefly to recoup our energies and spirits, but the word "camp" started my heart pounding in fear. . . . In Föhrenwald, our group was directed from the theater kitchen to our assigned quarters. Survivors of all ages, wearing torn clothes or concentration camp stripes, were passing us on either side. . . . Other survivors who had arrived there before us invited us into their crowded quarters . . . that first night, we had exchanged much information about the death camps, and also learned that no one had yet been transferred from Camp Föhrenwald. Our stay would not end tomorrow, and probably not next week or next month, something we had not really expected. . . . We were very tired after a long, hot, and active day and evening. . . . For us, sleep was not a respite, but a reliving of tragedy in our nightmares. As soon as I fell asleep, the horrible tales of the skinny concentration camp survivors tormented my rest. . . . I was unable to sleep for night after night. . . . The caged-in environment forced a constant reliving of scenes from our horrible pasts.[6]

The Jews' sharing of quarters with non-Jews caused major psychological problems for the Jewish survivors, especially since many non-Jewish DPs made no secret of their anti-Semitism and worked to make life in the camps as difficult as possible for the Jews, who were in a weakened state and desperately trying to find out whether any of their relatives were still alive. There is a report, for instance, of a Polish Jewish couple who had lived through the war as members of a partisan unit. Upon returning to their village, they found only six surviving Jewish families (out of a prewar community of 1,600). The party given to celebrate their return was broken up by murderers, and only the couple themselves and a ten-year-old boy survived and made their way to a DP camp—where they were immediately placed in the section reserved for their "fellow nationals," the Poles.[7]

"Army officials admit that the former group [the Jews] needs special care . . . but at the moment this cannot be given," noted a terse summary of an American Friends Service Committee meeting in the summer of 1945.[8] The refusal to make a distinction between Jewish and non-Jewish victims of the Nazis was carried to such absurd lengths that German Jews released from the concentration camps were not entitled to DP status. In fact, as "ex-enemy nationals" they were to be treated like any other citizens of the former German Reich. The Supreme Headquarters Allied Expeditionary Forces (SHAEF) handbook stipulated in 1944 that "as a general rule, military Government should avoid creating the impression that the Jews are to be singled out for special treatment, as such action will tend to perpetuate the distinctions of Nazi racial theory." A SHAEF memo of 16 April 1945, which was supposed to form the legal basis for the treatment of Jewish DPs in the years that followed,[9] ordered that ex-enemy nationals persecuted because of race, religion, or activities on behalf of United Nations (UN) countries be accorded the same care as UN DPs. However, the order was generally ignored. This meant that German Jewish as well as Austrian and Hungarian concentration camp inmates were in fact treated by Allied soldiers as Germans and thus as former enemies. Hungarian and Austrian Jews were handled in the same fashion.[10]

Another bitter experience for the survivors was the fact that they could not expect to receive help from Jewish relief organizations until the late summer of 1945, that is, three months after liberation. Josef Rosensaft, the future chairman of the Central Committee of Liberated Jews in the British Zone, expressed his personal disappointment: "Before liberation, a hope kept us alive. We dreamed about the day of liberation and had our ideas of what it would look like. And then the day came, and we saw before us a new kind of world, cold and strange. The free Jews came to us months later, and many liberated Jews, who were too far gone to survive, died without a '*Gut Morgn*' or a '*Shalom*' from our free brethren. . . . But many months went by before the first signs of effective help appeared."[11]

The first "free" Jews encountered by the survivors were Jewish military chaplains and Jewish soldiers serving in the Allied armies. Because Jewish relief organizations had arrived late on the scene and had to clear a number of bureaucratic hurdles before they could begin their work, Jewish soldiers played an especially important role. They were familiar with the mentality of their coreligionists, understood their language, and were therefore of inestimable value in helping survivors rebuild their lives. After regaining their health, survivors understandably were first interested in discovering the fate of their relatives and, if possible, locating them. Since the civilian postal system was not yet operational, a number of Jewish soldiers, together with almost all of the twenty-five or so Jewish chaplains in the U.S. Zone, set up their own postal and parcel delivery service for the DPs. Apart from these kinds of measures, the very presence of Jewish clergymen in uniform was a factor of immense psychological importance. For the survivors, they became the representatives of world Jewry, and through their personal efforts they managed to create a sense of hope in the Jewish future among the DPs. When news spread that a rabbi had arrived in Bergen-Belsen, a frenzy of joy erupted. Many of the survivors wanted to touch him, because they could not quite believe that he was real and that they had actually been liberated.

One military chaplain, Abraham J. Klausner, became especially famous. Born in 1915 in Memphis, Tennessee, this young Reform rabbi was not quite thirty when he arrived in Europe in 1944. Called to serve in the 116th Evacuation Hospital Unit (part of the U.S. Seventh Army), he reached Dachau in May 1945. Klausner was unequipped for his encounter with Holocaust survivors; he especially lacked training in psychology. His first task was to bury those whom the medical teams could not save. They were placed in mass graves; often the names of those who died were unknown, and there was no way of identifying them. After this sad introduction to his work, Klausner visited a number of DP camps in the vicinity of Dachau. The Jewish DPs were concentrated in southern Germany, since many of them had escaped from the death marches or been liberated by the Americans in that part of the country.[12]

A man so sick that he could not raise himself asked Klausner about a brother of his who had gone to America many years before to become a rabbi. This prompted Klausner to establish a tracing service for the survivors. By remarkable coincidence, the man's brother was not only known to Klausner but was actually serving as a chaplain in the neighborhood. When he brought the two brothers together, he saw how the sick man was revived by the meeting and realized how crucial his tracing service was to restoring the mental health of former concentration camp inmates. He made the rounds of the newly established DP camps in the vicinity of Munich, produced a list of inmates, and left a copy of his list of names in every camp he visited. In Dachau he collected all the lists and used them as the basis for setting up his system for locating survivors.

Rabbi Klausner identified fully with the Jewish DPs, and they in turn accepted him as one of their own. He supported them in their struggle to be independent and to restore their dignity as human beings and admired their ability to fight further discrimination. He frequently helped them circumvent the heavy-handed army bureaucracy, and, more important, he shared the view of nearly all survivors that only a national home for the Jewish people—that is, a Jewish state in Palestine—could solve the Jewish DP problem. A wholehearted supporter of Zionism, Klausner did not shrink from using unorthodox methods to achieve his aims. This inevitably led to a series of run-ins with the U.S. military authorities. His efforts remain an impressive example of the work undertaken to secure the rights of the Jewish DPs.[13]

Apart from the military chaplains and the Jewish soldiers serving in the Allied armies, it was the Jewish Brigade that provided the first help to the survivors. Formed in September 1944, the Brigade was composed of 25,700 Jews from Palestine who had volunteered to join the British Army. Before that time, Palestinian Jews had not been allowed to fight at the front, because the British feared they might fight well and thus be in a position to exert political pressure on Great Britain to relax its mandate over Palestine and liberalize its rigid immigration restrictions. The Brigade sailed for Italy as part of the British Eighth Army. Its first encounter with Holocaust survivors took place in May 1945 in the northern part of Italy. Until then there had been only unsubstantiated reports regarding the existence of Jewish survivors in the liberated concentration camps. The initial details and data regarding the survivors were forwarded to the Brigade by Martin Hauser of the Royal Air Force, who had visited the camps around Munich and in the Tyrol under the auspices of the Red Cross. On 20 June 1945 a delegation from the Brigade went to visit several DP camps in order to determine how many Jews were still alive north of the Italian border and whether any relatives of Brigade soldiers could be discovered among the survivors. What they found were thousands of Jews, poorly fed and inadequately clothed, subjected to overt anti-Semitism in the camps, and living under constant threat of repatriation to their "homes." The first delegation was followed by others.[14] Many of the soldiers stayed on for weeks or even months to help the surviving Jews.

The DPs greeted with wild enthusiasm the arrival of soldiers bearing the Magen David who were fighting as Jews, not as Americans or British. These soldiers gave up their rations and other supplies for the DPs. Although the help given by the Brigade was necessarily minimal because their numbers were so few, their very presence provided enormous moral support. Many of the Brigade soldiers stayed on beyond the term of their military obligations. They encouraged their fellow Jews and gave them strength and renewed hope through their advocacy of Zionism.

It was partly as a result of the Brigade's work in the camps that the Zionist way of looking at things grew in popularity among the Jewish DPs and that Palestine (later Israel) became the land to which they most often wanted to immigrate. As early as July 1945, one of the activists in the Brigade predicted the consequences that would ensue from this wave of immigration: "Hundreds of thousands of Jews from She'erit Hapletah in Europe will find their way to the shores of the Mediterranean, where they will be organized in groups and sent on to Erets Israel. This will be a war of the desperate for their future and their survival; this will be the powerful hammer that will shatter to bits the White Paper."[15]

The Military and the Difficulty of Dealing with the DPs

Since most of the Jewish DPs were concentrated in the U.S. Zone, the job of providing for them fell largely to the U.S. Army, which, however, was completely unprepared to carry out the task. Though they had a thorough knowledge of military service and practices (they could fight and carry out orders), the soldiers were not equipped to deal with the survivors of Nazi terror, that is, with physically and psychologically abused human beings who were in need of urgent care. Major Irving Heymont, the Landsberg commandant, stated that "the Army came to Europe to fight Nazis and not to stand guard over their victims."[16] A positive development in the U.S. Zone was the recognition of the Jews as a special category who were to be treated differently from the multitude of other victims of the war. This was reflected in a series of political decisions. Jewish DPs did not, for instance, have to submit to an eligibility review in order to receive the benefits of DP status. And they were allowed to return to the U.S. Zone even after having been repatriated. In some cases they had been unable to locate relatives in their home countries or they were simply made to feel unwelcome there and were subjected to further persecution. Despite rules to the contrary, they were accorded DP status a second time, an option that was not available to any other group of DPs; once a displaced person left Germany, he or she was never to be granted DP status again.

As against the practice in the French and British Zones, Jews in the U.S. Zone received a higher ration of calories than other DPs. And in the fall of 1945 the ration was increased from 2,000 to 2,500 calories; however, because of the general deterioration in the supply situation, it was reduced again to 2,000 in June 1946. Nonetheless, it was still comparatively high and underscored the preferential treatment accorded to the Jewish DPs.

The most important American political leaders and senior U.S. Army officers were, as a rule, favorably disposed toward the Jewish survivors and sympathetic to their special needs. The ordinary soldier, on the other hand, was often at a loss for how to deal with the Jews. He did not have the necessary background knowledge or psychological training to understand their unique situation. The soldiers and the survivors had little in common; often they did not understand one another's language.[17] Consequently, the army reverted to the things it knew best: maintenance of law and order and rigid discipline in the camps.[18] The army's actions, however, were resisted by the Jews, who regarded such treatment as proper for the vanquished Germans but not for the liberated inmates of the concentration camps.

Moreover, the long tradition of ghetto life served only to exacerbate relations between the army and the DPs. The mainly Eastern European Jewish residents of the DP camps had lived in ghettos for centuries (in general, the few Western European Jews were quickly repatriated), and inside the ghettos they had been largely autonomous. This system of self-government, however, was alien to the army. The military felt it could ignore age-old traditions and create a well-organized community by exerting pressure from the outside. However, it was precisely this kind of interference that the survivors resisted. Establishing a modus vivendi between the army and the DPs called for a great deal of empathy, understanding, and patience—not military discipline and force.[19]

In addition, redeployment of forces and reorganization of the military structure led to a continual change in staff. Army men had no sooner developed some knowledge of DP circumstances than they were transferred and replaced by raw recruits who proceeded on the assumption that the Jewish DP camps should be organized along strictly military lines. In October 1945 a United Nations Relief and Rehabilitation Administration (UNRRA) official in the American-administered DP camp at Wildflecken complained that "the 'new broom' officers came through camp and made suggestions that kept us crazy for weeks at a time, undoing past work, redoing it in the new way and revamping all reports to fit the orders in the sheaves of directives which we had to study at night because we still had fifteen thousand people to take care of during the day."[20]

Given the long years of persecution, the innumerable hardships, and the suffering to which they had been subjected, the Jewish DPs were not easy to handle.[21] The new GIs were put off by their behavior and "found it difficult to understand and like people who pushed, screamed, clawed for food, smelled bad, who couldn't or didn't want to obey orders, who sat with dull faces and vacant staring eyes in a cellar, or concentration camp barrack, or within a primitive cave, and refused to come out at their command."[22] This and many other descriptions illustrate the wide gulf that separated the soldiers and the liberated displaced persons. Though the soldiers were clearly aware of the fact, they generally could not bridge the gap. A young intelligence officer who took a tour of the liberated Dora/Nordhausen concentration camp conducted by one of the Jewish prisoners described this feeling of alienation: "You know what I'm standing on?" the prisoner asked him when they reached the crematorium and his guide climbed up and stood on a pile of white ashes. "I'm standing on the bodies of. . . ." "I screamed at him to get off," the young officer remembered, "and he looked at me very puzzled, like what kind of morality is that? I realized I didn't understand him, and he didn't understand me, and there was a great barrier between us. . . . I really felt alien, more than alien, it was through a wish that I wasn't fully aware of to disassociate myself: That is different . . . those people are different . . . I don't belong there."[23]

Death had become a part of daily life. In many cases, the inmates of the camps had lost any sense of community, personal hygiene, or discipline. People who had had to fight for every scrap of food, every piece of clothing, every inch of living space, even their lives, were incapable of changing their attitudes overnight; they had slowly to reaccustom themselves to the norms of civilized behavior. As a rule, the soldiers had only a limited knowledge of the many forces that had been at work in Europe over the several preceding years and found it difficult to work up any sympathy for the behavior of the survivors. Why did they push and shove when food was being served, even though there was obviously enough of it to go around? Why did people still walk around the camps naked, even though they had been provided with clothes? Was it too demanding to ask that they use the sanitary facilities in the camps? Why didn't the residents of the camps work more to help improve the condition of their own surroundings?

Impressions such as these were often bolstered by the anti-Semitism that existed among the Allied troops. The Balts, it was frequently argued, were polite and clean. How come the Jews weren't? What the Allied soldiers tended to forget was that although the Balts had suffered deprivations during the war, this was hardly the sort of treatment common in the concentration camps. Most had lived in German workers' quarters or with farm families; many had actually served in the German army or the SS. So most had survived Nazism in much better circumstances than the Jews.[24]

Generally, the frontline troops who either had participated directly in liberating the concentration camps or had served in the days immediately following liberation had much more sympathy for the victims than the soldiers who succeeded them and had not seen the concentration camps. The former understood the reasons for the behavior of the Jewish DPs and had seen with their own eyes the residue left by the Nazi reign of terror—the piles of corpses, survivors who were indistinguishable from the dead, and the epidemics that claimed the lives of thousands even after liberation. Numerous reports attest to the kindness and help showered on the DPs by the liberating troops.[25] The fresh military personnel who replaced the frontline troops in the fall of 1945 found it difficult to put themselves in the position of those who had actually seen the concentration camps.[26]

The German civilian population also played a critical role in shaping relations between the army and the liberated DPs. Based on the negative image of the Germans that had been propagated during the war years, Americans assumed that what they would encounter in Germany was a horde of wild beasts: they "expected to see savages but what they found were friendly old people and pretty girls."[27] American soldiers quickly began to feel at home in Germany. "The average soldier of our Army," wrote a GI in 1945, "cannot understand that the nice and clean-looking people with their well-kept homes and their sense of law and order could be dangerous or guilty of any crime . . . they strike most Americans in Germany as decent, pleasant, rather kindly people, who respect their parents, love children, and lavish affection on pets."[28]

Despite the nonfraternization order and the anti-German propaganda to which they had been exposed before beginning their tours of duty, the GIs were more likely to establish contact with Germans than to deal with the problems of the DPs, let alone associate with them. As the U.S. Army's film *Your Job in Germany* shows, American soldiers had been instructed only about their "contact with the enemy." In other words, they had been prepared solely for their role as an occupying force in a conquered Germany, the essence of which was "Don't trust any Germans."

The Nazi Party may be gone—Nazi thinking, Nazi training and Nazi trickery remain. The German lust for conquest is not dead, it's merely gone under cover. Somewhere in Germany there are the SS guards, the Schutzstaffel, the Gestapo gangster—out of uniform. You won't know them—but they know you. Somewhere in Germany . . . there are 2 million ex-Nazi officials out of power but still there and thinking, thinking about next time. . . . The doctors, technicians, clockmakers, postmen, farmers, housekeepers, toymakers, barbers, cooks, dockworkers, practically every German was part of the Nazi network.

Guard particularly against this group. These are the most dangerous. German youth . . . practically everything you believe in, they have been trained to hate and destroy. They believe they were born to be masters, that we are inferiors, designed to be their slaves.[29]

The longer the troops stayed on in Germany, the more conspicuous became the differences between the Germans and the Jewish DPs. The Germans strove to rebuild their cities as quickly as possible. They were noticeably well dressed and cooperated with the occupying power. The DPs, by contrast, were housed in barracks or similar accommodations, were poorly dressed, and were less inclined to bow to the will of the occupiers. They had been forced to remain in Germany against their will and viewed the country as merely a stopping-off place on their way to the land of Palestine, for which they had yearned so long. For all these reasons, they were met with a lack of understanding and aroused feelings of hostility among American soldiers.[30] The Jewish DP problem gradually became a nuisance for them. On the other hand, the GIs were becoming increasingly friendly with the Germans as the political realties of the Cold War made it more and more apparent that Germany had become America's ally.

However, due care must be exercised in generalizing about the attitude toward the Jewish DPs among members of the U.S. Army. Military commanders had a comparatively large measure of decision-making authority and could therefore act in accordance with their own way of viewing things, so long as it was not in serious conflict with the orders and directives issued by the leaders of the army. General George Patton, commander of the U.S. Third Army headquartered in Bad Tölz, gained a certain sad notoriety in this regard. Patton's command contained the single largest concentration of Jewish DPs in the U.S. Zone. Patton, who made no effort to hide his anti-Semitism, insisted that every camp be surrounded by barbed wire and manned by armed guards to watch over the detainees as if they were prisoners. He wrote in his diary on 15 September 1945 that "if they were not kept under guard they would not stay in the camps, would spread like locusts over the country, and would eventually have to be rounded up after quite a few of them had been shot and quite a few Germans murdered and pillaged."[31]

When Patton visited the DP camp at Feldafing for a second time at the end of September 1945, after General Eisenhower had cajoled him into attending Yom Kippur services in the camp synagogue, he once again gave vent to his anti-Semitism, saying that there was much that remained to be done, primarily "because the Jewish type of DP . . . is a sub-human species without any of the cultural or social refinements of our time. I have never looked at a group who seem to be more lacking in intelligence and spirit. Practically all of them had the flat brownish gray eye . . . which, in my mind, indicates very low intelligence."[32]

Patton's anti-Semitism reached its zenith when he asserted that others may "believe that the Displaced Person is a human being, which he is not, and this applies particularly to the Jews, who are lower than animals."[33] Patton was thus becoming more and more of a political liability. Finally, General Eisenhower relieved him of his command and directed him to assume command of the Fifteenth Army at Bad Nauheim, where he died as the result of a traffic accident on 21 December 1945. Although Patton may have been unusually open about expressing his anti-Semitism, his values and attitudes clearly coincided with those of other American military officials.

When the Jewish survivors were forced to live under the command of such officers, they had little reason to expect sympathy for their plight. On the other hand, when they were treated properly, their morale improved, as happened, for instance, in the area of the Seventh Army commanded by General Patch. Patch permitted the residents of the assembly centers to come and go at will and treated the displaced persons in a humane fashion.[34] The examples of Patton and Patch show that the influence of the army's top leadership was limited and did not extend much beyond general orders and directives.

In the British Zone, where the Jewish DPs fared much worse than in the U.S. Zone, it was not the attitude of the officers and men that was responsible for their situation but rather the restrictive policies adopted by the government in London and the top British military leaders in response to the British mandate in Palestine. At first, the British permitted Jews to enter their zone and gain entry to the DP centers. However, with the growing infiltration of Jews into Germany from Eastern Europe beginning in the fall of 1945, rumors circulated that the survivors streaming into the British Zone were part of a well-organized Zionist scheme, financed by American Jewry, to force Britain to open the gates of Palestine to the survivors. So, as early as 5 December 1945, the British prohibited the further movement of Jews into or through their zone via Berlin and subsequently ruled that those who infiltrated by any route would no longer be admitted to their DP centers. After protracted negotiations between the British occupation authorities and UNRRA, an agreement was finally hammered out, according to which the roughly 2,000 Jews who had entered the British Zone on or before 10 August 1946 were to be registered as DPs. Anyone who reached the British Zone after that deadline was obliged to seek his or her own accommodations (not in the camps, though) and was denied any welfare. Therefore, most Jews, after arriving in the British Zone, quickly continued on to the U.S. Zone. And since crossing zonal boundaries required a special permit that could be obtained only by going through a long, drawn-out bureaucratic process, they were forced to enter the U.S. Zone in the same way they had immigrated to Germany, namely, illegally.

Assistance from the United Nations: UNRRA

In their work with the Jewish DPs, the Allied armies received support from the United Nations Relief and Rehabilitation Administration, the international welfare organization. Preliminary work, on the creation of UNRRA was completed on 9 October 1942 in Atlantic City. On 9 November 1943, the representatives of 44 nations met in the White House and agreed to its establishment. UNRRA concentrated on registering, caring for, and repatriating displaced persons resident in the member states of the UN, including the survivors of the concentration camps. If everything had gone as planned, UNRRA would have taken on its assigned tasks immediately after liberation. The military authorities, however, were loath to permit civilian organizations to operate in the occupied areas and preferred to handle the DPs themselves, believing that the involvement of civilians would only complicate an already difficult situation.[35] However, many more DPs remained in the liberated countries than had been anticipated. The military requested 450 UNRRA teams, but the organization could not supply the requisite number. Each UNRRA team should have had thirteen persons and was intended to work with 2,000 DPs, but sometimes just seven to ten people had to deal with between 8,000 and 10,000 DPs. UNRRA hurriedly recruited additional staff, many of whom were poorly trained. The best UNRRA personnel came from France, Britain, the Netherlands, Norway, and Poland, where many of them had experienced the savageries of war, understood the problems of the DPs, and were familiar with Nazi terrorism.[36] However, serious problems arose in dealing with the Jewish DPs whenever UNRRA people did not speak the DPs' languages, had not even heard of Dachau, or spent more time trying to profit from black market activities than help camp residents.[37]

The DPs' interactions with the UNRRA teams, as with the occupation forces, varied widely. The results of a team's work were largely a function of the UNRRA workers' attitudes. Because of the lack of understanding of each other's problems at Föhrenwald, for instance, disputes arose continually between UNRRA and the residents of the DP camp. At the beginning of November 1945, for example, UNRRA officials, without any prior warning, reduced the supplementary rations given to residents employed in the camp. After a series of violent protests by the Föhrenwald workers, an UNRRA employee said that if the rations were not reduced, Germans would have to go hungry, too. This produced an angry response from the Jewish DPs: "We starved for six years—let them feel what it's like to go hungry." The UNRRA worker tried to calm the incensed residents. He told the protesters that they ought to be grateful for having been given clothes to wear, whereupon someone in the crowd shouted: "We've simply gotten back a few of the things the Germans stole from us."[38] A resident of the Föhrenwald camp felt that UNRRA officials treated the survivors like escaped criminals who had disobeyed Hitler's law to be exterminated.[39] Disputes such as these poisoned the atmosphere and only made it more difficult for the DPs and those who sought to aid them to work together.

At the end of the war, the DP camps came under the control of the military. About six months later, on 15 November 1945, UNRRA assumed responsibility for administering the DP camps in the U.S. Zone; in early March 1946 UNRRA took over the administration of those in the British Zone as well.[40] In every area other than administration, UNRRA was subordinate to the military, which continued to be responsible for housing and security in the assembly centers as well as for the provision of food, clothing, and medical supplies. UNRRA's tasks included administering the camps and providing

supplementary supplies, health and welfare services, recreational facilities, self-help programs, and vocational guidance. In addition,
UNRRA assisted in the process of repatriation and operated a tracing
bureau.[41] Further, it was responsible for coordinating the activities of
the Jewish relief organizations in the camps.[42]

UNRRA established a central headquarters for Germany at Höchst
in September 1945, which was subsequently moved to Arolsen in
December. On 1 October 1946 Lieutenant General Sir Frederick E.
Morgan, the former deputy chief of staff of SHAEF, was appointed
chief of UNRRA operations in Germany. However, purportedly anti-
Semitic remarks by Morgan quickly put his appointment in jeopardy.
During a press conference in Frankfurt on 2 January 1946, he had
reportedly said that a general exodus of Jews from Eastern Europe was
in progress and that when they arrived in Germany the Jews were
well dressed, well nourished, and well supplied with money. In the
hysterical comments which greeted Morgan's statement in the press,
fragments of his remarks were taken out of context. He was not only
misquoted but accused of being an anti-Semite, which he clearly was
not. Because of his prominence, Morgan was made a scapegoat for
British DP policy, a policy for which he was in no way responsible.
Morgan had merely tried to discuss certain facts concerning the influx
of Eastern European Jews into western Germany and to increase
awareness of the associated problems. Following the uproar created
by his public remarks, Morgan was obliged to discuss the situation
at UNRRA's American headquarters in New York, in particular with
Herbert Lehman, UNRRA's director-general. It was not until February 1946 that Morgan was able to resume his duties in Germany.[43]
General Morgan was ultimately in charge of the three subordinate
zone headquarters—at Pasing in the U.S. Zone, at Haslach in the
French Zone, and at Lemgo in the British Zone.[44]

❖

The Harrison Report and Its Repercussions

In the summer of 1945, the liberated Jews were still in a desperate state. The survivors were forced to live in hurriedly erected, over-filled camps, where they were frequently exposed to the anti-Semitism of non-Jewish DPs and often lacked sufficient food and clothing. Further, their treatment by the U.S. Army was often deplorable. Reports on their situation soon began to reach the United States. Among other things, the American public and in particular Jewish organizations were alarmed by various press reports, the letters of Rabbi Klausner to Stephen S. Wise of the World Jewish Congress and Secretary of the Treasury Henry W. Morgenthau, and the many rumors circulating at the time. Morgenthau persuaded President Truman, who had been in office since April 1945, to order an immediate investigation into the reports coming out of Germany. On 22 June Truman authorized Earl G. Harrison, formerly United States commissioner of immigration, dean of the University of Pennsylvania Law School, and the American representative to the Intergovernmental Committee on Refugees, to travel to Europe on behalf of the State Department. Harrison was to pay special attention to the condition of the Jewish DPs in the camps. He left in early July and was accompanied by Joseph J. Schwartz, European director of the American Jewish Joint Distribution Committee, Patrick J. Malin, deputy director of the Intergovernmental Committee, and Herbert Katzki of the War Refugee Board. The group made the rounds of about thirty DP camps. Schwartz went to visit northern Germany and other areas, while Harrison concentrated on the U.S. Zones in Bavaria and Austria. Harrison submitted his report on 24 August. Its criticisms of the U.S. Army were devastating:[1]

Many Jewish displaced persons . . . are living under guard behind barbed-wire fences (built by the Germans for slave-laborers and Jews) including some of the most notorious concentration camps, amidst crowded, frequently unsanitary and generally grim conditions, in complete idleness, with no opportunity, except surreptitiously, to communicate with the outside world, waiting, hoping for some word of encouragement and action in their behalf . . . many of the Jewish displaced persons, late in July, had no clothing other than their concentration camp garb—a rather hideous striped pajama effect—while others, to their chagrin, were obliged to wear German S.S. uniforms. It is questionable which clothing they hate more. . . . Beyond knowing that they are no longer in danger of the gas chambers, torture, and other forms of violent death, they see—and there is—little change. The morale of those who are either stateless or who do not wish to return to their countries of nationality is very low. They have witnessed great activity and efficiency in returning people to their homes but they hear or see nothing in the way of plans for them and consequently they wonder and frequently ask what "liberation" means. This situation is considerably accentuated where, as in so many cases, they are able to look from their crowded and bare quarters and see the German civilian population, particularly in the rural areas, to all appearances living normal lives in their own homes.

The most absorbing worry of these Nazi and war victims concerns relatives—wives, husbands, parents, children. Most of them have been separated for three, four or five years and they cannot understand why the liberators should not have undertaken immediately the organized effort to re-unite family groups. Most of the very little which has been done in this direction has been informal action by the displaced persons themselves with the aid of devoted Army Chaplains, frequently Rabbis, and the American Joint Distribution Committee. . . . Even where, as has been happening, information has been received as to relatives living in other camps in Germany, it depends on the personal attitude and disposition of the Camp Commandant whether permission can be obtained or assistance received to follow up on the information. Some Camp Commandants are quite rigid in this particular, while others lend every effort to join the family groups. . . .

In many camps, the 2,000 calories included 1,250 calories of a black, wet and extremely unappetizing bread. I received the distinct impression and considerable substantiating information that large numbers of the

German population—again principally in the rural areas—have a more varied and palatable diet than is the case with the displaced persons. . . . Many of the buildings in which displaced persons are housed are clearly unfit for winter.[2]

In inveighing against the deplorable state of affairs and the general mismanagement in the camps, Harrison held the U.S. Army to be chiefly responsible, and his words hit their target. His accusations culminated in the observation that "we appear to be treating the Jews as the Nazis treated them except that we do not exterminate them. They are in concentration camps in large numbers under our military guard instead of S.S. troops. One is led to wonder whether the German people, seeing this, are not supposing that we are following or at least condoning Nazi policy." This statement hit Washington like a bombshell and led to a scurry of activity for change even before the final version of the report appeared.

One important result of the report was the understanding that additional aid was practical only if the Jewish survivors were recognized as Jews. Harrison was very explicit on this point:

> The first and plainest need of these people is a recognition of their actual status and by this I mean their status as Jews. . . . While SHAEF (now Combined Displaced Persons Executive) policy directives have recognized formerly persecuted persons, including enemy and ex-enemy nationals, as one of the special categories of displaced persons, the general practice thus far has been to follow only nationality lines. While admittedly it is not normally desirable to set aside particular racial or religious groups from their nationality categories, the plain truth is that this was done for so long by the Nazis that a group has been created which has special needs. Jews as Jews (not as members of their nationality groups) have been more severely victimized than the non-Jewish members of the same or other nationalities. . . . Refusal to recognize the Jews as such has the effect, in this situation, of closing one's eyes to their former and more barbaric persecution. . . . I recommend urgently that separate camps be set up for Jews.[3]

SHAEF commander General Dwight D. Eisenhower reacted with alacrity to Harrison's report and issued a series of directives on 22

August 1945. Stateless Jews and Jews who did not wish to return to their homelands were to be housed in special separate camps. Particular attention was to be paid to improving the quality of their accommodations. If necessary, housing for them was to be requisitioned, even if it meant displacing Germans. Nationals of ex-enemy states who had been persecuted because of their race, religion, or activities on behalf of the United Nations were to be recognized as UN DPs. This latter directive applied mainly to German and Hungarian Jews.[4]

Other directives ordered subordinates to increase the daily rations received by Jewish refugees to 2,500 calories, twice that of German civilians. DPs were to be given priority in employment over Germans, thereby reducing the number of Germans working in the DP camps. Cooperation with voluntary agencies was to be expanded and a tracing bureau set up to help reunite families.[5]

The American officials' rapid reaction to the Harrison Report may be explained by the fact that some of the investigation's findings reached Washington at the end of July or at the latest in early August, that is, about three weeks before the president received the final version on 24 August 1945. And from Washington, word quickly spread to the army's senior officers in Germany.[6]

A further result of the Harrison Report was the selection of an adviser on Jewish affairs as a liaison to the U.S. Army. Although Eisenhower had at first (May 1945) opposed the idea, he ultimately gave his consent. The four most important American Jewish organizations—the American Jewish Committee, the American Jewish Conference, the American Jewish Joint Distribution Committee, and the World Jewish Congress—plus representatives of the Jewish Agency for Palestine recommended a candidate for the position to the secretary of war, who then officially named the adviser.[7] Pending the appointment of a permanent liaison officer, Rabbi Judah P. Nadich had assumed the position of special consultant on Jewish problems. He had played a major part in the creation of the post of Jewish adviser to the U.S. theater commander in Europe.[8] Prior to that time, Nadich had served as a chaplain in the U.S. Army and had taken up the cause of the Jewish survivors. His vaguely formulated charge as special consultant was to coordinate activities in connection with the Jewish DPs. The duties of the adviser would not be defined in any more precise terms for Nadich's successors, who were to determine on the spot which questions should be given priority and how to direct their attention to the problems that seemed most important to them.

On 20 October 1945 Nadich was replaced by Simon H. Rifkind, who served as the first adviser on Jewish affairs to the American Command in Germany, first under Eisenhower until November 1945 and then under Eisenhower's successor, General Lucius D. Clay. Until his appointment, Rifkind had worked as a judge in New York and been vice president of the New York City Board of Higher Education.

Rifkind's successor, Rabbi Philip S. Bernstein, served longest in the office of adviser for Germany and Austria, from May 1946 to August 1947. His extraordinary involvement on behalf of the Jewish DPs probably made him the most prominent individual to occupy the post.[9] During his tenure, the mass infiltration of Jews from Eastern Europe and Austria in the summer of 1946 added a new dimension to the DP problem. Before his appointment as adviser to General Clay, Bernstein had been the spiritual head of Reform temple B'rith Kodesh in Rochester, New York, and executive director of the Committee on Army and Navy Religious Activity of the National Jewish Welfare Board and had thus acquired experience in dealing with things military.

From August 1947 to January 1948, Louis E. Levinthal, a justice on the Pennsylvania Supreme Court and former president of the Zionist Organization of America, assumed the duties of adviser. He was succeeded in January 1949 by William Haber, a professor of economics and an adviser to the U.S. Social Security Board and the National Resources Planning Board. Harry Greenstein, who prior to his appointment had been executive director of the Associated Jewish Charities of Baltimore, state relief administrator for the Maryland Public Welfare Department, and director of welfare for the UNRRA Middle East Mission, held the office of adviser until October 1949.[10] Major Abraham S. Hyman of the field artillery, who had served as an assistant under Bernstein and his three successors, took over from Greenstein. Then, on 31 December 1949, in his capacity as acting adviser on Jewish affairs to both commands (Germany and Austria), Hyman closed the office of the adviser in Frankfurt.

Though all the advisers held the rank of major general, they were not army officers. What the position called for was a civilian with wide experience in public affairs and administration as well as an understanding of the difficult task of coordinating efforts between the Jewish victims of Nazism and the military.[11] The advisers were readily given access to the zone commanders and their assistant chiefs of staff—the directors of the Civil Affairs Division (G-5) responsible for the DPs—as well as to the regional military offices. They were thus entrusted with the important task of acting as liaisons between the responsible authorities and the Jewish displaced persons. They sought to create understanding in the military for the plight of the Jews. Bernstein, for example, published a number of articles in the army newspaper *Stars and Stripes* and in the *Bulletin for Troop Information and Education Services* about the DPs, their life in the camps, their hopes and aspirations, and the reasons for their predicament.

One can gauge the impact the advisers had on Middle East policy by the fact that Rifkind was called to testify before the Anglo-American Committee of Inquiry on Palestine and Bernstein before the United Nations ad hoc Special Committee on Palestine, where they expounded on the history and current situation of the Jewish displaced persons. Both committees were instrumental in deciding to partition Palestine into Jewish and Arab states. Palestine—in the opinion of all the advisers on Jewish affairs—was the only real solution to the Jewish DP problem.[12]

The British zonal authorities also retained an adviser on Jewish affairs. Unlike the American adviser, however, he did not serve the military but rather the British government. Consequently, he had his official residence at the Control Office in London. The position he assumed in March 1946 (that is, much later than his counterpart in the U.S. Zone) turned out to be quite problematic because of the complicated situation stemming from the British mandate in Palestine. The incumbent, Colonel Robert Bernard Solomon, an attorney, had until 1937 been president of the Jewish National Fund in Great Britain and was regarded as one of the leading British Zionists. He expended a great deal of effort mediating between the Jewish DPs and His Majesty's government. Even in the days of Ernest Bevin, an avowed anti-Zionist, Bevin himself received Colonel Solomon and Josef Rosensaft, the chairman of the Central Committee of the Liberated Jews in the British Zone; as a result of the negotiations, some 200 children went to Erets Yisrael outside the quota. At least in this case, Solomon's efforts were crowned with success.[13] In a number of other instances, however, his recommendations were ignored. He therefore resigned his position in July 1947[14] and was not replaced.

Although the treatment given the Jewish DPs continued to vary according to the personal attitudes of the army authorities responsible for their care, the Harrison Report did produce a fundamental change in the U.S. Zone and over the long term in the British Zone as well. After having been considered merely a matter of peripheral importance in the chaotic conditions that prevailed after liberation, the fate of this persecuted group moved to center stage—at least so far as the U.S. military and President Truman were concerned.[15] Aside from the positive effects that the report had on the lives of the Jewish survivors, a major part of its significance lay in the higher priority given to the Jewish DP problem in general. Even Samuel Gringauz, the chairman of the DP camp at Landsberg, emphasized the change in policy that accompanied the transition from the "military police" period, as he put it, to the humanitarian period.[16]

President Truman's personal interest in the Jewish DP question was reflected in a letter he wrote to General Eisenhower on 31 August 1945: "I know you will agree with me that we have a particular responsibility toward these victims of persecution and tyranny who are in our zone. We must make clear to the German people that we thoroughly abhor the Nazi policies of hatred and persecution. We have no better opportunity to demonstrate this than by the manner in which we ourselves actually treat the survivors remaining in Germany."[17]

The demand in Harrison's report for 100,000 immigration certificates for Palestine became an explosive issue in relations between the United States and Great Britain. Palestine, according to Harrison, was the only realistic solution to the Jewish DP problem:

> [M]ost Jews want to leave Germany and Austria as soon as possible. That is their first and great expressed wish and while this report necessarily deals with other needs present in the situation, many of the people themselves fear other suggestions or plans for their benefit because of the possibility that attention might thereby be diverted from the all-important matter of evacuation from Germany. . . . They want to be evacuated to Palestine now, just as other national groups are being repatriated to their homes. . . . The Jewish Agency for Palestine has submitted to the British Government a petition that one hundred thousand additional immigra-

tion certificates be made available. . . . No other single matter is, therefore, so important from the viewpoint of Jews in Germany and Austria
and those elsewhere who have known the horrors of the concentration
camps as is the disposition of the Palestine question.[18]

The most important long-term consequence of the Harrison Report was the recognition that Palestine had become the focus of Jewish attention and that only a relaxation of the rigid British immigration restrictions (just 1,500 certificates were being issued worldwide
each month) could defuse this source of conflict. However, Britain
was in no mood to relinquish the remaining bastions of its former
empire and weaken its position in the Middle East, especially after its
influence over India had diminished and it had been forced to grant
independence to the subcontinent in January 1948. Allowing more
Jews into Palestine, the British believed, would necessarily undermine Britain's influence in the Middle East and risk stirring up
Arab disorders.

Precisely why Harrison demanded 100,000 additional immigration certificates is not known. In August 1945 there were only about
50,000 Jews in Germany and Austria. The emigration of 100,000
would have solved the DP problem not only in these two countries
but would also have benefited most of the approximately 80,000 Jews
still living in Poland by providing them with a new home. One possible explanation is that Harrison's demand was not based on the report's findings but on inflated figures provided by the Jewish Agency,
which had in effect declared war on the British in the dispute over
opening Palestine to Jewish immigration. In any case, on 31 August
1945 President Truman urged the British to allow 100,000 displaced
European Jews into Palestine.

The U.S. recommendation was at the heart of a long-standing
British-American dispute that also manifested itself in the differen-
tial treatment accorded the Jewish DPs in each country's zone of occupation. The British wanted to draw a line between the liberated Jews
who remained in Europe and the Palestine question. The cabinet
therefore approved of Foreign Secretary Bevin's proposal that Jewish
immigration to Palestine be kept, as in the preceding months, at
1,500 persons per month. The cabinet was led to its decision by the

fear of Arab attacks. British officials thought that the Jews were the weaker group and would offer less resistance. Immediately following the British decision, however, the Jews launched a series of terrorist attacks against British installations. Thus began the long and violent struggle to open the gates of Palestine to the Jews that finally ended in the establishment of the state of Israel in May 1948.[19]

The ill feelings reflected in the exchange of notes between Great Britain and the United States did not leave British DP policy unaffected.[20] The British continued to draw a sharp distinction between German Jews and Jewish DPs. They regarded German Jews as Germans and refused to grant them the benefits of displaced person status. Further, the British military, as a matter of policy, did not accord Jews special privileges. Unlike the Americans, the British did not recognize the Jewish DPs as a separate group but only as members of nationalities. A memorandum from the chief of staff's office of the British Zone Command explained the reason—or perhaps the pretext—for the refusal to grant Jews separate status: "It is undesirable to accept the Nazi theory that the Jews are a separate race. Jews, in common with all other religious sects, should be rated according to their nationality rather than as a race or a religious sect. . . . Jews should be accommodated in camps appropriate to their nationality rather than to their race or religion. Any form of racial or religious segregation will only give rise to anti-Jewish feeling and may well have far-reaching consequences."[21]

British Foreign Secretary Ernest Bevin went so far as to say at a press conference that the Jews "with all their suffering" were not the only victims of fascism. This triggered anti-British demonstrations in both Germany and Austria[22] and severely strained relations between British officials in charge of the DP camps and representatives of the some 13,000 Jewish displaced persons in the British Zone, most of whom were in Belsen-Hohne. Even after the demonstrations ended, the conflict over Palestine, an issue of overriding importance to the Jewish survivors, stood in the way of any understanding or settlement between the two parties.

When compared to the situation of Jewish refugees in the British Zone, the effects of the Harrison Report for the Jewish DPs in the U.S. Zone were far-reaching and positive. In his "Final Report on Jewish

Displaced Persons in Germany," dated 5 November 1945, General Eisenhower informed President Truman of the changes that had taken place in the conditions of the Jewish survivors:

> Since Mr. Harrison's visit in July many changes have taken place with respect to the condition of Jewish and other displaced persons. Except for temporarily crowded conditions . . . housing is on a reasonable basis. Nevertheless, efforts to improve their condition continue unabated. Subordinate commanders are under orders to requisition German houses, grounds, and other facilities without hesitation for this purpose. . . . Displaced persons have absolute preference over Germans for housing. . . . Special Jewish centers were established for "those Jews who are without nationality or those not Soviet citizens who do not desire to return to their country of origin." . . . Necessary guard should be done by displaced persons themselves on the volunteer system and without arms. . . . I have recently raised the daily calorie food value per person . . . for racial, religious and political persecutees to a minimum of 2,500. . . . Clothing and shoes are available in adequate amounts and of suitable types.[23]

Thus the U.S. Army had fulfilled a substantial number of the demands made by Harrison in his report.

Even though the British occupation authorities did not, as a matter of principle, distinguish between Jewish and non-Jewish DPs, they did at least agree that Jews who had been repatriated and who then returned to the British Zone on or before 15 January 1946 would not be denied care. In no other respect, however, did Jewish DPs in the British Zone—or in the French Zone, for that matter—enjoy any special status. This applied also to the rationing of commodities, especially food. In the beginning, the ration of food supplies in the British and U.S. Zones was roughly equal—between 2,300 and 2,600 calories per person per day—but during the first postwar winter of 1945 to 1946, the British cut their ration to 2,170 calories. And in March 1946 they drastically reduced it again for those in the camps to 1,850 calories per day. Finally, in July the British zonal authorities slashed the ration for displaced persons to a low of 1,550 calories, which they maintained throughout the following year. The reductions were due in part to the ineffective distribution system in the British Zone. Germany's industrial nerve centers along the Rhine and the Ruhr had been more devastated by the war than any other areas in the country. And since Britain itself had suffered terribly as a result of the war, it was unable to supply even its occupation army in Germany with sufficient quantities of food. Although the area around Hanover, where the great majority of DPs in the British Zone lived, was largely agricultural and offered the best opportunities for correcting the supply situation, the displaced persons were not in possession of German ration cards and were therefore obliged to obtain their rations from inadequate British Army and UNRRA supplies. The irony was that the Germans—and the DPs living outside the camps—were actually better fed than the DPs residing in the camps.

Immediately after the war, the DPs in the French Zone had to contend with conditions nearly as harsh as those that had obtained in the British Zone during the spring of 1946. The French Army supplied its soldiers in Germany from food stocks it had secured in its zone of occupation. Further, it demanded reparations (in kind) to make up for shortages in France. Rations in the French Zone were at a semistarvation level during the winter and early spring; however, the French authorities raised the calories per person from 1,390 to 1,685 by October 1946, that is, to a level higher than that obtaining in the British Zone during the same period.[24]

❧

The Mass Exodus of Jews from Eastern Europe

Causes and Effects

The situation of the Jewish DPs changed fundamentally in 1946, the main reason being the constant movement of Jews from Eastern Europe, primarily from Poland, into Germany and Austria. The influx reached its zenith in the summer of 1946 following a pogrom in Kielce. In January 1946 there were some 36,000 Jewish DPs registered in the U.S. Zone; in October of the same year the number swelled to 141,000.[1] At the Belsen-Hohne camp in the British Zone, there were roughly 9,000 Jews in January 1946; by 17 August the number had risen to 11,139. On 15 June 1946 UNRRA determined that there were 19,373 Jewish DPs in the whole of the British Zone, and in November 1946 the American Jewish Joint Distribution Committee (AJJDC, or JDC for short) estimated a total of 50,000. For the French Zone JDC recorded a figure of 1,200 Jewish DPs in January 1946; by 15 June, according to UNRRA, the number had climbed to 1,454, dropping in November to 1,202, only 602 of whom were housed in camps.[2] These figures illustrate that the greatest impact of the mass exodus was in the U.S. Zone.

By 15 November 1946, 111,139 Jews had sought refuge in the U.S. Zone of Occupation in Germany.[3] It was one of the paradoxes of history that for a brief period after the war a defeated Nazi Germany, the cause of the Jewish tragedy, became the largest and safest sanctuary for Jewish refugees waiting in DP camps for the opportunity to emigrate. In the fall of 1945 there were some 80,000 Jews in Poland[4] out of a prewar population of 3.3 million. Some had been liberated from the concentration camps or had survived the war in hiding; others had returned from Germany to search for relatives; and about 13,000 had come from the Soviet Union with the Polish Army. Their situation in Poland was desperate. The country was like a huge Jewish graveyard. The returnees generally turned out to be the sole survivors from their families. The once-flourishing Jewish communities had been eradicated. It was virtually impossible to think of rebuilding Jewish life in Poland. Numerous reports bear witness to the despair that awaited the few survivors of the Holocaust. Lipman Sznajder put his feelings into words:

> After the time of terror had passed . . . I decided to return to Chelm, the city where I was born. . . . The happiness I felt upon reaching the city limits was indescribable. What I would have most liked to have done was wave to everyone and shout at the top of my voice: "I'm alive, I'm alive, me, Lipman Sznajder, Shlomo Sznajder's son . . . I escaped from hell and I've come back." . . . At any rate, that's what I wanted to do—but couldn't. I turned and looked everywhere but there was nothing to see. . . . The Chelm I had known no longer existed. The city to which I returned was unfamiliar; it appeared like a silent, gray, colorless, meaningless desert of stone. My whole family had been exterminated and my city had become a different place. I felt as though I were walking through a cemetery: every building a gravestone memorializing the venerable Jewish communities that had flourished here and perished. . . . I wandered down the streets of Chelm like a sleepwalker. . . . My feet took me to the building we used to live in on Lwowska Street. I stepped into the interior courtyard and stopped suddenly as if struck by lightning. Nothing but ruins. Not one brick rested on top of another. . . . All that remained was a gigantic pile of rubble; a monument and a memorial to my family which had been wiped out forever. I went on roaming through the streets of Chelm, lonely and abandoned, without parents, without brothers or sisters or friends to share the joy of having survived. The war was over, but so was my dream of a Chelm I had once loved; gone as well were my childhood and my youth.[5]

Not only were the returning Jews often unsuccessful in locating surviving family members, but many Poles refused to return Jewish property. This effectively deprived the survivors of the wherewithal to rebuild their lives. The greatest problem the Jews faced, however, was the resurgence of anti-Semitism, a threat from which the Polish government was unable to protect them. The leaders of the new regime tried their best to integrate the Jews into postwar Poland, but they lacked the support of any significant segment of Polish society and were powerless to prevent anti-Semitic outbreaks.

Small-scale pogroms erupted in a number of cities, for example, in Kraków in August 1945, when Polish children began throwing stones at Jews as they were attending synagogue. A Polish Jewish soldier ordered the children to stop, but they simply started shouting at the top of their voices that the Jews had tried to kill them. A crowd gathered outside the synagogue, then broke into the house of worship and set it ablaze. Ten Jews were killed and some thirty seriously wounded. In the same period at Rabka near Kraków, anti-Semites planted a bomb in a sanitarium for Jewish children who had lost their parents during the war. Since most of the children were not in the building when the bomb exploded, "only" four persons were killed. The sanitarium was destroyed in the fire.[6] In May 1946 a group of twenty-six kibbutzniks on their way from Kraków to the U.S. Zone was stopped by armed Polish soldiers near the Czech border. The soldiers opened fire on the kibbutzniks, some of whom were just children. Several managed to escape, but thirteen were killed and a number wounded. Not long after the soldiers had left the scene of the crime, villagers appeared and robbed the corpses. The only reason the wounded were not butchered was that they had pretended to be dead.[7] Medieval Christian anti-Semitism was alive again in Poland. An official government summary estimated that between November 1944, that is, after the withdrawal of the Germans, and October 1945, 351 Jews had been murdered in Poland.[8]

Some 200,000 Polish Jews who had sought refuge in the Soviet Union at the outbreak of the war and had survived in Russia were unaware of these anti-Semitic outrages. The Soviet and Polish governments had been negotiating since the summer of 1945 over the repatriation of Poles living in the USSR. At the beginning of 1946, the two sides agreed that Polish citizens would be allowed to decide whether they wished to remain in Russia or return to Poland. Of the 200,000, an estimated 175,000—that is, the great majority—chose to return to Poland.[9] After having spent long years in forced-labor camps and undergone severe privations, as a result of which many had died, the Jewish repatriates hoped to find their families, recover their possessions, and begin new lives in Poland. Then came the shock. They faced the same atmosphere of gloom, the same problems in trying to recover their property, and the same virulent anti-Semitism that was making life difficult, if not impossible, for the Jews who were already living in Poland. A family of five, for instance, returned to Przemyśl from Russia only to receive anonymous letters asking all five to leave the city. They nevertheless decided to remain. Three days later ten men entered their home and murdered the entire family.[10]

The campaigns against the Jews culminated in an armed pogrom in Kielce in July 1946. Kielce is a medium-sized city, 190 kilometers (114 miles) southeast of Warsaw with a population of some 50,000. When war broke out in 1939, 25,000 Jews lived in Kielce; after the war 200 Jews returned.[11] On the evening of 3 June 1946, the father of nine-year-old Henryk Blaszczyk reported to the Kielce police that his son had been missing for two days. The next morning Henryk and his father appeared at the local police station. The story Henryk told was that he had been held captive in the Jewish Committee's house at No. 7 Planty Avenue, where he had been sent to deliver a parcel. He went on to say that he had been held there in a cellar and that he had seen other Christian children murdered there by the Jews. Fortunately, he had managed to escape. The police commander ordered his men to go to the committee's house. The boy, who had accompanied the police, expounded his story to an assembled crowd. The mood quickly turned ugly and a pogrom ensued. Forty-two Jewish men, women, and children were murdered, including a "kibbutz" group of youngsters who were preparing to leave Poland at the first opportunity. The Polish government was shocked, and official representatives took part in the funeral ceremony. After a quick trial, nine of the perpetrators were sentenced to death; they were executed on 12 July 1946. Henryk Blaszczyk had admitted earlier, on 5 July, that his story was a pure fabrication. It had been concocted by Polish anti-Semites who had forced Henryk to learn the story by heart and tell it to the police. They had threatened him with severe punishment if he refused to play along with them.[12]

In the city of Kielce, in broad daylight, a ritual murder story had caused a massacre, something few had believed was still possible in postwar Poland. The Polish government stood helpless in the face of the violence. Nor could the Jews expect assistance from the Church, which had failed to offer a sharp and explicit condemnation of the pogrom. Polish Jewry reacted swiftly. Nothing could prevent them now from leaving Poland; a mass exodus was the only answer. The flow of Holocaust survivors was directed by Brichah (Hebrew, "flight" or "escape"), a semiclandestine Jewish organization that helped Jews get out of Eastern Europe. The name applied both to the organization itself and to the mass movement of refugees.[13] Soon after their liberation in 1944, survivors in Poland began to establish contact with one another. Given the hopelessness of their situation in Eastern Europe, their natural destination after liberation was Palestine. However, the prospects of an individual reaching the promised land by himself or herself in war-ravaged Europe were not good and the chances of doing so legally were virtually nil. For this reason, the survivors established an underground refugee service organization whose job it was to secure means of transportation and, most important but also most difficult, find ways, mainly illegal, to cross national borders. For this purpose, Brichah groups were smuggled into railway junctions and other places where Jews had assembled to effect their escape. For reasons of security, the Brichah people knew one another only by their first names. Their task was to provide safe passage and accommodations for the refugees during their often long journeys across Europe.

Until August 1945 Brichah had sought to bring Jewish survivors to Italy, from whose coasts they hoped the prospective emigrants could embark for Palestine. However, Italian authorities soon realized that they were unable to control the situation created by the large influx of DPs, so they clamped down on illegal border crossings. By the end of the year, Brichah had no choice but to put the Jewish refugees up in Allied-occupied Germany and Austria. The political aims of Brichah became increasingly evident during 1946: the more Jews brought into the U.S. Zone of Occupation and the more pressure put on the Americans to feed and house the refugees, the more the United States would urge Britain to relax its restrictions on emigration to Palestine. At the same time, Brichah continued to transport Jews illegally by ship to the promised land. It is estimated that in July and August 1946 alone 90,000 to 95,000 Jews from Eastern Europe, Germany, Austria, and Italy reached Erets Yisrael.[14]

In 1946 Brichah operated two main routes for Jews fleeing Eastern

Europe—one via Náchod, Bratislava, Vienna, Linz, and Salzburg to the DP camps in the U.S. Zone and the other leading from Stettin (Szczecin) to the American sector of Berlin. Most chose the first route, since the one to Berlin required them to cross the Soviet Zone of Occupation, where the refugees could expect little sympathy and where Soviet soldiers might steal their belongings when they crossed the border. There were also a number of other routes. Frequently they had to be changed at short notice or new routes opened up because part of an established route had been discovered and it no longer seemed safe to cross the border at that point. The success of Brichah operations depended largely on the attitude of the American occupation authorities toward the huge flow of refugees. If American officials had not kept their zone boundaries open, Brichah's undertakings would have had little prospect of success. The Americans could not, of course, have completely stopped the flow of these desperate human beings. However, families with young children or elderly relatives might not have risked a dangerous journey, associated as it was with illegal border crossings, if they had not considered their chances of reaching their destination reasonably good.

With the continuous flow of Jews into the U.S. Zone in the late summer of 1945, the DP camps were quickly becoming overcrowded. The U.S. Army at first adopted a wait-and-see attitude. The military refused to improve conditions in the camps on the theory that if they did, it would encourage infiltrees to move into the zone in even larger numbers. On the other hand, after the Harrison Report, the army was in no mood to provide fodder for further negative newspaper headlines or to provoke another scandal.[15]

An incident that took place in August 1945 illustrates the tense relations between the army and the refugees. On 21 August Brichah people smuggled some 650 Jews into Germany in four trainloads across zone boundaries near Pilsen (Plzeň) in Czechoslovakia. The Eighth Armored Division tried to force the refugees back to Poland. However, they again infiltrated Germany on foot and in small groups. This was the first and the last time that U.S. authorities in Germany tried to use force against Jews to prevent them from entering the zone. Further use of force would have provoked an outcry and possible presidential intervention, as had happened in the case of the Harrison Report. In any event, the movement of refugees into Germany could have been stopped only by the application of brute force. But no American general would have dreamed of ordering his troops to fire on Jewish persecutees in 1945, so soon after the defeat of Nazism, a fact that Brichah had obviously factored into its calculations. The rethinking of the army's position, however, was not motivated solely by the fear of an outcry in the American press but also by the benevolent attitude of senior military commanders toward the survivors of the Holocaust. For many, it had become a matter of principle to provide these human beings with a more or less secure place to stay.[16]

All Jews within the boundaries of the U.S. Zone as of 18 February 1946 were to be considered DPs and to have the same rights to housing, food, and clothing as did the "old" DPs,[17] even though the refugees from Eastern Europe did not fit the true definition of displaced persons, namely, civilians driven out of their country by reason of war. Since they had not fled liberated Eastern Europe before the end of the war, in the strict sense they were "persecutees."[18]

The refugees who arrived in the fall of 1945 and the early summer of 1946 were put up in existing DP camps. However, the mass influx that came in the summer of 1946 completely overwhelmed the capacity of the already overcrowded camps. After some initial hesitation, the U.S. Army set up thirty-eight new assembly centers in its zone.[19] Some were nothing more than transit camps, such as Landshut and Cham, which were located near the Czech border; the army regarded these camps as temporary shelters to give refugees an opportunity to rest and regain their strength after weeks of arduous travel before moving on to the DP camps. Nevertheless, the army was forced to build new camps so as to provide longer-term housing for the seemingly endless flow of refugees, until they were ready to leave Germany.[20]

Britain refused to adopt the liberal American attitude toward the problem. Any willingness on Britain's part to accept refugees and so provide even indirect support for Brichah ran counter to London's policy of preventing the immigration of Jews to Palestine. The British dismissed reports of the Jews' plight in Poland, anti-Semitic outbreaks, and discrimination as nothing more than Zionist atrocity propaganda used by Brichah to frighten Holocaust survivors into leaving the country and moving to Palestine. Although it is true that Brichah propagandized the cause of Zionism and that all its members were Zionists who were prepared to sacrifice their lives for the dream of a

Jewish state in Palestine, the organization could never have contrived
to persuade over 100,000 people to flee once again if they had not felt
seriously threatened. Moreover, the anti-Semitic outrages were not a
figment of people's imaginations; they were a bitter reality. Brichah
did everything in its power to engender enthusiasm among the refugees for emigrating to Palestine; however, Brichah could never have
been as successful as it was if the survivors had not also genuinely
believed in a Jewish state. No Jew would have fled from Eastern Europe to Germany after the war solely on the basis of Zionist propaganda.

Unfortunately, the mass exodus from Poland reached a peak at the
same time as did the terrorist attacks of the Irgun Tsva'i Le'umi (National Military Organization) in Palestine. The British reacted swiftly,
taking strong measures both in the Holy Land and in their occupation
zone in Germany. The British High Commissioner for Palestine pres-
sured the cabinet in London to stop illegal immigration since Brichah
was continuing to recruit new members from among recently arrived
immigrants. After prolonged discussions with the General Staff, the
British cabinet decided on 7 August 1946 to deport illegal immigrants to Cyprus. Just one week later the first 1,200 persons were
shipped from Haifa to Cyprus. The high cost of maintaining the nine
detention camps set up on the island plus the risk of confrontations
with the Arabs led the British to curtail the flow of refugees into their
occupation zone. British diplomats became active in an effort to stop
the movement of Jewish refugees into the other zones of occupation
as well.[21]

As a result, a greatly reduced number of Jews from Eastern Europe
("infiltrees") entered the British Zone in northern Germany. Aside
from a few small camps, there was only one big DP camp in the British Zone—the Bergen-Belsen DP Hohne Camp, or "Belsen" for short.
DPs from Berlin who had arrived in Germany via Stettin (Szczecin) were directed by Brichah to the Belsen camp; unlike those who
settled in the U.S. Zone, however, they were not officially recognized
as displaced persons. In order to receive DP status, they had to show
proof of having been in Germany at the time of their liberation. Most
of the "infiltrees" therefore came within the jurisdiction of the German
authorities and were not entitled to extra rations or assistance from
UNRRA. Furthermore, they were prohibited from seeking housing

in camps administered by UNRRA; the only accommodations available to them were in German refugee camps or in the local Jewish communities. Nevertheless, many Eastern European Jewish immigrants managed to get into Belsen "illegally," though they were then dependent for their support on the DPs who were living there "legally."[22]

Following a series of protracted negotiations, UNRRA managed to have 2,273 "illegals" declared eligible for assistance as DPs. However, only persons who had reached Belsen on or before 1 July 1946 could actually qualify. The process of deciding on eligibility was supposed to have been completed by 22 July. By that date, however, only half of the infiltrees had been registered, mainly because officials had to determine precisely who had arrived at the camp before 1 July and who arrived there after 1 July, that is, who was in Belsen illegally. Thus, the deadline for deciding was extended to 10 August 1946.[23]

On 1 July 1946, the British further tightened their restrictive policy on infiltrees and Jewish DPs. Belsen became, in essence, a "closed" camp; infiltrees were not given any status at all. Refugees were prohibited from entering Belsen or any other DP camp in the British Zone and were denied assistance from external relief organizations. In other words, they were treated like German expellees. "Old" DPs were entitled to assistance only if they lived inside the camps and were forced to return to the camps if they wished to retain the benefits of DP status.[24] According to the British ruling, there were only three groups of Jews in their zone: German Jews without DP status who were excluded from UNRRA assistance; DPs who were in Germany at the time of their liberation; and infiltrees without DP status who were under German administration.[25] These distinctions were not merely a bureaucratic exercise; they affected people's lives directly and in very negative ways. Consequently, Brichah made every effort to direct Eastern European Jewish refugees into the U.S. Zone as quickly as possible.

The flow of refugees from Eastern Europe had far-reaching consequences for the makeup of the Jewish DP camps in the U.S. Zone. Very few German Jews lived in the camps. They had either survived the war in hiding or had returned to their homeland from the concentration camps. In any event, the majority had decided in favor of a life outside the camps. They tried to reintegrate themselves into German society and establish new Jewish communities.

Eastern European Jews, on the other hand, represented the overwhelming majority in the DP camps. They may be roughly divided into three categories: (1) concentration camp survivors consisting almost exclusively of men and women between the ages of eighteen and forty-five. There were hardly any children or old people in this group. A JDC analysis estimated that among 900 persons surveyed, there were no children under six years of age and only 3 percent were between the ages of six and seventeen; 0.2 percent were over the age of sixty-five.[26] (2) The second group was made up of young men and women who had escaped from the ghettos or death-camp transports and had subsequently joined partisan units. Surprisingly, many of these young people had managed to take their children with them. Despite a hard life in the forests, they often had been able to keep their families intact, bring new children into the world, and adopt orphans. As a rule, they were mentally and physically more fit than the former concentration camp inmates. In general, they had not had to endure the torments and humiliations to which the inmates of the concentration camps had been subjected. (3) The last and by far the largest group consisted of refugees from Eastern Europe: Jews—mainly from Poland but also from Russia and other countries—who had never been in Germany before, who saw no chance to rebuild their lives in their homelands, and who regarded Germany as a way station on the journey to Palestine. These "infiltrees" were often Orthodox Jews who were in better physical condition than those comprising the first two groups. They often had large numbers of children and thus altered the age profile of the DP camps. The above-mentioned JDC study reported that at the end of December 1946, 20.3 percent of those surveyed were children (4.3 percent of whom were infants, 4 percent children ages one to five, and 11.8 percent children of school age) and 79.7 percent adults, of whom most were between the ages of eighteen and forty-four. Fewer than 2 percent were older than sixty.[27] The refugees from Eastern Europe also included a large number of intellectuals, who were later to play an important part in the cultural life of the camps.[28]

In November 1946 UNRRA surveyed 127,000 Jews in the U.S. Zone as to their nationality. Seventy-one percent had come from Poland, 6 percent from Hungary, 4 percent from Czechoslovakia, 2.5 percent from Germany and Romania, respectively, 2 percent from

Austria, and over 10 percent had arrived from other countries or were stateless.[29] The Eastern European Jews, who were clearly in the majority, distanced themselves from their German surroundings and built their own society inside the DP camps, a society that encompassed every sphere of life—politics, government, police, law, culture, education, vocational training, and the press. Each camp created its own little state within the state, an artificial Jewish "ghetto" that maintained as little contact as possible with its German milieu. The displaced persons regarded the DP camps in Germany merely as stopping-off places; they all agreed that after the Holocaust Germany could no longer be a home to Jews. However, the dream of a rapid departure from Germany was not to be realized quickly. During 1946 and 1947, the camps began to appear less and less like temporary shelters. The survivors of the Holocaust were bitterly disappointed that the world seemed so oblivious to their fate, that it barred them from reaching their longed-for home in Palestine, and that the other countries to which they might have immigrated had closed their doors to them.

❊

The Joint

American Jewish Assistance from Overseas

It was not until the fall of 1945 and partly as a result of the Harrison Report that the major Jewish organizations from abroad, including Palestine, were able to establish offices in Germany and build a social-welfare network adapted to the needs of the Jewish DPs. Smaller teams of relief workers had been operating in Germany since the summer. However, to the Jewish survivors who had waited so eagerly for these organizations to arrive, the fact that they had not come earlier was difficult for them to understand. In some cases, the DPs reacted with outright bitterness because of the delays in providing assistance.

The most important of the voluntary relief organizations was the American Jewish Joint Distribution Committee (AJJDC, JDC for short), popularly known among *She'erit Hapletah* as "the Joint." JDC was founded in the United States after the outbreak of World War I in 1914. Alarmed at the suffering of Jews during the war, JDC distributed funds to its coreligionists in Europe. In addition, it sent food and other commodities to Palestine and Poland. Ultimately, JDC became active wherever Jews were subjected to persecution or pogroms. From 1924 to 1938, JDC supported Jewish farm settlements in the Soviet Union. During World War II it concentrated on aiding the persecuted Jews of Europe, distributing food and offering subvention to various assistance programs. After 1945 the Joint contributed more than any other Jewish organization to the support of Holocaust survivors. Even now it is among the largest and most important Jewish social-welfare organizations.

The First JDC Teams Arrive in Germany

On 13 June 1945, the first JDC workers entered the concentration camp at Buchenwald, 11 kilometers (5 miles) northwest of Weimar, which had been liberated two months earlier and housed some 4,000 inmates. At that time the camp was still within the U.S. Zone. The JDC team focused first on caring for the nearly 1,000 Jewish children in the camp. They were in desperate straits, having arrived in Thuringia after being evacuated from Auschwitz. JDC arranged for the transport of 441 of these children to France along with 92 other children who had been liberated en route to Bergen-Belsen. Of those who remained in the camp, most immigrated to Switzerland or Palestine. Some of the children and adults who stayed on at Buchenwald—forty-seven persons in all—joined a kibbutz that had been established on 3 June at Egendorf, 30 kilometers (18.6 miles) from the camp. Before Soviet occupation forces entered Thuringia, the members of the kibbutz left Egendorf and established a new collective at Geringshof near Fulda. Founded by Mizrachi, the principal political party of Orthodox religious Zionism, Geringshof had been operated as a training farm since 1924. It was shut down by the Nazis in 1941. When the kibbutz members from Weimar arrived in Geringshof on 21 June 1945, they found the farm completely destroyed. However, seventy kibbutzniks under the direction of two former staff members of the prewar training facility soon managed to expand the first *hakhsharah* (Hebrew, literally "preparation," that is, for agricultural work in Palestine) built in Germany after World War II into a first-class vocational education center. The first "graduates" left Geringshof in August 1945 to seek a new home in Erets Yisrael.[1]

In the meantime, the JDC team had left Buchenwald. Although the Soviets were about to take over the administration of the camp, the team's departure was not connected to the arrival of the Russians but rather to the fact that the Allies had not extended official recognition and support to JDC workers, thereby impeding them in the performance of their duties. The JDC teams that had been working in Hesse and Württemberg-Baden since June labored under similar handicaps. However, these teams had far fewer Jewish DPs in their charge. The first officially recognized JDC team did not reach Bergen-Belsen until 29 July 1945. It was led by Maurice Eigen. A few days later, on 4 August, a JDC team under Eli Rock received permission to begin working in Bavaria. However, even before then, in July 1945, two JDC representatives, Dr. Henri Heitan and his wife, Ruth, had established a medical program in the camp at Feldafing. It was not until the arrival of Eli Rock, though, that assistance was significantly expanded. Like the Heitans, Rock and his people resided for a time at Feldafing.

JDC headquarters in New York tried repeatedly to obtain permits from the Allied armies to enter their respective zones; however, American and British military leaders rejected any civilian interference in their command areas. Since UNRRA was anxious not to jeopardize relations with the occupation authorities by supporting "private" welfare organizations, it endorsed the military's position. In a letter to UNRRA dated 7 May 1945, one day before the surrender of all German forces, JDC expressed its concern regarding the need to assist Jewish DPs as quickly as possible and to provide a staff of well-trained social workers. Besides pointing out the important role it could play as an intermediary between the DPs on the one hand and the army and UNRRA on the other, JDC proposed "to provide . . . welfare and medical staff members for work, . . . where large numbers of displaced persons (i.e., stateless displaced persons in Germany or persecuted Jewish displaced persons now in Germany or former enemy countries) have been found." The letter also referred to JDC's long years of experience in dealing with "problems of relief, reconstruction, and displaced persons in the European area." Above all, it stressed the nonpolitical nature of the organization.[2] JDC's request to enter Germany was approved, but representatives of the teams were required to obtain separate permits from each army.

Some of the teams—in the British Zone and the northern part of the U.S. Zone, for instance—obtained permission relatively quickly. On the other hand, the Third and Seventh Armies (in Bavaria) turned down applications to enter their zones, fearing that nongovernmental civilian relief workers would be an unwelcome intrusion on their authority.[3] Thus, when Eli Rock arrived in Feldafing, he obtained permission to work only in that camp and nowhere else. It was not until the middle of August that he and his team were able to expand their activities so as to provide assistance to the many other DP camps in the vicinity.

JDC's relief efforts gradually developed into a comprehensive social-welfare program that helped ease the Jewish DPs' resentment at the lack of support they had received from world Jewry immediately after liberation. As late as the end of May 1945, in an appeal issued to the World Jewish Congress, Dr. Zalman Grinberg, the future chairman of the Central Committee of Liberated Jews in the U.S. Zone and at that time a doctor at the Jewish hospital at St. Ottilien near Landsberg, criticized the delay in providing assistance: "Four weeks have passed since our liberation and not a single representative of world Jewry, not a single representative of any Jewish organization has come to talk with us about the gravest ordeal ever endured by any people, or to comfort us, to ease our temporary distress or give us immediate assistance. We have been obliged to use our diminished strength to try to help ourselves. This was our first and greatest disappointment following liberation. These are the sad and incomprehensible facts, as we see them."[4]

Though relations between the DPs and the Joint were not always smooth, there was great joy when the JDC workers finally arrived. In subsequent years, the displaced persons and the Joint worked as partners to resolve all questions involving day-to-day living.

Organizational Structure of the Joint in Germany

Jacob L. Trobe set up the Joint's first German headquarters toward the end of July 1945 at the Belsen DP camp. During September, JDC moved its headquarters to Höchst, after UNRRA had established its headquarters there. And in December both UNRRA and the JDC moved their headquarters again, to Arolsen. UNRRA had moved as the result of agreements that it had reached with the three military zonal authorities, specifying, among other things, that voluntary welfare organizations were to be subordinate to UNRRA. The agreement for the British Zone was signed on 27 November 1945; those for the French and U.S. Zones were signed on 18 and 19 February 1946, respectively.[5] JDC and its activities were thus overseen by UNRRA and later by its successor, the International Refugee Organization (IRO). The Joint was obliged to set up quarters wherever UNRRA or IRO did. Proximity to these two organizations allowed JDC to talk directly to those with overall responsibility for the care of displaced persons whenever problems arose.

During the second half of August 1945, Eli Rock and his group obtained from the U.S. Army a building in Munich that was to be the central headquarters of JDC for the next few years. When Trobe stepped down from his post as the Joint's director for Germany in January 1946, JDC's activities were growing apace; hundreds of its workers were fanning out from Germany's major cities into every part of the country. It became a matter of necessity for the Joint to divide Germany into regions. On paper JDC continued to establish its regional offices in tandem with UNRRA. In the U.S. Zone, for instance, the official mailing address of its headquarters was the Munich suburb of Pasing. In actual fact, however, the organization operated from a building on Siebertstraße in the Bogenhausen section of Munich, where the American zonal authorities had their headquarters. In the British Zone, JDC directed its activities from Belsen and Hamburg, even though it came under UNRRA's subordinate zone headquarters at Lemgo. In the French Zone, the Joint had its headquarters at Konstanz, although it came under the control of the UNRRA office at Haslach.[6]

After Trobe left his post, Herbert Katzki assumed responsibility for JDC's activities in Germany, operating out of the Joint's New York headquarters. Katzki had been working for the U.S. War Refugee Board (WRB) in 1944 and 1945 and had accompanied Earl G. Harrison on his mission to investigate DP camps in Germany. After Katzki resigned, JDC sent Lavy M. Becker, a Canadian, to take charge of the entire U.S. Zone. He was followed in April by Leo W. Schwarz and a year after that by Charles S. Passman. Apart from these personnel changes, JDC established regional offices and appointed field representatives in a number of towns and camps with heavy concentrations of displaced persons. The process of decentralization was carried out to keep JDC in conformity with UNRRA practices. In the British Zone, the Joint continued to direct its activities from Belsen. The office of director in the British Zone passed successively from Maurice Eigen to David B. Wodlinger, Rabbi Schwarz, Samuel Dallob, and Egon Fink. In 1945 Henri Laufer was named head of the JDC office at Konstanz in the French Zone. He remained director until the office ceased coordinating JDC's local welfare program on 1 January 1950, transferring responsibility to the Joint's headquarters in the U.S. Zone. Only the Emigration Department remained in Konstanz, continuing to provide direct assistance to the few Jews living there. In the Soviet Zone there were some 1,200 Jews in the *Kultusgemeinde,* or local Jewish community, which the Joint "unofficially" supplied with food and clothing.

Under Samuel L. Haber, JDC, headquartered in Munich, centralized its operations for all of occupied Germany in October 1949. Beginning at the end of April 1947, Haber became director of JDC's operations in Bavaria and in December was given responsibility for the entire U.S. Zone. A few months later, Haber also became director of JDC's operations in the Western occupation zones in Austria, remaining in that position until the DP problem in Austria was finally resolved in 1952.[7] Haber was the Joint's country director for Germany until the end of 1953. Except for Föhrenwald, all the DP camps in Germany had been shut down by that date. Haber left Germany on 1 January 1954 to continue his work for JDC in Morocco. Following his departure, JDC limited itself to providing for the welfare of the DPs at Föhrenwald, the last operational DP camp in Germany— initially under the directorship of James Rice and finally under that of Theodor Feder—until it closed its offices in Germany in March 1957. As early as 1951 the Joint had focused its efforts in Germany on the Föhrenwald camp and was concerned mainly with the emigration of so-called hard-core cases, most of whom were mentally or physically disabled.

Generally, the Joint's departments in Germany received their directives from JDC New York. The New York office also maintained close contact with the Joint's European Executive Council in Paris. In New York, the JDC secretary responsible for European operations, Moses A. Leavitt, was determined to translate the organization's humanitarian and philanthropic principles into direct action. Joseph J. Schwartz was the chairman of the Executive Council. Schwartz was born in Ukraine and had been taken to the United States as a child. Though he had Orthodox religious training, he eventually moved away from Orthodox Judaism and studied Semitic languages and literatures. He had the ability to speak half a dozen languages, including German, French, Yiddish, Hebrew, and Arabic. A scholar and a man of vision with a warm personality and a profound understanding of people, Schwartz possessed precisely the qualities needed to fill JDC's important post in Paris. JDC had sent him to the French capital in 1939, where he became director of the Joint's European departments. After German troops occupied France, Schwartz moved to Lisbon, where he continued to carry out his duties and assisted persecuted Jews fleeing the Nazis.[8] It was Schwartz who, in the course of protracted negotiations with SHAEF, succeeded in having the first JDC teams brought to Germany.

Schwartz visited Munich on 25 October 1946 to get a firsthand impression of the DPs' situation inside the camps. Meeting with representatives of the Central Committee of Liberated Jews in the U.S. Zone, he was favored with the first positive comments regarding JDC's activities. Until that time, survivors had voiced continual— and in part justified—criticism of the Joint's ineffective methods of operation. Except for managerial staff, the first JDC employees in Germany were run-of-the-mill social workers who had come from a bewildering variety of countries. Since they had not been properly trained to deal with the problems at hand, these workers were unable to cope with the demands of the job. Furthermore, the lack of sufficient financial resources and of an adequate transportation system, together with the various restrictions placed on crossing zonal boundaries in occupied Germany, made it impossible to import enough supplies from other European countries or from the United States to care for the DPs. The situation changed for the better in the spring of 1946, when the first shiploads of supplies finally arrived from overseas and the first imports came in from neighboring Switzerland, allowing JDC to distribute enough food and other commodities to meet the DPs' needs. Moreover, the increase in the number of staff and the hiring of better-trained JDC workers also had a positive effect on the Joint's European operations.

In retrospect, the policies practiced by JDC while it operated in Germany proved to be sound. The Joint issued general guidelines and gave its local officials a free hand to make decisions based on their personal experience and the knowledge they had acquired in dealing with the special problems of the Jewish DPs. JDC personnel in Germany were responsible solely to their respective regional directors, not to the department heads in Paris or New York.

American Jews provided the necessary funds, mainly in the form of individual donations but also from money raised by the United Jewish Appeal, which had been founded in 1939 as a humanitarian relief organization to aid Jews in Europe and Palestine.[9] Examining JDC's annual expenditures for its work in Germany and Austria during the period 1945 through 1948, one begins to grasp the magnitude of the services the organization rendered to the Jewish DPs. In 1945 the Joint spent $317,000 to provide relief for the DPs in both countries; by 1946 expenditures had increased more than tenfold to $3,979,500, and in 1947 they reached a maximum of $9,012,000, a staggering amount of money for the time.[10]

The Joint's activities included the importation and distribution of food and clothing as well as the provision of funds for supporting the DPs. JDC was further involved in rebuilding communities and their associated institutions: it organized emigration; performed social work; operated a tracing bureau and an information service; supported cultural, educational, and religious programs; and expanded the provision of health care for the DPs.[11] Soon after JDC people arrived in Germany, special departments were established for each of the above-mentioned areas of responsibility, and in the spring of 1946 each department was staffed with the necessary number of trained personnel. However, not all DPs viewed the expansion of the staff as a positive development; they were critical of the fact that the new workers had not been recruited from the ranks of the DPs themselves. This problem was soon resolved.

By 1947, only 108 out of the 560 Joint workers in the U.S. Zone were still so-called foreign personnel. Jewish DPs now formed the majority of those employed by JDC in the camps. And of the 452 Jewish workers, 126 were designated as so-called Class II employees; they wore the same uniforms as their JDC colleagues and enjoyed a number of other privileges, including, for example, permission to use military hotels and military transportation.[12] In April 1948 there were 700 Jewish DPs working for JDC in the U.S. Zone. Their compensation consisted of additional food rations and other commodities, though the actual amounts were negligible when compared to the rations received by other DPs. Since only foodstuffs and other commodities were being sent to Germany and cash was unavailable, JDC could not reimburse the DPs in hard currency.[13]

In the French Zone, the reluctance of the DPs to find employment was a source of considerable concern for the Joint. As in the other zones, Jewish survivors in the French Zone were reluctant to help rebuild the German economy. Furthermore, a representative of the Organization for Rehabilitation through Training (ORT) did not arrive in the French Zone until March 1947, whereas in the British and U.S. Zones ORT had begun a program of vocational schooling and training in the DP camps as early as the fall of 1945. ORT's extensive vocational education program in these zones allowed survivors to learn a trade outside the German industrial-education system, an opportunity that was available only in limited measure to DPs in the French Zone. The Joint had realized early that only when the DPs were employed could their attention be diverted from the desperate conditions in which they lived. Therefore, JDC determined that DPs in the French Zone between the ages of sixteen and thirty-five would continue to receive rations only if they were gainfully employed, even though the Joint itself had no job vacancies; the ruling took effect on 1 May 1947.[14]

The Growing Number of Jewish DPs: New Problems for the Joint

As the influx of Jews from Eastern Europe began in the fall of 1945 and increasingly assumed the character of a mass exodus, both the Joint and the occupying powers found themselves facing a set of nearly insoluble problems. The DP camps were overcrowded and the relief programs were becoming unmanageable. In the Munich area, rations for Jewish DPs were reduced near the end of 1945. Red Cross parcels that had been sent by JDC in Switzerland were distributed not as additional supplies but as a substitute for rations. The U.S. Army decided not to pay Jews with food for labor they performed, whether in the camps or outside them, if they were inmates of such camps. Clearly, these restrictive measures were not introduced because of any impending scarcity of resources but rather as an attempt by the occupying powers to limit the movement of Jews into their respective zones. They had deluded themselves into believing that, by leaking information about the lack of adequate food and housing in Germany for Jewish DPs, they could somehow prevent the further migration of Jews into the Western zones. It quickly turned out, however, that the military had completely misjudged the situation of the Jews in Eastern Europe. Jews there felt so threatened by the outbreaks of anti-Semitism that no news about living conditions in Germany, however dire, was going to stop them from fleeing to the West.[15] At the same time, JDC tried to avoid adding fuel to the rumors being circulated about the impending arrival of between 250,000 and 350,000 new "infiltrees."

The enormous problems caused by the mass influx from Eastern Europe during the second half of 1946 induced JDC to reexamine its operations. The administrative structure of the organization was found to be effective and was left untouched. Rather, further emphasis was to be placed on increasing the organization's flexibility, especially on enhancing its cooperation with UNRRA. First, as stipulated by UNRRA, the Joint divided the U.S. Zone—the zone most affected by the influx—into five administrative regions with headquarters in Stuttgart, Frankfurt, Bamberg, Regensburg, and Munich. Then it established a liaison office with UNRRA. This new opportunity for exchanging information contributed to a further improvement in relations between UNRRA and JDC; it also enhanced the effectiveness of the UNRRA Council for Jewish Affairs, which had existed since February 1946 and to which all organizations working with the Jewish DPs, including the Central Committee of Liberated Jews, belonged. Further, the chief of UNRRA operations for Germany had acceded to JDC's request to be allowed to confer directly with the U.S. military on certain questions rather than first having to enter into negotiations with UNRRA as prescribed by the official guidelines. Finally, JDC's director and the Joint's liaison officer were invited to participate in UNRRA senior staff conferences.

UNRRA began a dramatic reduction in the size of its staff toward the end of 1946, a move that had serious implications, especially for the DP camps where UNRRA had neglected to prepare residents to perform jobs for which they were ultimately made responsible. Consequently, JDC was forced to expand its assistance program. In principle, UNRRA's policy of helping the DPs to help themselves was sound, but it could be implemented only with the support of JDC. The responsibilities assigned to JDC, along with the associated financial and staffing problems, mushroomed when UNRRA finally ended its work in Germany on 30 June 1947.[16]

The International Refugee Organization (IRO) took over UNRRA's responsibilities and inherited its remaining personnel, that is, about half of its former staff. In one important respect, however, IRO's charge differed from that of UNRRA. The focus was now on resettlement and the care of so-called hard-core refugees, not on repatriation. Furthermore, according to an agreement with the occupation authorities, IRO was to assume total responsibility for DP operations, which were then still under the command of the U.S. Army. When it came to implementing the agreement, however, the military relinquished its control only with great reluctance; it was not until August 1948 that responsibility for the displaced persons camps was actually transferred to IRO. IRO's employees only took over the management of the camps, assigning the job of administration to the DPs and thus giving them greater responsibility than they had had under UNRRA. IRO—and the U.S. Army—refused to distribute rations to camp inmates who had entered the U.S. Zone on or before 21 April 1947. Initially, the army prohibited the entry of Jews into the U.S. Zone as of that date; however, it eventually relaxed its regulation and permitted Jews who had already moved into the zone to remain there. Nevertheless, the "infiltrees" received no assistance and were not allowed to reside in the camps. The nongovernmental relief organizations— in particular, the Joint—were obliged to provide for their care.[17]

Time and again disputes arose between IRO and JDC. For financial reasons, IRO was progressively reducing its operations. Sam Dallob reported in April 1948 that for several months the Joint had been obliged to pay for telephone service, telegrams, and transportation as well as for the maintenance of the dining facilities in the camps. He pointed out that no one could foresee how far IRO would go to reduce its expenditures. IRO's money-saving measures, he wrote, would only shift the financial burden to JDC.[18]

With the termination of IRO, JDC redrew its district boundaries inside the U.S. Zone. In October 1947 the U.S. Zone (Charles S. Passman was JDC's director at the time) was divided into three administrative regions. The Eastern Military District No. 1, headquartered in Munich (director: Maurice Lipian), comprised the state of Bavaria and included the former JDC regional offices at Munich, Regensburg, and Bamberg. The Western Military District No. 2, with its headquarters in Frankfurt (director: Abraham Cohen), encompassed the states of Hesse and Württemberg-Baden and included the former Joint offices at Stuttgart and Frankfurt (including Kassel). The third military district—Berlin—remained unchanged and came under the direction of Joseph Fink. The directors of the three districts reported directly to the JDC director for Germany. There were also eight so-called zonal advisers, who were in charge of JDC's various departments and who likewise reported to the director for Germany. The departments they managed covered the following areas: employment and vocational training; religious issues; medical and dental care; welfare (including personal services); education and rehabilitation; legal aid; supply and transportation; and emigration.[19]

JDC's Departments

Initially, medical and material assistance, that is, the Health Department and the Supply and Transportation Department, were the focus of JDC's attention. Then the Emigration Department and the Education and Cultural Activities Departments became the Joint's—and the survivors'—main concern.

JDC's Emigration Department was responsible for resettling refugees and displaced persons in the United States and other countries, except for Palestine. Beginning in December 1945, the Jewish Agency for Palestine assumed responsibility for emigration to Erets Yisrael. Before the establishment of the state of Israel, the agency had arrogated to itself some of the powers of an independent Jewish government, even performing de facto consular functions. Nevertheless, JDC still continued its financial support, for example, paying the cost of passage on ships chartered by the Jewish Agency. Of course, when the agency was involved in illegal activities, JDC was precluded from giving official support, though it could still supply food to the emigrants.

Even though its hands were often tied because of restrictions placed on immigration to the United States and other countries, JDC's Emigration Department nevertheless managed to find homes overseas for Jewish DPs. The Joint was determined not to let anyone miss the opportunity to emigrate for lack of money. The JDC arranged travel for all DPs in possession of a valid visa and, if need be, paid their passage and supplied them with the funds required by some countries as a token of their ability to support themselves after being admitted as immigrants.

The Joint's Emigration Department oversaw the entire process of resettling DPs in other countries, from procuring the necessary documents attesting to their financial status (affidavits of support) to placing them in transit camps and, ultimately, transporting them to their points of embarkation. The greatest problem was producing a birth certificate, which had to accompany any application for an immigrant visa. Most Jews had been relentlessly on the move during the Nazi period and had lost their personal papers. JDC helped the DPs correspond with the proper authorities in Eastern Europe to recover them and if need be even contacted the authorities directly on behalf of the DPs to obtain replacement copies.[20]

The first thing JDC had to do was to determine where the Jewish DPs wished to immigrate. In August 1946 Joseph J. Schwartz assumed that "a great number desired to go to Palestine since they realized that their chances of being admitted to the U.S. or other countries was slight or nonexistent."[21] Yehuda Bauer, on the other hand, was of the opinion that the majority of the Jewish DPs would have immigrated to America if the United States had relaxed its strict immigration policies before the establishment of the state of Israel.[22] It therefore remains to be determined to what extent the DPs were in agreement in calling for the creation of a Jewish state in Erets Yisrael. Surveys showed that although the majority named Palestine as their ultimate destination, in the end it was the political situation at the time and the personal circumstances of the DPs that determined to which country a person ultimately immigrated.

Whatever the original motivations or desires of the emigrants, the Joint, with offices in Belsen, Berlin, Bremen, Frankfurt, Munich, and Stuttgart, was confronted with the task of finding countries willing to accept literally thousands of Holocaust survivors. Facing the same challenge was the Hebrew Sheltering and Immigrant Aid Society, HIAS for short. Working out of Frankfurt at first, and then from early 1946 out of its newly opened office in Munich, HIAS helped potential emigrants resettle in every country other than Palestine. There was a good deal of overlap between the Joint and HIAS; both organizations served the same group of persons and sought to gain them entry to the same countries. These divided efforts on behalf of what was essentially a common concern led those in positions of responsibility to conclude much too late that only by coordinating their efforts could they optimize their effectiveness. After the Displaced Persons Coordinating Committee was created in 1949, the emigration departments of JDC and HIAS were combined in 1949 with the United Service for New Americans, which helped to facilitate the integration of new immigrants in the United States, to form United HIAS Service. At this point, however, the bulk of the Jewish DPs in Germany had already been resettled. The only remaining task was to care for the residents of Föhrenwald.

Starting in 1945, JDC and HIAS focused their efforts on resettling DPs in the United States. Nevertheless, the number of Jewish immigrants admitted to the United States was negligible, even though the Truman Directive of December 1945 had mandated the issuance of 39,000 immigrant visas for 1946, 90 percent of which had been set aside for DPs residing in Germany. The Joint facilitated the emigration to the United States of only 5,000 persons from the U.S. Zones in Germany and Austria during the first nine months of 1946, 2,758 of whom came from Germany. HIAS organized ships to transport a further 1,191 persons from the two countries. In 1947 2,665 survivors made the journey from Germany and Austria to the United States with the assistance of HIAS; the Joint brought over 3,856 DPs. In addition, JDC helped resettle 6,260 displaced persons in other countries during 1947, obtaining visas for them and providing them with clothing, food for the journey, and money. That same year HIAS managed to organize the emigration of 3,567 persons to South America, 1,435 to Australia, and 202 to Canada.[23]

The United States admitted relatively few Jewish displaced persons before 1948, so JDC was obliged to look elsewhere. After difficult and protracted negotiations, the Joint finally succeeded in persuading countries such as South Africa, Switzerland, Norway, and Sweden to admit Jewish DPs. Nevertheless, the morale of the Jews in Germany reached its nadir in the spring of 1948. Although the United Nations decision in November 1947 to partition Palestine paved the way for the creation of the state of Israel, the DPs were still waiting in the camps to emigrate. The majority continued to look for a place to resettle, for an *eitse* (some advice, a tip), as they put it. In April 1948 Samuel Haber reported that a leader of *She'erit Hapletah* had told him: "Take us to Madagascar until you can take us to some other place."[24]

By the end of June 1947, the United States had issued a total of 15,478 visas to Jewish DPs in Germany. In July 1948 the Displaced Persons Act became law, allowing 202,000 displaced persons and 3,000 displaced orphans to be admitted to the United States as non-quota immigrants. However, according to a special provision of the act, most of the admitted persons were to be ethnic German expellees and DPs from the Baltic states, thereby largely excluding Jews. Only those displaced persons who had entered the occupied zones of Germany, Austria, or Italy as refugees before 22 December 1945 were eligible. The date stipulation resulted in the automatic exclusion of the great majority of Jews who had fled from Eastern Europe in 1946. Further, because many suffered from tuberculosis, the strict health requirements eliminated another large group of Jewish DPs as prospective immigrants to the United States. Nor could they immigrate to Israel because of their inability to tolerate that country's climate. Another provision in the act stipulating that 30 percent of immigrants be "agriculturalists" also worked against Jewish DPs, most of whom were not farmers. A JDC analysis estimated that only 3.7 percent of the Jews in the U.S. Zone and 6.1 percent in the British-controlled territories might qualify as "agriculturalists."[25] President Truman, however, nominated immigration commissioners who were friendly to the Jewish DPs and used loopholes in the act to help them.

First, "Germany" was very loosely defined in the act and included the Reich's former eastern territories. Second, 40 percent of the immigrants had to be from "annexed areas" of Eastern Europe, that is, the Baltic states, eastern Poland, Bessarabia, and Bukovina. This, of course, fit the Jewish case, quite unintentionally.[26] Thus, the Displaced Persons Act of 1948, despite the provisions that discriminated against Jews, must be recognized as a landmark in the history of American immigration policy. It provided for the first time a specific agency to facilitate immigrant entry into the United States—the Displaced Persons Commission, which began formal operations in August 1948 and continued in existence until 1952. The main administrative stumbling block, however, concerned the 22 December 1945 cutoff date. When the date was advanced to 1 January 1949, Jews were no longer at a disadvantage in gaining entry to the United States.

The liberal amendments to the act came too late to help most of the Jewish DPs who had been waiting in camps in Germany. The majority had already gone to other countries and the Jewish DP problem had been largely resolved. From 1945 to 1949, however, what the Allies had originally planned as temporary residences for survivors in the Western occupation zones had evolved into something more permanent. *She'erit Hapletah* had become disillusioned as a result of the restrictive immigration policies in Palestine and elsewhere. They needed to be reenergized. Just as they were left to their own devices to accomplish things in the cultural sphere during their forced stay in Germany, the DPs ultimately had to rebuild their lives on their own. JDC workers laid the financial foundation and furnished the DPs with the habit of mind needed to reach their goal. Leading the way was the historian Koppel S. Pinson. Stationed in Frankfurt, Pinson was the JDC's educational director for displaced persons in Germany and Austria; he coordinated the Joint's cultural work in the Western occupation zones from October 1945 to September 1946. The first assistant director was Jacob M. Joslow, who was succeeded in the fall of 1946 by Dr. Philipp Friedman. Both men directed JDC's educational activities in the U.S. Zone out of the Munich office. In November the Joint organized its educational and cultural activities in the French Zone out of Munich as well. This helped the few Jews living there to expand their limited contact with Jewish relief organizations and the DPs in the U.S. Zone.

Shortly before his arrival in Germany, Pinson criticized JDC New York's lack of preparation: "We could hardly make any concrete plans in advance because we received practically no relevant information from the office." A month later he summed up the situation: "The achievements of the Education Department . . . are, to put it simply, nil . . . mainly because we lack the requisite resources."[27] However, already at the end of July 1946 Joslow was able to report that the work of the previous nine months had produced results of a more positive nature: "An appreciable increase in staff now permits proper organization and division of responsibilities with adequate attention to a few of the many problems facing the department."[28]

However, trained personnel alone did not ensure that the Joint's work in the area of education would be effective. Suitable instructional materials were needed, especially reading material. Pinson was at the forefront of the effort. In April 1946 he managed, through the intervention of Simon Rifkind, then adviser to the theater commander, to draw 20,000 books from among the hundreds of thousands in the so-called Rosenberg collection in the Offenbach Archival Depot. Alfred Rosenberg, the Nazi Party's chief "philosopher," had ordered the confiscation of books from Jewish libraries, archives, bookstores, and publishing houses. These collections included German Jewish encyclopedias; dictionaries and handbooks; classics of Yiddish and Hebrew literature; general literature in German, English, and French; and rabbinic literature. Further, the Joint financed the reprinting of numerous other books and soon set up libraries in almost all the major DP camps, with collections ranging from 500 to 4,000 volumes.[29]

The survivors had a lot to catch up on in the way of education. This was particularly true for children and young people, some of whom had never gone to school and many of whom had attended for just a few years. Hence, the Joint's main task, especially given the many children who had arrived in the camps with the adult refugees, was to establish schools, hire teachers, and acquire instructional materials.

Once the educational infrastructure had been put in place in the camps, instruction had to be standardized. In June 1946 the camp for displaced persons at Feldafing on the shores of the Starnbergersee in Bavaria was the first to require compulsory school attendance for all children between the ages of six and eighteen years of age. Furthermore, adolescents over the age of fifteen were required to spend half their day attending school and half receiving vocational training. Finally, in November 1946 the Joint announced that, together with the Central Committee of Liberated Jews and ORT representatives, it had worked out a curriculum for the first five grades and introduced compulsory education throughout the DP camps. To help make up for the shortage of instructional materials, JDC, the Jewish Agency, and the Cultural Department of the Central Committee decided at the end of 1946 to contract with two German printers to publish their own books.

Despite collaboration in specific areas such as those mentioned above, the Jewish relief organizations had not yet managed to coordinate their various efforts. It was not until February 1947 that JDC Europe, the Jewish Agency, and the Central Committee of Liberated Jews concluded an agreement establishing a Board of Education and Culture. The Board's initial meeting was on 26 March 1947, and its first director was Nachum Lewin, the representative of the Jewish Agency. Its various subcommittees covered everything from publishing, culture, and leisure-time activities to school inspection; they were staffed with equal numbers of workers from the participating organizations. Henceforth, the board was responsible for designing the cultural and educational programs for *She'erit Hapletah*.

At a country directors conference in April 1948, Samuel Haber described the Board of Education as JDC's "crowning jewel." In spite of all the difficulties, wrote Haber, "we now have some 10,000 youngsters attending schools throughout Germany. We have every conceivable kind of training a child should have. Is it as good as it should be? The answer is 'No.' It is, however, much better than anyone a year ago would have had the foresight to predict."[30]

At the beginning of the 1947 to 1948 school year, the Board of Education could boast of having hired 600 instructors and provided educational opportunities for almost 9,000 students taught in Jewish DP schools located both inside and outside the camps. The Joint had supplied not only the funds and the instructional materials but, together with the other participating organizations, had helped ensure that school would become an institution strongly rooted in the lives of the DPs.

The same desire animated the cultural activities of *She'erit Hapletah*, particularly the many theater groups that were formed in the DP camps, especially the Münchner Jüdisches Theater (Munich Jewish Theater), which was popularly known as MIKT, an acronym for Miniatur-Kunst-Theater (Miniature Art Theater). MIKT was founded in March 1946 in Reichenbach (Dzierżoniów) in Lower Silesia. Under the direction of Israel Becker, the ensemble moved to Munich in July 1946, where it became particularly well known for its outstanding productions of the plays of Sholem Aleichem. Apart from such classics of Yiddish literature, the group staged dramas based on themes that directly touched the lives of the Jewish DPs, for example, Moisei

Pinchevskii's *I'm Alive: A Hero's Drama in Three Acts,* which told the
story of Jewish survivors who had joined a partisan unit after escaping
from a concentration camp. Pinchevskii's play showed that not all
Jews were led like lambs to the slaughter and that there were examples of Jewish resistance against their persecutors. In reviewing *I'm
Alive,* the *Süddeutsche Zeitung* wrote that Jewish theater tended to be
different from theater in general. The actors not only performed and
spoke their lines; they also captivated their audience with songs
and dances. Spectators were treated to a magical world where reality
and fantasy combined:

> The stage designs are rarely sets in the traditional sense; they are rich in
> atmosphere. Those who attend a Jewish theater performance for the first
> time will be stunned by what they see and hear. . . . They will be baffled
> . . . , as the action switches from naturalistic portrayals to melodramatic
> dances that suddenly turn lyrical and then come to an equally abrupt
> surrealistic end. Those who love the theater, who are prepared to let them-
> selves be carried away, will be delighted, will be drawn into and absorbed
> by this world of dreams acted out. The Jewish theater—though it may
> perhaps be childlike and naive—is nothing if not elemental. In this sense,
> Israel Becker's production . . . is an outstanding example of Jewish
> theater.[31]

In addition to aiding larger theater companies in the towns, the
Joint and the Board of Education subsidized smaller amateur dra-
matic groups in the camps, employed mobile cinema units, and orga-
nized guest appearances for well-known foreign musical artists. In
May 1949, for example, Leonard Bernstein conducted the former
Kowno (Kaunas) ghetto orchestra and gave two concerts in the camps
at Feldafing and Föhrenwald. The orchestra had reconstituted itself
at St. Ottilien immediately after the war ended in May 1945. The
JDC and the Board also helped support the Professional Jewish Actors
Organization, founded in 1947, and the Jewish Writers and Artists
Association, established in August 1946.[32]

Despite their mutual respect and the massive assistance provided
by the Joint in the cultural sphere, it was precisely in this area that
the fundamental political differences between the Jewish survivors
and JDC, which was not an avowedly Zionist organization, came to

the fore. The seeds of conflict between the Joint on the one hand and both the prolabor DPs—who were in the majority—and the well-represented Orthodox religious minority on the other had already been sown. JDC held its first Country Director's Conference after World War II in February 1947 in Paris. In his address to the directors, Joseph J. Schwartz noted that Orthodox Jewish organizations in America exercised a powerful influence over the Orthodox Jews living in Germany. He went on to say that JDC could not resolve its problems with these organizations by simply excluding them from Jewish life. To illustrate his point he referred to Va'ad Hahatzalah (Rescue Committee), a rabbinic organization originally established in 1939 as a subsidiary of the ultra-Orthodox Agudat Israel, whose mission was to save Orthodox Jews during the Holocaust:

> The Vaad Hazala exists and let us not try to talk ourselves out of it, for regardless of what the JDC says and how forthright the JDC is about it, with the Vaad Hazala you will always find a lot of people in the United States who would rather trust a Rabbi with a beard than Mr. Paul Baerwald [JDC New York] who does not have a beard and does not observe the Sabbath. It is the same way as a lot of people will support the Jewish Labour party and not the JDC and that is because they are labourers and they don't want to have anything to do with the JDC because somebody who is a capitalist is on the JDC Board. You have got to have in a country like the United States, which is organized the way it is, special interest groups. . . . It may take another three or five years to put the Vaad Hazala out of business. In the meantime we have to realize that we have to go on with our work. . . . The policy of the JDC is not to do a direct job but to work through local existing organizations . . . and as soon as we have semblance of good decent local organization in places like Germany and in Austria, we are going to work through them. We have worked with the Central Committee and we will continue to work with them. There will be frictions because the committee is new and the JDC is new to that situation and it will take a little time.[33]

In essence, the problems were due to the fact that Va'ad Hahatzalah focused exclusively on promoting the interests of the Orthodox survivors and their religious concerns, whereas the Joint, given its basically liberal political and religious outlook, was committed to supporting all the Jewish DPs. Differences arose mainly with regard to emigration. U.S. immigration laws allowed the entry of rabbis and rabbinical students without regard to quota limitations, that is, treatment that was preferential when compared to that given to other DPs. Further, it was assumed that a number of those who had placed themselves in the care of Va'ad Hahatzalah had done so simply with an eye to gaining entry to the United States. The Joint, on the other hand, was obliged to provide for the majority of emigrant DPs, and they gave JDC a taste of the anger they felt at the preferential treatment accorded to a select few. Since it was not enough to have a visa in order to emigrate, JDC ultimately had to charter ships and even arrange transportation to ports of departure for the nonquota emigrants. Try as it might, the Joint could not free itself from these obligations. Therefore, at the 1947 Paris conference, Joseph J. Schwartz proposed that JDC enter into agreements with Va'ad Hahatzalah and Agudat Israel that would relieve emigrants of the burden of having to apply for the necessary documents individually and allow them to expedite the process by applying for visas on a group basis. At the same time, Schwartz noted that the problem of preferential treatment for clergymen and religious students would soon resolve itself, since the number of rabbis and rabbinical students was not infinite.[34]

Va'ad Hahatzalah was at odds with both the Joint and the Central Committee of Liberated Jews, even though the Central Committee had no particular religious agenda. Despite these differences, the Va'ad managed to achieve some important things before it closed its offices in Munich in 1951, particularly in the area of education and especially under the leadership of Rabbi Nathan Baruch, who directed its activities from 1945 to 1949. The Va'ad established religious schools and yeshivas (institutes of Talmudic learning) in practically every DP camp. In the towns of Aschau, Bad Nauheim, Hogeismar, Lindenfels, Munich, Rosenheim, Ulm, and Wasserburg, it set up children's homes. At Deggendorf the Va'ad opened the first and only home for the elderly inside a DP camp in Germany.[35] The Joint was actively involved with the Va'ad in setting up these facilities, and like the DP camps JDC included them in its supply and distribution network.

Regardless of the degree to which JDC was involved or not involved in the cultural sphere, it continued to deliver needed supplies and provide relief for as long as it remained active in Germany. In May and June 1947, for example, the Joint distributed 1.2 million pounds of food and 471,830 packs of cigarettes. A year earlier JDC had determined that it would distribute rations strictly on the basis of need rather than arbitrarily. In March 1948 the Joint reorganized its relief operations in order to preclude the discretionary distribution of rations by the camp committees responsible for receiving and issuing supplies. Until then the committees tended to give preferential treatment to their political cronies. At that time the Joint was feeding 85,000 persons in the U.S. Zone (excluding Berlin) from the 500 to 550 tons of food that it imported every month from abroad and stored in its ten warehouses in Germany. Of these 85,000 DPs, 30,000 were placed in the so-called laborer category; they performed various services in the camps or worked in trade schools. The remaining 55,000 were classified according to specific social categories—for example, pregnant women, nursing mothers, disabled persons, and so on—and food rations were allocated accordingly.[36]

Strangely enough, until 1948 the Joint complied with the request of the Central Committee in the U.S. Zone to exclude from its distribution network Jews living in the Jewish communities (*Kultusgemeinden*) in Germany. In the British Zone, on the other hand, German Jewish communities had from the outset been included in JDC's relief program, because the local Jewish communities were on better terms with the Central Committee of the British Zone than their counterparts in the U.S. Zone were with their central committee. In any case, the fact that most German Jews were excluded from JDC's relief efforts cannot be attributed solely to a negative attitude on the part of the Central Committee of the U.S. Zone. Part of the reason was that the *Kultusgemeinden* refused to accept Jewish DPs who wished to become members of their communities. Without looking more deeply into the causes of the problem, however, the Joint uncritically sided with the Central Committee, bolstering the position of other non-German relief organizations, which—like the majority of the DPs—completely rejected the idea of rebuilding Jewish life in Germany.

After receiving numerous complaints from German Jews and their relief organizations—for example, the Bayerisches Hilfswerk für die von den Nürnberger Gesetzen Betroffenen (Bavarian Aid Society for

Those Affected by the Nuremberg Laws), which had been active since May 1945—JDC finally began to provide proper rations for German Jews as well.[37] Up to that time the German Jews had been given extra rations only on the Jewish High Holy Days. On 1 January 1948, disregarding the Central Committee's interventions, the Joint included German Jews in its food distribution network.[38]

The DPs Learn to Help Themselves

The Central Committees of Liberated Jews

With the late arrival of the Jewish relief organizations, the survivors soon realized that they themselves would have to shoulder the responsibility for shaping their own future. In the British Zone, Josef Rosensaft and nine other survivors, including Rosensaft's future wife, Hadassa Bimko, and Rabbi Zvi Azaria, established the first Temporary Committee of Liberated Jews in April 1945, just a few days after liberation. The committee remained active until the First Congress of *She'erit Hapletah* met in the British Zone from 25 to 27 September 1945. Rosensaft was born in 1911 in Będzin, Poland. He had survived the concentration camps at Auschwitz and Dora/Nordhausen before being liberated at Bergen-Belsen in April 1945.

For their part, the survivors in the French Zone did not establish a Central Committee until December 1945. The local Jewish communities (*Kultusgemeinden*) and DP camps sent one person each to represent them on the committee. The committee was headed by Abraham Hochhäuser and headquartered in Konstanz in the southern sector of the French Zone, where Eastern European Jews made up the majority of the DP population. Most of the surviving German Jews lived in the northern sector. The German Jews felt that they were adequately represented by their newly established communities, located in Koblenz, Kreznach, Landau, Mainz, Neuwied, Saarbrücken, and Trier, as well as by the Landesverband der jüdischen Gemeinden Rheinland-Pfalz (Association of Jewish Communities of the Rhineland-Palatinate).[1] Following the Central Committee elections of August 1947, Hochhäuser was replaced by Chaim Erenberg, a native of Warsaw. Erenberg presided over an executive committee of five, whose four subcommittees were responsible for the care and feeding of some 600 Jews.[2] However, with only several hundred Jews to provide for, the Central Committee for the French Zone was relatively insignificant.

Zalman Grinberg, a young doctor from Kowno (Kaunas), and Abraham J. Klausner, a U.S. Army chaplain, were instrumental in establishing a separate organization for *She'erit Hapletah* in the U.S. Zone. Along with 500 other Jewish inmates of Dachau's satellite camp at Kaufering, Grinberg was liberated at Schwabhausen in Bavaria as he was being transferred by the Nazis in a railway freight car headed to the Tyrol. After the train had been strafed by American warplanes and the SS men guarding the transport had taken flight, Grinberg managed to get his 500 fellow inmates, some of whom had been seriously wounded, to the nearby Benedictine monastery of St. Ottilien near Landsberg. During the war the Germans had transformed the monastery into a military hospital. When Grinberg arrived, the monastery was still in German hands, and he found a number of wounded German and Hungarian soldiers there. Thanks to Grinberg's determination and resolve, the German medical director was persuaded that if he wished to facilitate relations with the Americans before they actually took over the hospital, he would be well advised to admit Jewish survivors. After the evacuation of the non-Jewish patients, the former Kowno ghetto doctor succeeded in establishing a smoothly running Jewish hospital at St. Ottilien that continued treating people until 1948, when the monastery was returned to its monks.

The interaction between Grinberg and Klausner, two dynamic individuals who were present "at the creation," as it were, marked the beginning of their collaboration on the political level. Both considered it essential that the army provide the liberated Jews with food rations, medical care, and financial assistance. However, they also felt that only an organization built by the survivors themselves could truly meet the DPs' special needs.

The first meeting organized by *She'erit Hapletah* took place on 27 May 1945 at St. Ottilien. The former Kowno ghetto orchestra gave a concert of Yiddish and Hebrew songs for the patients. Of its forty-five original members, only its conductor, Michael Hofmekler, and eight other performers had survived the Holocaust. In his welcoming address Grinberg expressed the feelings of those present: "We have met here to celebrate our liberation. However, this is also a day of mourning. We are free but we do not yet grasp what it really means to be free, perhaps because we still stand in the shadow of death."[3] The concert symbolized and demonstrated not only what Isaac Rattner, editor of the soon-to-be-published Yiddish newspaper *Unzer Veg* (*Our Way*), meant when he said, "*Mir zeinen do*" ("We are here"). It also reflected the first stirrings of an emerging self-confidence among Jews living on German soil. In his 27 May address, Grinberg pointed the way to the deliberations that five weeks later would lead to the establishment of the Central Committee of Liberated Jews in Bavaria, or ZK for short (an acronym derived from its Yiddish name, Tsentral-Komitet, the German Romanization of the Yiddish original being Zentral Komitet). On 1 July 1945 representatives from forty-one large and small Jewish DP camps throughout Bavaria met to set up a permanent committee. Since the American military had not yet extended official recognition, it was obliged to call itself an "information bureau." For the time being, the committee established its headquarters in what had been a barracks for German antiaircraft units. When UNRRA appeared on the scene, the committee moved to the Deutsches Museum and finally to the Munich headquarters of the Joint on Siebertstraße.[4]

A resolution passed at Feldafing on 1 July 1945 reflected the events of the recent past:

> In the shadow of the gas chambers and the fires of the crematoria, in view of the Jewish blood that has been spilled, we call upon the former Jewish [concentration camp] inmates in Bavaria, upon the *yishuv* in Erets Yisrael, upon the whole Jewish people, to unite and forget the partisan struggles that have deprived the Jews of so much of their strength and blood, so that together we may build a Jewish state! During the darkest days in the ghettos and concentration camps, we who bore the brunt of the suffering kept our common dream alive. Now we wish to see that dream become a reality. When we arrive in Palestine we intend with all our strength to support the sacred work of unification![5]

Yet the unity for which the Central Committee was pleading would remain a utopian wish. The growing politicization of *She'erit Hapletah,* which had begun as early as 1946, together with the differences between the two Central Committees—the committee that had been established in the British Zone and its counterpart in the U.S. Zone—showed that, despite their common suffering, the gaps separating the Jews had not been bridged. Moreover, to these conflicts was added the problem of discrimination against German Jews by the Central Committee for the U.S. Zone.

The seeds of conflict are to be found not only in the differences between Western European and Eastern European Jewry and the traditional Jewish agreement to disagree but also in the nature of the various survivors' experiences during the period of persecution. *She'erit Hapletah* had made the ideals of Zionism the focus of their efforts. However, differing views as to how to realize those ideals and the attempt by some German Jewish survivors to rebuild their lives in their former homeland soon caused frictions. The ZK, however, never publicly debated its differences with the German Jews; rather, it concentrated its energies on becoming the sole representative of the Jewish survivors. According to its charter, the Central Committee of Liberated Jews in Bavaria was to represent all Jews living in or resident on the territory of the state of Bavaria. Yet, without even introducing an amendment, it went on to assume responsibility for the "Jewish communities in the other south German states (Hesse and Württemberg-Baden)."[6] Thus, by 1 July 1945 the ZK had laid the foundation for expanding its influence over the entire U.S. Zone.

Six months later, on 27 January 1946, at the First Congress of Liberated Jews, held in the Munich city hall, the ZK was formally given responsibility for the whole of the U.S. Zone. Incidentally, David Ben-Gurion, who would later become Israel's first prime minister, attended the congress. The first chairman of the Central Committee of Liberated Jews in the U.S. Zone was Dr. Zalman Grinberg, who had occupied the same position on the Temporary Committee. He was followed in July 1946 by David Treger, an accountant and journalist, also from Kowno. Grinberg subsequently immigrated to Palestine, where he became the medical director of the Beilinson Hospital in Petach Tikva. Dr. Samuel Gringauz, a lawyer and leader of the DP camp at Landsberg, became the chairman of the Council of Liberated Jews, the second most important body within the ZK after the Presidium. He, too, was from Kowno and had worked for the Zionist underground in the Kaufering concentration camp. He held the office of chairman until he immigrated to the United States in 1947.

Planning for a Single Organization to Represent the Jewish Survivors in the Western Occupation Zones of Germany

Jewish Brigade soldiers organized a General Jewish Survivors' Conference that met at St. Ottilien on 25 July 1945. Participants were brought in from all over Germany and Austria. Ninety-four delegates, including Josef Rosensaft from Belsen, were present, representing some 40,000 Jews from thirty DP camps. Separate committees had already been set up both in occupied Germany and Austria. The purpose of the conference was to lay the foundation for a single central committee of liberated Jews throughout western Germany. As it turned out, the French Zone played no part in the negotiations. The delegates elected an executive committee of five, a preparatory committee of eight, and a "Temporary Central Committee" that was set to meet in Munich for two months.[7]

It had become apparent at the fourth meeting of the Temporary Central Committee in Munich in early August that the Belsen committee's willingness to be run by a committee representing all of Germany was quickly evaporating. The members of the Temporary Central Committee therefore let it be known that they would not take part in the Congress of Liberated Jews in the British Zone, planned for the fall, unless the British committee declared the congress an extension of the general conference of 25 July. Despite their misgivings, the members of the Temporary Central Committee nevertheless sent a delegation to a preparatory conference held at Belsen in early September 1945,[8] during which an agenda was worked out for the forthcoming meeting of delegates from the Western zones of occupation.

Despite a ban by the British military authorities, Josef Rosensaft nevertheless opened the First Congress of Liberated Jews in the British Zone at the Belsen DP camp on 25 September. The participants included representatives of the British Labour Party and the Jewish Brigade as well as the well-known London-based mathematics professor and Zionist leader Selig Brodetsky. However, the Central Committee of Jews in Bavaria never received an invitation to attend the three-day meeting. At a gathering of the Bavarian Central Committee on 7 October, Isaac Rattner said that the reason the committee had not taken part in this major event was that it had not been informed when the congress was to be held. After admitting their oversight, the Belsen people apologized, citing a "communications breakdown." Rattner acknowledged that the most important decision to be made at the congress was to "establish a Joint Central Committee for Germany," consisting of five representatives each from Belsen and Munich plus two representatives from Hesse-Nassau. After he had finished making his remarks, Rattner announced that six delegates from Munich would travel to Frankfurt for the first meeting of the Joint Central Committee on 10 October 1945.[9]

However, after a fruitless second meeting on 19 November 1945 in Frankfurt, the plan to establish a Joint Central Committee was postponed pending the meeting of the First Congress of Liberated Jews in the U.S. Zone, which was to be held from 27 to 28 January 1946. The subject of a Joint Central Committee once again came up for discussion at the first meeting[10] of the newly elected Central Committee for the U.S. Zone on 29 January. Participants included a seven-member delegation from the Central Committee for the British Zone together with the delegation's leader, Josef Rosensaft; all had been invited to attend the congress. Though they decided to have another meeting later, cooperation between the DP representatives in the American and British Zones was nominal, until the U.S. and British Central Committees were finally dissolved in 1950 and 1951, respectively. Contemporary witnesses such as Leo W. Schwarz and Samuel Haber attributed the failure to implement a Joint Central Committee—an idea that had been pursued with such energy at first—to Josef Rosensaft's indecisiveness. Rosensaft feared that the Munich committee would become too powerful and therefore refused to participate in the project.[11]

Relations between the Central Committees
in the American and British Zones

Rosensaft's fears may not have been totally unfounded, however. Since the end of 1945, the Central Committee for the U.S. Zone had represented a significantly larger number of Jewish survivors and would certainly have demanded a correspondingly greater role in decision making. At the same time, Rosensaft must have realized that the Central Committee for the U.S. Zone was more democratic, better organized, and possessed greater legitimacy than the Belsen committee.[12]

The debates at the first joint meeting on 25 July 1945 made it clear that what some on the British committee disapproved of most was the democratic structure of the American committee. The people in Munich, the seat of the ZK, firmly believed that the camp committees should be organized on a democratic basis, modeled on the DP camp at Feldafing, which in early July 1945 had become the first camp in Germany to carry out elections for chairman. The Belsen representatives, on the other hand, feared that such actions would serve only to limit the power of the local zonal groups. This is probably the reason why the Belsen camp did not actually have its own committee until the spring of 1947 and why the ZK was for a time the only DP committee operating in the British Zone. Even when the Belsen DPs finally elected a local committee in March 1947, there was no guarantee that it would be independent or able to make decisions freely, despite the fact it was composed of representatives from nearly all the major political parties. Once again, Rosensaft assumed the position of chairman. But Rosensaft was not alone in keeping in his own hands the reins of power over both the camp committee and the zonal committee; Samuel Weintraub, for instance, served as the head of the provisioning office for both committees.

Harry Viteles, a JDC worker who lived in Palestine and visited the British Zone in April 1946, was critical of developments there. In his summary report he wrote that the

Central Committee of the Federation of Liberated Jews in the British Zone appeared to have less competent men, and a poorer administration than the Central Committee of its counterpart in the U.S. Zone. Whatever the reasons for this difference may be the fact remained that the Committee in the British Zone was less well thought of both by the people themselves [the DPs] and by the Authorities. Complaints against it were that it showed partiality to the residents of Belsen in the distribution of supplies; that it was badly organized and bureaucratic; that nepotism prevents able and honest people from joining the Committee and that the Committee was not democratically elected. Some of these allegations were not without foundation. It might be added that the accounts of the Central Committee in the U.S. Zone were submitted and audited by its own Auditing Committee while the accounts of the Committee in the British Zone had not been submitted.[13]

The Auditing Committee, which consisted of five members, had been established at the same time as the Central Committee for the U.S. Zone, that is, in January 1946. Besides carrying out audits of the Central Committee's books, the Auditing Committee was responsible for reviewing the work of the committee in general. At the Second Congress of Liberated Jews in the British Zone, which took place from 20 to 22 July 1947 in Belsen and Bad Harzburg, the newly elected Central Committee—once again under the chairmanship of Josef Rosensaft—established a three-member Control Commission.[14]

Congress delegates also instituted a new council. Forming part of the Central Committee of Liberated Jews, the council was composed of thirty-six members representing all the Jewish communities and committees in the British Zone. The inclusion of the local Jewish communities and the influence exercised by their representatives over the British Central Committee by way of the council highlights one of the major differences between it and the Central Committee for the U.S. Zone. In the British Zone of Occupation, the survivors, in particular the Central Committee, played a decisive role in rebuilding German Jewish communities in postwar Germany. From the outset, cooperation between the DPs and German Jews produced positive results. The British Zone was largely untouched by the mass influx of refugees from Eastern Europe; most of the Jews who infiltrated into the British Zone of Germany were in transit to the U.S. Zone. So Eastern European Jews had relatively little impact on conditions in the British Zone, making it easier for the DPs and the local Jewish communities to develop closer ties—ties that in the U.S. Zone were more often the exception than the rule.

Josef Rosensaft was a pivotal figure in promoting a forward-looking policy of cooperation. Rosensaft and Norbert Wollheim, the vice chairman of the Central Committee for the British Zone, established contact with German Jewish survivors, championed the establishment of federations of Jewish communities in the various German states, and played a prominent role in creating the Zentralrat der Juden in Deutschland (Central Council of Jews in Germany), which was inaugurated on 19 July 1950 in Frankfurt. Members of the first directorate of the Zentralrat included the following persons: Philipp Auerbach, the Bavarian state commissioner for the racially, religiously, and politically persecuted; Heinz Galinski, who was to head the Berlin Jewish community for many years to come and later became chairman of the Zentralrat; Benno Ostertag, a lawyer specializing in compensating the victims of Nazism; Pesach Piekatch and Chaskiel Eife, two members of the Central Committee for the U.S. Zone; and finally Rosensaft and Wollheim.[15] Together they laid the foundation for the most important organization of Jews in Germany. At the same time, the Central Committee for the British Zone managed to break through the barriers of "ghetto" life in the DP camps. The Jews living in the DP camps of the U.S. Zone, however, had an ideal environment for preserving the Eastern European Jewish way of life; the isolated atmosphere—set apart from German society and the traditions of German Jews—obliged them to recall their traditions.

Official Recognition of the Central Committee for the U.S. Zone

By focusing its attention on the DPs living in the camps, the Central Committee for the U.S. Zone was in effect discriminating against Jews who opposed its ideas. This is the reason why articles 9 and 10 of the charter of the First Central Committee for the U.S. Zone, adopted after the election of 28 January 1946, became a matter of dispute. In its charter the committee claimed to be successor to the former German Jewish communities, associations, and federations, including successor to the rights of their assets. Basically, the ZK sought to finance its operations from proceeds derived from property in the U.S. Zone formerly owned by the Reichsvereinigung der Juden in Deutschland (Reich Organization of Jews in Germany) as well as from the personal assets once held by German Jews. Further, the committee wished to be awarded reparations for crimes committed against the Jews and to be given both the property of the former German Jewish communities and the assets of Jews who had died without leaving heirs.[16] This would have effectively precluded Jews from receiving reparations had they refused to become members of the Central Committee. The newly established Central Committee of Liberated Jews in Bavaria in fact enacted guidelines to this effect at its 19 August 1945 meeting. The resolution it passed stated that the committee would not deal with the local Jewish communities and that only Jews who—as was laid down in February 1946—had joined a Jewish committee would be accorded the same rights as displaced persons.

On the surface, the arguments advanced by the Central Committee sounded quite convincing; JDC, in fact, was sufficiently persuaded at first to abide by the resolutions passed by the ZK. The Joint as well as UNRRA unhesitatingly recognized the Central Committee as the sole representative of the Jewish survivors, despite the fact that its claim to be the leader of the Jewish DPs was not based on democratic principles. Recognition by UNRRA and JDC, however, did not confer full legitimacy on the Central Committee; the ZK could achieve that status only with the approval of the military authorities. Articles 9 and 10 of the charter turned out to be major obstacles to official recognition of the ZK. Members of the staff of General Joseph T. McNarney, Eisenhower's successor as the commanding general of U.S. forces in Germany, studied the charter and were appalled at the political and financial demands it imposed. They reported that the Central Committee would not be formally recognized until it had written a new democratic charter and had renounced its claim to be the sole representative of the Jewish survivors.

After the Central Committee amended the articles as requested, General McNarney signed the document on 7 September 1946 in Frankfurt in his capacity as U.S. military governor. The amended charter laid out the committee's areas of responsibility in three articles.[17]

The granting of official recognition to the Central Committee for the U.S. Zone marked a turning point in American policy toward the DPs. Despite the unsatisfactory conditions in which the DPs were forced to live, the U.S. military was persuaded that they had nevertheless made sufficient progress toward democracy to take the first steps in the direction of self-government.[18] Given the restrictive policy of the British with regard to the DPs, it is hardly surprising that the Central Committee in its zone was unable to secure official recognition, even though it had made numerous representations to the British military authorities and had been accepted by them as the de facto representative of the Jews in the British Zone.

In spite of the fact that the U.S. Army continued to keep a watchful eye on the ZK's activities and was intent on keeping it out of politics and confined to the social sphere, its power grew. The ZK ultimately regarded itself as the official representative of the Jews in the U.S. Zone. In fact, the committee's influence increased to the point that ORT, which had been operating independently, eventually had to subordinate itself administratively to the ZK. Starting on 23 October 1946, ORT was even obliged to call its training facilities "ORT schools attached to the Central Committee." The Central Committee henceforth viewed itself as a kind of Jewish government inside the U.S. Zone. In gaining administrative control over ORT, the ZK harked back to the prewar period, when ORT had come under the purview of the education ministries of the countries in which it operated.[19] Interestingly, the Central Committee for the British Zone could more legitimately lay claim to be the sole representative of the Jews living in its zone, since, unlike its U.S. counterpart, it refused to exclude the local Jewish communities in Germany.

Both committees gradually developed into states within the state in their respective zones, with their own elected "government," a kind of "parliament," and their own "ministries," together with their various administrative subdivisions. As specified in the charter, a congress was held annually and officers were elected to the Presidium and the council. First, though, elections were held in the camp and regional committees. The winning candidates then formed a group of electors, who selected the delegates to the congress. The procedure resembled the electoral college system in the United States. There was one delegate for every 500 Jews. Finally, the ZK Congress chose the thirty members of the Presidium, the council and its chairman, and the

nine-member Executive Committee, whose chairman was simultaneously appointed head of the Central Committee. The council in its
turn nominated the three members of an Auditing Committee, all of
whom were prohibited from serving on the council or the Executive
Committee.[20] The Central Committee for the British Zone followed
similar procedures. After its Second Congress in July 1947 in Bad
Harzburg (which turned out to be its last), the Central Committee
for the British Zone ended up with nine members plus Josef Rosensaft, the chairman, Norbert Wollheim, the vice chairman, and Berl
Laufer, the general secretary. Further, the congress appointed a council consisting of thirty-six members plus a chairman and a vice chairman as well as a control commission made up of three members.[21]

The differences between the two Central Committees consisted in
the number and kind of administrative divisions that came under the
Presidium. Nevertheless, both committees had a cultural department
and a rabbinate as well as their own health department, even though
the British committee's health department was not a separate entity
but came under the council's vice chairperson, Dr. Hadassa Bimko-
Rosensaft. In addition, the ZK had the following special divisions: a
public relations department with its own radio and news service; a
provisioning department responsible for distributing goods supplied
by JDC and other relief organizations; a department of labor and industry to which the ORT had to report beginning in October 1946
and responsibility for which was transferred to the Jewish Agency on
18 November 1947; a legal department; an athletic and transportation department; and a locating service.[22]

Politicization and Dissolution

In the British Zone, the Second Congress of She'erit Hapletah, which
met in July 1947, was the last to be held there; that is, the composition of the Central Committee remained essentially the same until it was finally dissolved on 15 August 1951. Any changes that took
place were made without the elections called for in the charter. In the
U.S. Zone, on the other hand, the Second Congress of She'erit Hapletah,
held in February 1947, was followed by a third, which met from 30
March to 2 April 1948 in Bad Reichenhall.

As early as the Second Congress it was clear that *She'erit Hapletah* were becoming deeply politicized. After the World Zionist Organization's congress in Basel in December 1946, twenty-seven political leaders from Palestine entered the U.S. Zone to teach survivors about the principles of Zionism. The result was that by early 1947 thirteen branches of the traditional Jewish political parties—from the right-wing Revisionists to the religious groupings to the various labor parties—had been formed in Munich and had considerable influence on the outcome of elections to the congress. However, politicization also led to serious confrontations that ultimately undermined the power of the committee to hold its constituents together.

Sharp disputes arose over questions regarding the establishment and structure of the future Jewish state. The Central Committee's ability to influence the decision-making process with regard to the creation of the state of Israel had diminished markedly, particularly when compared to the role it had played at the Second Congress. The January 1946 congress in Munich had put the demands for a Jewish homeland in Erets Yisrael on the world stage. David Ben-Gurion's speech, aimed at Truman, Stalin, and Bevin, was especially important in helping to arouse world opinion and inform the public about the plight of *She'erit Hapletah*.

Since charismatic leaders such as Ben-Gurion did not attend the Second Congress of *She'erit Hapletah* in Bad Reichenhall, it failed to attract the same international attention or have much of an impact beyond the Jewish DPs themselves. Further, the fate of the Jewish survivors was no longer the focus of negotiations regarding the establishment of the Jewish state. The political interests of the governments in London, Washington, and Moscow now took precedence over any humanitarian concerns.

The elections of 27 February 1947 in Bad Reichenhall were won by a labor coalition under the leadership of the moderate socialist Labor Party (Mapai); old-line members of the Central Committee were no longer a factor. Political interests sometimes even overshadowed the practical work of the committee. People complained increasingly about its lack of effectiveness and its authoritarian leadership style. The main reason for the growing dissatisfaction, of course, was the fact that the DPs were still waiting in the camps after having pinned their hopes in vain on the Central Committee to facilitate their emigration. Their disaffection was clearly reflected in the elections to the Third Congress of *She'erit Hapletah* in March 1948. Just 7 percent of those eligible to vote actually went to the polls; the Mapai won only 20 percent of the votes cast, losing to the left-wing United Zionist Socialists List (UZSL). UZSL eventually formed a coalition with the Orthodox religious Zionist Mizrachi Party, which had captured 59 percent of the delegates' votes.[23] After the founding of the state of Israel in May 1948, the best and most influential members of the Central Committee—men such as David Treger and Leon Retter—left for Israel in the first wave of emigration in order to participate in the building of their new homeland. Criticism of the Central Committee only grew more vociferous. In spite of its considerable differences with and lukewarm support from the DPs, the Central Committee still regarded itself as the representative of all the Jewish survivors in the U.S. Zone.

At the Third Congress and for the last time, delegates elected a new Presidium according to the rules of the charter and chose David Treger as its head. It was not long, though, before the first signs of disintegration appeared. After the proclamation of a Jewish state in Palestine, the Central Committee began transferring its funds and sending the archives of its Historical Commission to Israel. The committee had created the commission on 4 November 1945 as a division of its cultural and education departments. In addition to its other work, the commission published a periodical called *Fun letstn Churbn* (*From the Last Catastrophe*), which dealt with the history of the Jewish people during the Nazi period. One of the first attempts to document the Holocaust, the journal contained articles ranging from reports on the wholesale destruction of Jewish communities to descriptions of life in the concentration camps to eyewitness accounts of the liquidation of the ghettos and extermination camps. The editorial committee, which was also in charge of the Historical Commission, was concerned primarily with documenting how, despite their persecution, the Jews were still capable of cultural achievements. The editors published songs that had been written in the concentration camps and ghettos as well as personal records of work done in the ghetto schools and other facilities. Particularly impressive was a series of reports in which children described their experiences during the war. JDC director Leo W. Schwarz published excerpts from the recollections of these children in his 1949 book *The Root and the Bough*.[24] For three years the Historical Commission collected documents—nearly 5,000 statistical surveys and over 1,000 eyewitness accounts—archiving them in its Munich headquarters and its thirty-seven branch offices. Some of the material was published in *Fun letstn Churbn*. In December 1948 all the documents were shipped to Israel, where they became part of the Yad Vashem Archives in Jerusalem.[25]

The employees of the commission immigrated to Israel in 1949. Incidentally, the Central Committee in the British Zone also had an Historical Commission, headquartered in Göttingen. David Treger, who had served as chairman of the ZK since July 1946, immigrated to Israel on 1 November 1948 and handed over his office to Pesach Piekatch. Piekatch was born in Łódź, Poland, had survived the war in Siberia, and came to Germany during the mass exodus of Jews from Eastern Europe.

At a meeting of the council in February 1949 at the Hofbräuhaus in Munich, it was decided that there would be no more elections to *She'erit Hapletah*'s main governing bodies; that is, there would not be a fourth congress. A year later, on 16 March 1950, a resolution was passed setting up a "Liquidation Committee" to gradually close the ZK's various departments and end its work in Germany. On 17 December 1950, the ZK officially ceased its activities in the U.S. Zone. In a solemn ceremony at the Deutsches Museum in Munich, Rabbi Samuel Abba Snieg, the only one of the ZK's original members still remaining in Germany, delivered a farewell address in which he pointed to the Central Committee's efforts in helping to set up the DP camps, establish schools and social institutions, and organize religious life in the U.S. Zone. Together with Boruch Leiserowski and Samuel Jacob Ros, Snieg had for five years directed the work of Va'ad Harabanim, the Rabbinate of the Central Committee of Liberated Jews in the U.S. Zone.[26]

It was during this period of dissolution—or, as *She'erit Hapletah* called it, using the old Nazi term, the "liquidation phase"—that the Jewish DPs achieved perhaps one of their greatest successes: the reprinting of the Babylonian Talmud in nineteen volumes, which came to be known as the Survivors' Talmud. The idea of printing Judaism's most important religious book (after the Bible) in the very country responsible for the destruction of nearly all the monuments of Jewish

culture in Europe originated in the winter of 1945 as the brainchild
of the Orthodox rabbis of Va'ad Harabanim. The project was initiated
by Rabbi Snieg and the younger Rabbi Ros, who, like so many of the
leaders of *She'erit Hapletah,* came from Kowno (Kaunas) and had been
liberated in Dachau or its satellite camps. In carrying out their duties,
the rabbis were particularly concerned with the training of Orthodox
Jews and students of the Talmud. Wherever they established institutions of religious study and worship, however, they could no longer
find a complete set of the Talmud, the basis of any course of Jewish
religious study. With the support of the Central Committee, the two
rabbis entered into negotiations with the U.S. Army, since only the
military could locate a photoengraving firm with appropriate film
and equipment and procure the tons of paper—a very rare commod-
ity at the time—necessary to complete the project. After a series of
protracted discussions and a number of setbacks, the Central Committee finally contracted with a Heidelberg firm to do the job. The
first fifty sets of the complete edition, based on the Vilna Talmud,
appeared in 1949. Each set was dedicated to the United States Army
of Occupation in Germany. On page 1 of each volume were sketches
of camps and barbed wire, of palm trees from the Holy Land, reminis-
cent of the trees symbolizing *She'erit Hapletah,* with the underside of
their trunks lying lifeless on the ground while the stumps sprouted
fresh shoots. Not only was it astounding that such an enormous project originated in Germany, but also that it received DM 200,000
from various German sources. The Joint invested an equivalent amount
in order to print an additional 1,000 sets for distribution worldwide,
shipping them in 1951 to major libraries in the United States, Canada, South Africa, Europe, and Israel.[27]

Föhrenwald

A description of life in the camp at Föhrenwald is an ideal way to gain insight into the complex history of the Jewish DPs. This "waiting room" for displaced persons, as Zalman Grinberg once called the DP camps, continued to function until February 1957—longer than any other DP camp in Germany and nearly twelve years after the Jews had been liberated from Nazi rule. Since the Nazi regime itself had lasted about twelve years, some displaced persons ended up spending nearly the same amount of time in surroundings that evoked the terrible memories of the concentration camps, robbed them of any sense of privacy, and subjected them to the stringent rules of camp life. Worst of all, however, the residents of the camps were forced to live on German soil for twelve years and watch as the country that had caused the Jewish tragedy grew increasingly prosperous and was again accepted into the family of civilized nations, while they, the DPs, had to struggle simply to rebuild their lives. The residents of Föhrenwald endured all the joys and suffering that characterized the history of the Jewish DPs in general: from the bitter and nerve-racking struggle to obtain more entrance certificates for Palestine— their destination of choice—to the euphoria that accompanied the creation of the state of Israel and finally to the difficult transition to German administration and the long-drawn-out process of closing the camp and finding other places for the old and the sick to stay.

The Föhrenwald "assembly center" was situated some 25 kilometers (17 miles) southwest of Munich near the village of Wolfratshausen, currently the Waldram section of the town of Wolfratshausen. I. G. Farben had built Föhrenwald at the beginning of the war in 1939 as a planned community for its workers. The German chemical giant operated several hidden munitions factories in the woods outside of town. Under the Nazis, Föhrenwald rarely exceeded the maximum of 3,200 residents for which it had been designed.[1] In July 1944, there were just 1,390 employees still residing there, half Germans and half foreign workers.[2] Immediately after liberation in May 1945, the U.S. Army set up an international DP camp at Föhrenwald. At first the army used the camp to house the families of former Soviet slave laborers. After the Russians left in June, some 3,000 non-Jewish DPs from Poland, Yugoslavia, Hungary, and the Baltic states moved in.[3] During the summer of 1945, they lived in the camp together with approximately 200 Jewish DPs, most of whom had come from Lithuania. Allied air attacks had enabled these Jews to escape from the infamous Dachau Transport, the "death march" from the Dachau concentration camp to the Tyrol, where Hitler planned to establish an Alpine republic (*Alpenrepublik*).[4]

In the late summer of 1945 it had become clear that the Landsberg and Feldafing camps, already exclusively Jewish, were seriously overcrowded and that the housing problem could be solved only by establishing another Jewish camp in the vicinity of Munich. This was when the spotlight first fell on Föhrenwald. At the time, however, UNRRA and the U.S. Army advocated placing orphans and families of all nationalities in the Föhrenwald camp, since the accommodations there were better than those in other camps, where housing often consisted of nothing more than poorly insulated barracks. The groups of four small row houses at Föhrenwald, on the other hand, were equipped with central heating and shared bathroom facilities and thus were well suited for winter conditions. Consequently, the housing development did not require any structural alterations or the investment of additional funds. Outwardly, the only change from the Nazi period occurred when the streets were renamed in honor of the states of the United States of America.

In September 1945, after the results of the Harrison Report had induced U.S. commanders to change their policy toward the Jewish DPs, the Americans once again directed their attention toward Föhrenwald. On 17 September General Eisenhower visited Feldafing to attend Yom Kippur services and expressed his outrage at the overcrowding and poor conditions in the camp. The general's visit provided the impetus needed to establish a third major Jewish DP camp in the vicinity of Munich. After the Americans announced their decision to set up the camp, the non-Jewish residents were evacuated within twenty-four hours and Föhrenwald was declared an exclusively Jewish camp. Thus, the Americans had laid the groundwork for the development of yet another tiny insular Jewish state inside Germany, a state that had virtually no contact with the surrounding German population. Föhrenwald was surrounded by a two-meter-high (six-and-a-half-foot-high) mesh wire fence[5] that was symbolic of the camp residents' desire and intention to distance themselves from their German milieu. Behind these "walls," a virtual Eastern European Jewish shtetl came into being, with its own administration, political parties, police, law courts, religious institutions (synagogues, a *mikvah* [ritual bath], kosher food), health care system, newspapers, vocational training facilities, schools, kindergartens, theater groups, orchestras, sports clubs, and so forth. Föhrenwald became an important shelter for the many refugees who had entered the U.S. Zone of Occupation since October 1945. In the final days of October and the first days of November 1945, 1,080 of the 1,400 Eastern European Jews who had entered Bavaria were sent to Föhrenwald.[6]

The Camp Administration

The way in which the Jewish DP camps were administered was crucial to their development. On 15 November 1945 UNRRA was made officially responsible for running the so-called DP assembly centers. Early on, however, the Jewish DPs made vocal their demand to govern themselves. The residents of the camps elected their own committees. However, since there was no official policy regulating their authority, the power and influence of these committees depended on which UNRRA director was in charge at the time. Jean Henshaw, the first director of the twenty-two-member UNRRA team responsible for Föhrenwald, faced a number of serious problems in her relations with the DPs. She apparently treated the residents of the camp in a very condescending manner, "with a little sarcastic smile pasted on her face, as if we were some kind of vermin or pest," as one resident put it.[7] Her anti-Zionist attitude added to her problems in communicating with the overwhelmingly Zionist-oriented Jews. Clearly, it was

asking too much of a trained child-welfare worker to run a large displaced persons camp such as Föhrenwald—a camp in which the number of residents grew from some 3,000 in October 1945[8] to 5,300 in
January 1946.[9] From the outset, Henshaw was assisted by a Jewish
committee. Its chairman, Nachum Bakstansky, an elderly gentleman
with a talent for administration, had championed the interests of the
Jewish DPs in the camp since May 1945. It should be noted, though,
that the committee had been appointed by Jean Henshaw; it had not
been chosen in an open and free election.

Henshaw ultimately acceded to the Jewish DPs' request for a democratically elected representative body. The date of the election and
the way in which it was to be administered were announced in *Bamidbar* (*In the Desert*), the camp newspaper. The election of the camp administrator and six committee members was scheduled for 16 December. Prospective candidates for the post of administrator had to
collect the signatures of at least 150 camp residents among those who
were eligible to vote. Those who signed the nominating petitions had
to print their name and the number of their voter registration card
next to their signatures. To run for membership on the committee,
candidates needed to collect only 75 signatures. Eligible voters included all men and women residents eighteen years and older who
were properly registered in the camp. UNRRA workers were precluded from voting. The entire electoral process was to take place
under the supervision of the U.S. Army.[10] Thus, before the election,
the army called for the committee to be expanded to eight members
so as to ensure broader and more democratic representation. Further,
it stipulated that the date of the election be postponed until 7 January
1946. Prospective candidates could thus file a nominating petition
with the chairman of the electoral commission, Avigdor Rubinstejn,
at his residence, No. 3 New York Street, as late as 16 December
1945.[11]

The Zionists emerged the clear winners in the election. Four of
the old committee members who had run for reelection without the
support of the Zionists received an average of just 342 votes each.
The other two members of the former committee were pro-Zionist
and were reelected with 1,080 of the votes cast. The six new members
received an average of 1,235 votes each; they, too, were members of
the Zionist group.[12] Nachum Bakstansky, the former chairman of the

Jewish Committee, was elected chairman of the camp. At the beginning of 1946, Henry Cohen took over the position of director of UNRRA's team at Föhrenwald from Jean Henshaw. As a Jew, Cohen had a better understanding of the survivors' needs and was a strong advocate of Jewish self-government. Cohen assigned a number of important duties to the residents, hoping that this would promote a sense of responsibility and increase self-confidence among the Jews. Though Föhrenwald was still officially the responsibility of UNRRA, for all practical purposes the DPs were in charge of administering the camp. Regularly scheduled elections were held for the heads of the various departments in the camp. By early 1947 a clearly developed system of Jewish self-government had come into being, which showed just how well the camp could function without the intervention of the outside world. Below are the election results for early 1947:

1. Arje Zlotykamien—Chairman of the Camp Administration; Head of Security and Administration;
2. Benjamin Dawidow—General Secretary and Vice Chairman of the Camp Administration; Head of the Financial Department, the Post Office, and the Information and Health Departments;
3. David Glitzer, an engineer—Head of the Labor Office;
4. Leon Kaliszer—Head of the Cultural Department and Director of Physical Education (Athletic Department);
5. Nochem Singer—Head of the Provisioning Department;
6. Jakub Kaplan—Head of the Clothing Supply Department;
7. Lipe Szarc—Head of the Social Welfare and Religious Departments;
8. Pinchas Ostrowski—Warehouse Supervisor and Deputy Vice Chairman of the Camp Administration;
9. Szaja Kac—Head of the Food Department.[13]

UNRRA's successor—first the Preparatory Commission for the International Refugee Organization (PCIRO) and then IRO itself—also granted the Jewish DPs a wide degree of latitude in administering themselves. Although any decisions made by the DPs had to be approved by IRO representatives, IRO generally refrained from interfering in the administration of the camp, since all parties benefited when residents were organized on a self-governing basis. Administration, of course, involved more than merely providing food, clothing, and medicine. Much more important, but also immeasurably more difficult, was restoring the survivors' self-respect. In this regard, self-government allowed them to take control of their lives and demonstrate that Hitler's thugs had not banished them forever from the ranks of civilized humanity.

In the meantime, the policy of the U.S. Military Government had entered a new phase. Following its formal recognition of the Central Committee for Liberated Jews in the U.S. Zone on 7 September 1946, the military authorities were ready to establish guidelines for granting the Jews the right to administer themselves. The Americans had already granted IRO great freedom of action with respect to administering the assembly centers, which the organization in turn accorded the DPs employed in the general operation of the camps. The only thing IRO reserved for itself was the right of "general supervision."[14]

Children: The DPs' Main Source of Hope

The Jewish DPs focused much of their attention on the children in the camps. During the war the Nazis had killed a great many children. Since they could not easily be exploited as slave laborers, children were of no practical use in the eyes of their murderers. Thus there were very few children and adolescents living in the DP camps in 1945. Among 1,281 Jews at Föhrenwald in early October, there were only nine babies, four small children between three and six years of age, and thirty-nine children between the ages of six and fourteen.[15] Because of its physical layout and accommodations, the U.S. Military Government soon made Föhrenwald a center for Jewish children and adolescents in southern Bavaria. By 14 October approximately one-third of the camp's some 3,000 residents were children and young people. Consequently, the age profile at Föhrenwald differed markedly from that of the other Jewish DP camps.[16]

With the movement of Jews from Eastern Europe into the U.S. Zone of Occupation, the number of children increased significantly, since both the Jews who had escaped into Russia during the war and the partisans who had fought inside enemy lines often brought children with them. In spite of their difficult circumstances, the refugees from Russia had frequently been able to keep their families intact; the partisans often had managed to care not only for their own offspring but for other children as well—children who had been hidden in forests, caves, and basements. Time and again the partisans would take in children who had been thrown out of trains by their parents as they were being transported to the death camps.

In the next few years, the Jewish DPs became known as the Jewish community with the highest birthrate in the world. In late October 1946 the number of babies born in Föhrenwald increased spectacularly; camp officials registered 203 children under the age of one, 98 children between the ages of one and five years, and 239 children between six and thirteen years of age.[17] The high birthrate underscores the important part played by children in the life of the Jewish DPs. Many parents hoped that generating new life would make the past easier to bear; children became the focus of their every thought and action. In some instances—unconsciously, of course—they were imposing a heavy burden on the very children they so loved.

An account by a male camp resident from Matseev in western Ukraine shows what an important experience and at the same time what a psychological burden the birth of a child was for Holocaust survivors. On 24 October 1945 the man's wife, Eva, gave birth to one of the first DP babies born at Föhrenwald:

> Eva woke me up gently and said, "I think it's time . . ." We slowly walked to the hospital. . . . In those ten minutes of a silent, but heart-throbbing walk, my life, Eva's life, and our past of running, hiding, and losing our loved ones, flashed through my mind like a fast-running film. . . . In 1939 the Soviets occupied our territory. Before we had a chance to adjust ourselves to living under communism, the Germans attacked the Soviets. Our vicinity was occupied by the Germans during the second day of the German attack. After several weeks of German control, the Gestapo came to town. The first thing they did was to order every Jewish male from sixteen to sixty to come one morning at eight o'clock to the rabbi's house in the center of town, to register our passports. Shortly after we were assembled, a pack of the Gestapo suddenly came from all directions on motorcycles. They surrounded us and marched us away to an old monastery. There, they murdered most of us by torture and shooting. They buried three hundred and twenty-five Jewish men.

The remaining seventy-five were selected for hard labor. Ben, my oldest brother, and Eva's father were among those killed at the monastery. . . . Shortly after the mass murder that we later called the "first action," the terror became constant. . . . One early morning in the summer of 1942, my young Ukrainian friend, Pieter, rushed into the house to warn us that "the last action" was about to begin. We did not care much at that point for our own lives, but we wanted to save our son, Shalom, who was almost two years old at that time. Pieter managed to start an argument with the *militz* guarding the road, and we were able to escape through the back of the house to the road leading into the Siomaki forest, which was about ten miles to the north of Matzeev. In the forest we found other survivors. Ten of us hid together, deep in the woods, in a section called Tsyganka. The *militz* discovered us there and ambushed us. They shot a sixteen-year-old girl, a man—and our little boy, Shalom, in my arms, while we were running away from them. After this shock, Eva and I lost our desire to live. We made up our minds to go to the monastery where we knew the Germans would kill us. . . . On our way to the monastery, a Ukrainian farmer named Nazar, a friend who was also an evangelist, intercepted us as we passed near his farm. He persuaded us not to turn ourselves in. . . . From that point on, our struggle to survive encompassed three terrible years of constantly moving from place to place. . . . After the liberation, we returned to Matzeev, our town. We found it "clean of Jews." Our group of survivors, including two couples who had returned from an escape into Russia, numbered ten. The Soviets, wanting to please the West Ukrainians, let them "finish up" with the surviving Jews. On the run again, we escaped from West Ukrainia into Poland. From there, with the help of the *Bricha* . . . the ten us managed to escape from Poland through Czechoslovakia into West Germany. There . . . two Jewish Palestinian soldiers . . . picked us up at the Munich railroad station . . . [and] took us to Föhrenwald. . . . Two short stairs and a large, white door suddenly ended my recollections. A nurse approached us as we entered the hospital's hallway. . . . "Come with me," the nurse whispered to Eva quietly and separated us. . . . While sitting, nervous and tired, I often closed my eyes. Nightmares mixed with sweet dreams. . . . I was wakened from my nightmare by the cry of a baby, a sound that transformed horror into joy at once. . . . The birth of our son marked a new era and was a symbol of our life to be, of our continuation. Eva and I along with Rabbi Friedman decided to name our baby *Chaim Shalom Dov.* The initials represented some of the descendants of both of our families, and *Chaim* in Hebrew means "life." Chaim truly did bring hope and a new life to all of us. . . . The newborn meant a new beginning. Our love for our child was mixed with sadness, because of the fact that there was no family with which to share our cherished moments. But, with all the suffering we had experienced from being Jewish, we were now proud to introduce our son into the world in a Jewish religious ceremony.[18]

Education and Preparation for Life

The central importance of children in the lives of the Jewish DPs found expression in schools that began as temporary expedients and gradually developed into an outstanding educational system. The heavy concentration of children at Föhrenwald led to the creation of a wide variety of kindergartens, schools, and training facilities as well as a children's orchestra and chorus.

After arriving at Föhrenwald with the first JDC team on 19 September 1945, Miriam Warburg, herself a Joint worker, immediately began devoting her efforts to developing the camp schools. From the outset she faced a bewildering number of problems. Where was she to find qualified teachers, textbooks, pencils, and classrooms? There were not even enough chairs for the students to sit on. Further, the children's educational backgrounds varied widely, and the native tongues of the children were heterogeneous—Yiddish, Polish, Hungarian, Russian, and French. Since most of the children came from Poland, Yiddish was the language most familiar to the majority. So, when school opened, the language of instruction was at first Yiddish. It became clear, though, that the children had to be taught a common language. Hebrew was the obvious choice, for the schools were geared to preparing students for emigration to Palestine.

At that time there were only three JDC workers to teach Hebrew, English, and arithmetic. The children accepted the improvised facilities and curriculum without demur; they were so hungry for knowledge that they grasped at any opportunity to learn. After the first few classes the teachers were desperate: they realized they could not slake the children's thirst for knowledge, even though their improvised curricula covered more than the children had learned during the years of persecution. When Miriam Warburg handed out the first writing materials, one boy said: "You know, it is the first time in six years that I've held a pencil in my hand."[19]

As more and more children and young people arrived at Föhrenwald during the following weeks, additional teachers had to be found. And since it was out of the question at that time to employ German teachers in the camp, JDC was obliged to call upon camp residents or the employees of other relief organizations to act as instructors. It was no easy task, however, to find people qualified to teach from among the camp residents, since so few of them were trained educators. So JDC managed as best it could. The camp doctors, for instance, taught the children biology and UNRRA employees gave them English lessons.[20] Still, this was not enough to do the job. Ultimately the Joint had to enlist the aid of camp residents to instruct the children. This was often a trying psychological experience for survivors, some of whom had lost their own children during the Nazi period and some of whom found it impossible to adjust to a daily routine. They were driven by an inner restlessness, hoping against all odds to find lost relatives or friends. However, if they did decide to teach, they found that the work often raised their spirits. Miriam Warburg told the story of a very shy man who, when asked if he would like to teach, explained that although he would very much like to do so, he could not say for sure whether his nerves would hold out. She suggested that he try to teach for just an hour or two, since she felt that working with children might relieve him of some of his anxieties. Two days later, a changed man, he sought Mrs. Warburg out and told her: "Yes, . . . I can do it; please put me down for as many hours as you want. It was wonderful."[21]

Mrs. Ruskin, a third-grade teacher, so loved the children that even when she became seriously ill, she refused to leave her work. Finally, the doctor ordered her to stay in bed for several days. The next wintry cold morning, when her husband had to leave for work, in an attempt to make sure that his wife would not go to work in her condition, he locked the door of their one-room apartment from the outside. However, Mrs. Ruskin missed her class so much that she broke out of her room through a window and taught that day anyway.[22]

The first thing done by camp residents who were being considered for the job of teacher was to ask for books so that they could brush up on their subject knowledge. During the years of persecution, they had forgotten much of what they had learned. One of them explained to Miriam Warburg: "For five years I have had no books in my hands, and when I started to read a few months ago, the letters simply danced before my eyes and I could not read more than two lines. Now I can read again."[23]

Even trained educators would have been unable to solve all the problems facing the instructors at Föhrenwald. Although the children were eager to learn, teachers found it hard to place them in the proper grades because of their different backgrounds and varying levels of education. Some had attended school before the war but had forgotten most of what they had learned during the long years of persecution and running. Others had received a measure of schooling while they were in hiding. The most serious problem, however, was the effect on their lives of the horrors they had witnessed. These experiences made it difficult for teachers to predict children's reactions to events that occurred during the school day and created an underlying atmosphere of tension in the classroom. Teachers who were themselves just learning to cope with the past found it difficult to adapt themselves to this complex situation. The prime pedagogical tenet "relate it to life" did not apply in these circumstances. "One has to be so careful," said a young woman teacher at the Landsberg DP camp. Once she had begun to write "honor thy father and thy mother" on the blackboard. And then she remembered in time. Most of the children in her class had no father and mother. She hastily wrote another commandment for the children to copy. And another time, when the holidays came, she wanted to teach the children how to write notes of greeting to their families, but when she started to show them how to spell "Dear Mother" in Hebrew, she substituted "Dear friend." Despite their apparent self-possession and exemplary discipline, the undercurrent of tension was strong. The young woman teacher herself had spent the war years in a ghetto and had survived the horrors of the Ravensbrück concentration camp. Like the children, she was struggling to overcome the trauma of the Holocaust.[24]

As a result of what they had gone through during the years of persecution, the behavior of Jewish children differed fundamentally from that of other children their age. A woman visitor to the Landsberg camp described her impressions of a Bible study class:

A Bible class was studying the life of Moses; they were reading the part where the infant Moses is left by his mother among the bulrushes. The teacher wanted to know if the mother was justified in abandoning her child to an unknown woman, the Egyptian princess. Was that how a real mother would act? This was no problem for the children. They had to make no effort of the mind and imagination . . . in order to produce replies. Of course, agreed the children, that's how a real mother would act. One little girl mentioned mothers whom she had seen throwing children out of trains to save them from certain extermination. Perhaps a compassionate passer-by would pick up the child. Another child had been present when a baby had been thrown over a fence during an "action." And finally, a boy got up and said, "Some of us in this class were given by our mothers to Poles. That's how we escaped."[25]

In spite or perhaps because of the difficulties they encountered in dealing with their own past, the Jewish DPs focused their energy on educating the children and preparing them for life. In early November 1945, there were twenty-seven teachers at Föhrenwald instructing students in Hebrew, religion, the Bible, English, mathematics, drawing, and sports. Two hundred fifty children attended the main Tarbut (Hebrew, "culture") school, which was organized along the lines of elementary schools maintained between the two world wars in Poland by Tarbut, a Hebrew educational and cultural organization that began activities in Russia after the February 1917 revolution. The school was located at No. 3–7 Michigan Street in the northern part of the camp.[26] A Tarbut secondary school for older children was established in 1946; its director was Edmund Feuerstein.[27] Students attended school six days a week. The curriculum included classes in Hebrew, Jewish history, the history of Palestine, world history, English, arithmetic, geography, anthropology, drawing, music, and physical education.

Along with the DP camp at Feldafing, Föhrenwald was a center of Orthodox Judaism, so students also had an opportunity to attend a religious school. Rabbi Yehezkiel (Jekuthiel) Yehuda Halberstam, probably the only major Hasidic leader to survive the Holocaust, introduced the Hasidic way of life to a segment of the Föhrenwald population. Halberstam was born in 1904. He was a descendant of the famous Rabbi Hayim ben Leibush Halberstam, the founder of a Hasidic dynasty centered in the town of Nowy Sącz (Sanz) in southern Poland who became known as the Sanz Rebbe. Before he was deported by the Germans, Rabbi Halberstam worked in the city of Klausenburg (Cluj-Kolozsvar) and later became the Klausenburg-Sanz Rebbe. His wife and eleven children were murdered by the Nazis. Halberstam was liberated in the vicinity of the Feldafing DP camp, where he subsequently established religious schools and the first yeshiva in Germany. Rabbi Halberstam and 100 of his students moved to Föhrenwald after it had become the largest Jewish DP camp. This towering man with a flowing black beard and long earlocks attracted a large following at Föhrenwald, and he more than lived up to his adherents' expectations. He devoted his energies to reviving interest in religion and religious education. In early October 1945, for example, he helped establish an ultra-Orthodox Beth Jacob school for girls in the camp.

Twenty girls were taught by Sarah Abraham in a room at No. 48 New Jersey Street. On 15 October 1945, however, the room suddenly became too small to accommodate the students—thirty members of a kibbutz group that had just arrived from Poland were asking to be admitted to the school. The administration at Föhrenwald wanted to avoid teaching two classes in one room, even though this was more often the rule than the exception in many of the other displaced persons camps. So the school was moved to No. 8 New Jersey Street, where each class could have its own little homeroom. The school was very popular, and soon space had to be found for yet another group of students.

Evening courses were offered for girls who worked in the camp office or kitchen during the day. In February 1946 there were ninety girls studying Hebrew, Jewish history, the Bible, English, and anthropology five days a week.[28] The girls were also made responsible for arranging programs for the holidays, such as Hanukkah.[29]

In addition, facilities were set up for educating rabbinical students. One hundred fifty young men between the ages of fourteen and twenty-five attended the yeshiva that Rabbi Halberstam had established in February 1946.[30] It was kept open day and night so that the students could study the Talmud whenever they wished.[31] In addition, Föhrenwald became Rabbi Halberstam's headquarters for administering *She'erit Hapletah*'s yeshivas throughout the rest of the U.S. Zone.[32]

In 1947 and 1948 the school system seemed to be working toward sometimes incompatible goals. On the one hand, the camp administrators wished to maintain a variety of schools; on the other, they wanted to standardize and optimize the overall quality of instruction. During school vacations, in-services or "seminars" were held to improve teachers' skills. Between the middle of July and the beginning of August 1947, 160 teachers in the U.S. Zone took in-service courses at the Pürten I DP camp near Mühldorf. They attended lectures by the Palestinian Jewish geographer and writer Joseph Braslavski on the geography of Palestine and the origins of the Hebrew language and by Dr. Emanuel Gamoran (of Hebrew Union College in Cincinnati) on child psychology, the teaching of Hebrew, the Bible, and Jewish and contemporary history. Professor Baruch Graubard, the founder and director of the Munich Jewish high school, lectured on topics ranging from Hebrew grammar and literary themes to the history of the Enlightenment. Zvi Hellman devoted his lectures to the Hebrew language. Professor Lachser discussed mathematics, and Professor Spector spoke about problems in the natural sciences. Curricula were designed for each grade level and specified the number of hours for the subjects covered, Hebrew invariably receiving the lion's share.[33]

Continuing education courses were to be a permanent part of the teachers' professional development. The Board of Education and Culture planned to begin a series of seminars on 1 March 1948; however, the head of the board, S. Lewis Gaber, noted in his report for the month of March that the board had failed to meet its deadline.[34] However, it finally organized a ten-day seminar to be held from 12 to 21 April 1948 at Föhrenwald. Eighty instructors participated and took courses that dealt largely with the Bible, Hebrew literature and grammar, and teaching methodology.[35] In June 1948 a second in-service was held, this time for the entire U.S. Zone; it was also to be the last.[36]

In the meantime, the state of Israel had been established, and the teachers, many of whom had joined the illegal emigration underground for Palestine known as Aliyah Bet (Hebrew, "ascent two"; that is, Emigration Two), were gradually leaving Germany. Teachers represented some of the more activist Jewish DPs, who were ready to risk the hardships and dangers of illegal immigration to Palestine. Further, because many of the older and stronger students were leaving during the night for the journey to Erets Yisrael, classes had to be reorganized almost daily. In 1948 teachers often were the first to volunteer for the Israeli Army.[37] Their replacements were generally unqualified. This plunged the entire educational system into a crisis from which it never fully recovered. After the state of Israel was born and the War of Independence had ended, it was the poorer teachers who stayed on in Germany—those who were no longer inspired by the zeal and idealism that had helped shape this multifaceted educational system.

The high birthrate among the DPs was now beginning to have an impact; there were more and more children who were in need of care and supervision. Even though few small children had survived Nazi rule, a nursery school was opened at Föhrenwald during the first week of November 1945, just six months after the end of the war. Two well-trained woman teachers cared for twelve toddlers.[38] As of February 1946, there were some thirty children, ranging from three to six years of age, in the kindergarten at No. 1 Michigan Street.[39] The number continued to grow until, by June 1950, the school—divided into ten classes—was serving 250 children a day. In addition, there was a religious kindergarten in the camp, similar to the religiously oriented elementary schools in which children were educated according to the precepts of Orthodox Judaism. The fact that there were in-service courses for nursery school as well as elementary and high school teachers reflects the value placed on the care and education of the very youngest children.[40]

ORT Schools

Besides a general education, arrangements were made for the Jewish DPs to receive vocational schooling in order to prepare them for emigration to Palestine. The organization that provided the training is inextricably linked to the name Jacob Oleiski. Born in Sakiai, Lithuania, he attended the University of Halle in Germany and subsequently became director of the ORT schools in Lithuania. The acronym ORT (Organization for Rehabilitation through Training) in Russian originally stood for Obshchestvo remeslennogo i zemledelcheskogo truda sredi yevreev v Rossii, or Society for the Promotion of Handicrafts and Agricultural Work among Jews in Russia. In 1941 the Nazis "resettled" Oleiski in the Kowno (Kaunas) ghetto, where he set up a vocational school in 1942. When the Germans liquidated the ghetto in 1944, they sent Oleiski to Dachau, where he was liberated in 1945.[41]

Immediately after the end of the Nazi regime, Oleiski translated his ideas into action. Creative work, he felt, would help restore the surviving Jews' spiritual well-being. He stressed the fact that their stay in the DP camps was merely a temporary stage before they resumed a normal life—a life, however, that they would only really be able to handle after they had been trained for a vocation. "Creative Work—the Meaning of Life" is what Oleiski titled the speech he gave at the opening-day ceremony for the first vocational school at the Landsberg camp on 1 October 1945. In his address he outlined his goals and described his motivations:

> We the former inmates of the concentration camps who have gone through so much and have seen with our own eyes people driven to the limits of their endurance, we know and understand how difficult it is to restore a camp resident's mental equilibrium. However we would be negligent or even criminal if we simply watched people leading pointless and futile lives in the camps and did nothing but allow ourselves to be carried along by the current. We must give the camp residents a purpose; we must reorganize their daily lives and introduce them to every possible kind and aspect of work. They must have the feeling that everywhere there are things to do. This is the only way we can prevent our fellow sufferers from letting their minds and senses atrophy and become even more demoralized. . . . We are not going to remain in the camps forever; we must view them as a phase, as a transition to a normal life. . . . A normal life is a life with purpose and meaning, filled with useful and productive labor. Whenever I spend time in training workshops or visit vocational classes and look into the eyes of former concentration camp inmates, my faith [in the power of work] grows stronger and stronger. . . . We have much to do in the future building a new country. Erets Yisrael is waiting to receive spiritually and physically healthy people who know

how to use their strength for useful and productive purposes. So in the words of the poet Kulbak I call upon all men and women in the camp: "Let's go, let's go and leave the weak behind! The bells have tolled. Bronzed youth answer their call to still the anger at the loss of years." Indeed it is only through productive, creative work that we can lessen our anger at having lost so many years.[42]

To achieve his objectives Oleiski availed himself of the services provided by ORT, the organization born in St. Petersburg in 1880. Originally, ORT's task was to provide vocational training for those among Russia's six million Jews who wished to acquire specializations in crafts or agriculture. After World War I the headquarters of what ultimately became known as the World ORT Union were moved to Berlin, and the organization began to expand its activity to countries outside Russia. Thus, in 1922 American Jews established the American ORT Federation at a meeting in New York. The aim of American ORT was to train Jews for work in industry, agriculture, and various trades. Further, it established branches in major centers of Jewish life throughout the United States.[43]

When the war ended in 1945, ORT resumed its activities in Germany. Its first priority was to provide training for Jewish DPs adequate to qualify them for employment in their new homeland. Although it still stressed vocational education, ORT began to shift some of its emphasis to teaching the Hebrew language, general Jewish history, and Palestinian Jewish history.[44] The first vocational school was set up in the Landsberg camp on 1 October 1945 under the supervision of Jacob Oleiski, laying the groundwork for ORT programs in both the American and British Zones of Occupation. ORT enabled thousands of Jewish DPs to be trained for a trade. At first Oleiski set up vocational schools and classes from his headquarters at Landsberg. However, as more and more Jewish camps were established in the U.S. Zone, he moved his office to No. 10 Möhlstraße in Munich during the spring of 1946. From there he coordinated ORT's programs for the entire zone.

Under the supervision of Dr. Oswald Dutch, Hanover became the headquarters of ORT in the British Zone. In the summer of 1948, Mark Lister replaced Dutch, who had been posted to ORT headquarters for Germany and Austria. There were 470 students enrolled in the ORT program in the British Zone in January 1947. By the beginning of 1948, ORT's nearly 100 teachers were providing training to over 2,000 DPs, mainly at Belsen.[45]

In September 1946 ORT had established a headquarters office in Germany. It was administered by the World ORT Union. ORT's vocational schools received financial assistance and the necessary machines, instruments, and tools from both the ORT Union and JDC.

ORT, of course, had to overcome a number of obstacles during its initial period of operation, similar to those encountered by those who built the camp school system, namely lack of sufficient equipment and a competent teaching staff. With the influx of Jews from Eastern Europe, ORT was able to make up for some of the teacher shortage, since many of the survivors were graduates of prewar ORT schools. JDC was instrumental in procuring equipment. All this did not solve the real problem, however. Many of the DPs were in such poor health—especially at Belsen—that they were unable to spend an eight-hour day pursuing a regular course of study. Furthermore, none of the DPs could have imagined that after liberation the camps in which they were staying, located on German soil, would be anything more than a stopping-off place or that they might have to spend months taking courses to learn a trade. The DPs were quickly forced to disabuse themselves of any illusions, and many successfully completed the vocational training programs. Nonetheless, it is a sad fact that some DPs dropped out of programs before graduation due to a kind of agony of the soul and emotional instability.

None of these things, however, affected the variety of courses offered: 1,770 students received their diplomas in some thirty-two different vocational fields. The most popular trades were the traditional Jewish needle trades (tailoring, dressmaking, corsetry) and auto mechanics. In addition, a number of DPs were trained as electricians, locksmiths, cutters in clothing factories, radio technicians, dental technicians, and weavers. The courses ranged from goldsmithing, cosmetology, site engineering, and bookkeeping to trades such as projectionist, typewriter repairman, upholsterer, carpenter, photographer, lathe operator, men's fashion illustrator, and tanner.[46]

Strict standards were established for awarding diplomas so as to maintain the high quality of ORT training. A board of examiners consisting of the director of the ORT school in question, the master craftsman in charge of the particular department, an officially recognized outside expert—if possible from a German trade guild—and an UNRRA representative administered the final examinations. The school sent a copy of the completed test to ORT headquarters in Munich for grading. If the candidate passed, the headquarters office awarded a diploma. Those who passed received either a "very good," "good," or "satisfactory" mark on their examinations.[47] ORT diplomas were recognized in most countries as the equivalent of a master craftsman's or journeyman's certificate.[48] There were also courses, however, that were not officially recognized and for which graduates did not receive a diploma.[49]

Permission to use a course in order to fulfill the requirements for graduation and the award of a diploma was contingent on approval by ORT officials, whose most important criterion was to maintain the highest possible educational standards. To ensure that these standards continued to be met, ORT headquarters kept in touch with the various ORT schools in the larger cities and camps by sending out circulars on a regular basis. Some circulars spelled out conditions of employment, for instance, the ORT teachers' responsibility to keep attendance records for every student registered for a class or workshop, to maintain a class diary with a record of the material covered in class, and to give midterm examinations every six weeks.[50] Others contained recommendations on how to deal with course subject matter. Circular No. 40 for June 1947, for example, recommended that courses in tailoring, dressmaking, children's tailoring, corsetry, and hat making include theoretical subjects such as chemistry, geometry, and sewing-machine design.[51] From such recommendations one can infer the importance attached to theoretical instruction and the notion that vocational training could only be successful within the context of a technical education. ORT, of course, had to provide the materials to support its efforts. Thus, ORT headquarters in Munich maintained a publishing department that produced scientific texts in the Yiddish language. Further, ORT published a monthly periodical for teachers and students entitled *Teknik und arbet* (*Technology and Work*).

In September 1947, 7,225 students were attending 361 courses throughout the U.S. Zone. At that time ORT employed 622 teachers and 275 persons in various administrative capacities.[52] In January 1948 ORT expanded its activities again; its programs now included

8,412 students taught by 721 teachers in 496 classes covering 53 different trades.[53] This was the high point of ORT's work in the Jewish DP camps. In spite of all the difficulties ORT encountered along the way, its efforts proved to be a resounding success.

After the establishment of the state of Israel, ORT's programs, as well as other aspects of life in the Jewish DP camps, had to be reevaluated in light of the fledgling Jewish state's needs. New teachers had to be recruited and trained, and classes had to be restructured as more and more students left Germany for Israel. Over the next few years, the bulk of the workshop equipment was shipped to Israel and used to build ORT schools in the new state. Nevertheless, ORT continued its activity in Germany—albeit at a reduced level—offering many Jews the chance to learn a trade during the next few years.

A comprehensive vocational education program was soon set up at Camp Föhrenwald. One of the initial signs of an effort to provide the DPs with a skill was the opening on 26 August 1945 of the first driver-training school in a camp inside the U.S. Zone. During this three-month course for "chauffeurs," which had been organized without ORT's assistance, students learned, among other things, what a motor vehicle consisted of (its *gebei*), how to maintain and operate it (*oisnutsung/ekspluatatsye*), how the ignition system (*onstsindung*) worked, and how to drive in traffic (*gasbavegung*) while observing the rules of the road (*distsiplin*).[54] After having launched the first ORT programs in Landsberg, Oleiski began setting up vocational schools at Föhrenwald in November 1945. That same month the camp hired fifteen instructors and enrolled 265 trainees. Twenty-one girls began a six-month course in nursing, which they could complete by working in the camp hospital. Sixty boys and girls attended courses in tailoring. In addition, the camp offered DPs the opportunity to learn locksmithing (16 apprentices), shoe making (3), carpentry (8), the field of electricity (8), cosmetology (4 or 5), and the operation of a motor vehicle (60 boys). In the spring ORT planned to begin an agricultural program.[55] Josef Goldberg, an engineer, was the first director of ORT's school at Föhrenwald; he was succeeded by Jacob Fuchs, Georg Kalinsky, and Mathias Siegman, also an engineer.

Whenever feasible, the schools were to follow the curriculum and the strict guidelines worked out by the ORT program. To illustrate, let us look at the camp's six-month sewing course for women. In February 1946, eighty young women between the ages of fourteen and twenty-three attended the course.[56] Of the twenty-four hours a week students were required to be in class, eight were devoted to sewing by hand. During this part of the course students learned the blind stitch and other utility stitches such as the cross, chain, and herringbone. Students were also expected to gain proficiency in sewing on buttons, mending linen lingerie, and making buttonholes. During twelve hours of on-the-job training, the women were instructed in the use of the sewing machine. Finally, the curriculum called for students to make several articles of clothing so that they could practice the skills they had learned in the classroom. The clothing included an apron, a girl's linen blouse, a sporty blouse and skirt, a pleated skirt, pajamas, and dresses in various styles.[57] The course ended with an examination that tested the students' theoretical knowledge as well their practical skills. At the conclusion of the program, not only had the graduates received training to qualify them for employment in the countries to which they wished to immigrate, but the camp benefited by receiving the clothing produced by the trainees. In this connection, we might mention that the women managed to find some white silk—enough for six wedding gowns. Since the rabbis in the camp always seemed to be busy performing weddings, the students made the gowns in six different sizes, so that every bride could borrow one for her wedding.[58]

Other vocational training programs were also of practical value for camp residents—the watch-repair course, for example. According to the detailed curriculum, classes were to be held Sunday through Thursday from 9 A.M. to 6 P.M. with an hour's break for lunch. The practical part of the course furnished instruction in skills such as filing, polishing, taking apart a watch, and putting it back together again. The theoretical portion was devoted to the science of horology and covered the principles and art of constructing instruments for indicating time as well as methods of measuring time that pertained specifically to the watchmaker's trade. The subjects studied included the clock and its development, the barrel assembly, crown, cylinder (horizontal) and anchor (recoil) escapements, the various screw threads and metals used, the calculation of gear ratios, and methods for determining the weight of a weight-driven clock mechanism. The final week of the three-month course was devoted to a review and an intermediate examination.[59]

Work in the Camp

Motivating the residents of the Jewish DP camps to engage in productive work of any kind proved to be a major problem, at least in the early period. The reason was obvious: displaced persons who had been used as slave laborers by the Nazis no longer had a desire to work. For years they had been forced to toil in the concentration camps under the harshest conditions and to the point of total exhaustion, knowing always that the only reason they remained alive was that they continued to be of some use to the Germans. After liberation, many DPs decided that they had done enough work in their lives. Needless to say, they had no desire to help rebuild the German economy after the war. The idea of working together with Germans, after the humiliations the Jews had been forced to endure at the hands of Nazis, was totally unacceptable. Finally, some were simply too weak to work full time; it was all they could do to while away their days eating and sleeping.

Yet the camp was in urgent need of workers, even those who were only willing to do menial labor. After the non-Jews left Föhrenwald in the fall of 1945, the Jewish residents had to take over jobs such as timber cutting, washing, and cooking, even though they were not obliged to do so. To motivate them to share in the responsibility of maintaining the camp, the camp chairman, after consulting with UNRRA and the Military Government, decided to increase the food and clothing allowances for those who chose to work. As a result, residents were divided into four categories: (1) police, labor service, drivers, and camp administrators; (2) kitchen and warehouse workers; (3) teachers and employees of the camp administration; and (4) all remaining camp residents. Those in the first category received a food parcel every two weeks; those in the second were given a food parcel every three weeks. In addition, those in categories 1 and 2 were allotted a ration of ten cigarettes per day, which they usually bartered for other desirable consumer items. Category 3 residents were entitled to just one food parcel every four weeks and six cigarettes per day, whereas those in category 4 received a parcel every eight weeks and three cigarettes a day. Similar guidelines had been laid down for the distribution of clothing.[60] As a result of this system, more Jewish DPs evidenced a desire to work. Nevertheless, UNRRA was obliged to employ 190 Germans.[61]

Conditions at Föhrenwald changed with the arrival of Jews from Eastern Europe. Their attitudes and expectations differed markedly from those of the DPs who had been liberated in the concentration camps. Having been informed in Poland about the lack of opportunities to emigrate, the Eastern European Jews were more likely to be aware that their stay in the DP camps would be protracted. Moreover, many of the new arrivals were in much better health than the liberated DPs and therefore more willing and able to take over some of the jobs in the camp.[62] In time, however, camp residents who had refused to do jobs such as those described above realized that working in the camp for UNRRA was not the same thing as being a slave for the Germans. By the middle of August 1946, 1,042 residents—not including those who were teaching in ORT DP programs—were employed in the camp as office workers, instructors, cleaning people, DP policemen, kitchen helpers, timber cutters, drivers, auto mechanics, laundry workers, administrative personnel, and workers in the cultural sphere.[63] A further inducement to take jobs in the camp was the inauguration on 1 May 1947 of a social insurance program for workers that provided for paid sick leave and medical care. The decree, signed by the camp's work director, also specified the number of vacation days and grounds for dismissal as well as the employer's responsibilities.[64]

Although the DPs rarely took jobs outside the camp, there probably would not have been enough jobs for them in the *Landkreis*[65] of Wolfratshausen anyway. And even if there had been, district officials were clearly disinclined to secure employment for them there. By the same token, the residents of Föhrenwald had little if any desire to seek employment in Wolfratshausen. There were some camp residents who were "self-employed" and had opened their own little shops and businesses in the camp. The official photographer at Feldafing, for instance, was a DP who operated his own small business and had become one of the most popular men in the camp. Very few of the DPs still retained prewar photographs of themselves or their relatives. So the chance to have pictures taken of newly found family members and friends triggered a storm of enthusiasm among those at Feldafing.[66]

In November 1946, Henry Cohen, the director of UNRRA's team at Föhrenwald, reported that 90 percent of the residents were employed as laborers, students, or housewives.[67] However, given the fact that the move to regulate work inside the camp was still causing problems in spite of the inducements offered residents to assume various jobs, Cohen's figure is probably too high.

Cultural Life in the Camp: Music and Theater

The Jewish DPs were amazingly energetic in the cultural sphere. Regardless of nationality, they all wished to become engaged to a greater or lesser degree in the cultural activities that were so important for their spiritual rehabilitation. This desire manifested itself in the establishment of a number of theater groups both inside and outside the camp. These groups regularly performed the works of such classic Yiddish playwrights as Sholem Aleichem, S. Ansky, and Abraham Goldfaden. In addition to reviving old Yiddish songs, the groups dealt with the horrors of their recent history, presenting plays based on life in the ghettos and concentration camps. Of course, they also performed plays that evoked the dream of so many of the Jewish DPs—their future life in Palestine.

It was at Föhrenwald that the first Jewish theater group was founded after the war, even though the camp was still without a cultural department to provide assistance, equipment, or even moral support. At first there were no actors, no director, no stagehands or sets, no props—not even a stage. However, a small group of students under the direction of Jacob Biber managed to overcome these obstacles. They inspired Biber to begin theatrical performances even sooner than he had planned. While he was writing a play called *The Storm* for the group's first performance, other talented young people attracted his attention and volunteered to join the group. Biber then put together an evening variety show, which the group first performed at Föhrenwald on 28 October 1945. The performers ranged in age from ten to eighteen and were all very capable. The show began with three short one-act plays (comedies), which were followed by a medley of Hebrew and Yiddish songs and poems and several numbers performed on string instruments.[68] The audience was deeply moved when an eighteen-year-old girl who had survived the war in the area of Vilna sang about a woman who gave away her only child for safe-keeping to a Lithuanian family. She sang with exceptional feeling about the love between mother and son, the suffering of the little boy, and the deep anguish of the mother after the two were separated. Everyone in the audience had known such sorrow. The lengthy applause showed how much the audience appreciated the young singer's performance.[69]

In fact, the performance was so successful that the group was obliged to repeat it a week later. In addition, the players received an invitation to present the show at Camp Feldafing. Biber described the importance of these initial performances for the Holocaust survivors:

> The theater hall in Feldafing was large enough to accommodate most of the DPs (about two thousand individuals), but we were most touched by the rows of sick people lined up on hospital cots in front of the stage. Feldafing had a sanitarium for tubercular patients, and all the survivors with that illness had been transferred there. When the show was running, I looked out from behind the curtain and saw pleasant smiles on their skeletal faces. Some of them were still wearing their striped concentration camp clothes. Others were covered with white sheets, but their eyes peering out from the covers expressed their eternal gratitude and satisfaction once again to see Jewish children performing. I saw tears in their eyes rolling down the hollowed cheeks. Shedding a few tears myself, I breathed a silent prayer: "Thank you, God, for giving me the strength to accomplish some good." I suddenly felt a sensation of relief in my heart. The guilt I had carried in me for the sin of surviving, while so many of our loved ones had suffered and died, had somewhat diminished. I suddenly felt that my efforts were worthy, and that, perhaps, there was reason for all of us to hope again.[70]

In addition to his position as head of the theater group, Biber assumed the directorship of the Tarbut school. However, his health did not allow him to carry out both of these arduous responsibilities for long. He gave up the cultural leadership of the camp but remained director of the school.[71] Sjome Visokodvarsky became the theater group's new director. He put on two plays by Abram Fremd—*A Scandal at the Court House* and *The Commandant and His Last Breath*. Following the first elections to the camp committee in January 1946, the newly established Cultural Department assumed responsibility for the group, which had become known as Bamidbar (In the Desert). The name referred to the forty years the Israelites spent wandering in the wilderness before reaching the promised land. The point, of course, was to make a connection between biblical times and conditions in the DP camps, which to the survivors seemed like living in the wilderness before "returning" to Israel. After several performances, however, the company was disbanded for financial reasons in March 1946, and Visokodvarsky founded a new group with professional actors that also called itself Bamidbar.[72] The twenty-member company continued to put on plays at Föhrenwald, including Sholem Aleichem's *Tevye the Dairyman*[73] and in June 1948 *Hertsele Meyuhes* (*Hertsele the Aristocrat*) by Moses Richter. In each case, Visokodvarksy was the producer-director.

Föhrenwald's professional theater company often gave guest performances at other DP camps. In December 1946, for example, the group performed four times at Landsberg alone.[74] Meanwhile, a number of professional actors, directors, set designers, and other theater professionals arrived at the DP camps in the wake of the Jewish exodus from Eastern Europe. They contributed greatly to improving the quality of the performances and raising the standards of theatrical presentations in general.

A new group of amateur actors called Mapilim ("trail blazers" or "daring pioneers") was founded at Föhrenwald in March 1946. Its members lived in two of the kibbutzim attached to the camp, Brit Hakhayil and Herzliyah. The troupe put on two plays written by Shifra Trapsko and Gershon Goldenberg, both members of the ensemble: *On the Way to Palestine* and *We Are Here*. The literary quality of the plays was not particularly high; however, a talented director, Jacob Sandler, and the subject matter itself, which naturally appealed to the audience, made the presentations a success. Nevertheless, Mapilim soon passed from the scene: after its second performance at Föhren-wald and a tour of various other camps, it disbanded—probably be-cause of political differences among the members.

In June 1946 yet another theater group was formed; it called itself Bar Kokhba in honor of the Jewish leader who led a bitter but unsuc-cessful revolt against Roman dominion in Palestine in the second cen-tury C.E. The company gave its first performance in August 1946 under the direction of Israel Rubinek. The play performed by Bar Kokhba was a rather ambitious work called *The Brave Family,* which was based on the wartime experiences of P. Kazvan, a member of a kibbutz at Föhrenwald. It was a great success.

The members of Bar Kokhba and Mapilim joined together in the fall of 1946 to form a single theater company at Föhrenwald. Called Negev, the combined company was headed by Rubinek and Sandler and was officially recognized and funded by the camp administration. The newly formed group was quite successful, as shown by the public's re-sponse to its premiere performance, Sholem Aleichem's *Di Goldgreber* (*The Gold Diggers*), which was presented three times at Föhrenwald alone.[75] Negev specialized in the works of classic Yiddish writers. Aside from Aleichem's *Di Goldgreber,* which remained part of its repertoire until 1948,[76] the group staged *The Golem* by H. Leivick (the pseu-donym of Leivick Halpern) in the summer of 1947[77] and Jacob Sand-ler's production of *Grine Felder* (*Green Fields*) by Peretz Hirschbein.[78]

Negev alone, however, was unable to satisfy the camp residents' hunger for theatrical presentations. So guest performances by other groups became common. In June 1947, for instance, Max Mixer mit zayn kinstler ansambl (Max Mixer and his artists' ensemble) came from Stuttgart to perform in the camp.[79] The most well known com-pany to appear at Föhrenwald was doubtless the Münchner Jüdisches Theater (MIKT), which had been giving performances on a regular basis at the Munich studio theater (Münchner Kammerspiele) since November 1946. On 2 June 1948 the MIKT players presented Her-mann Heyermanns's *Die Hoffnung* (*Hope*) at Föhrenwald, a play they had already performed twice in Munich and twice in Landsberg.[80]

In addition to the various theater groups in Föhrenwald, there was also an orchestra and a chorus. Misha Hoch, who had survived the war in Russia and come to the camp as part of the mass exodus of

Jews from Eastern Europe, put all of his organizational skills at the disposal of a string orchestra. He himself was an accomplished violinist and did much to inspire young people to join the orchestra. The regular concerts in the camp theater were a big success with Föhrenwald residents.[81] Shlomo Zektzer, who had also escaped from Russia, organized sixty students into a fine chorus.[82]

The Camp Press

Like nearly all other large DP camps, Föhrenwald set up a library and a reading room. After so many years of being deprived of access to educational opportunities and resources, it was nearly impossible to satisfy the DPs' hunger for news and knowledge. Young and old filled the reading room day and night. There were very few books and magazines for camp residents until the Joint and other American service organizations provided reading material from the United States. After receiving assistance from voluntary relief agencies, the library was able to make available forty newspapers from the United States, Palestine, and Germany; it even checked out board games to patrons. The head of the library was Rubin Podkorzer,[83] and the collection contained about 700 volumes.[84] At least once a week various people gave talks in the library reading rooms; the talks were often followed by lively discussions.[85]

Holocaust survivors were passionate in their desire to establish their own Jewish press, which was actually quite astonishing given the conditions prevailing at the time: paper was rationed, and typewriters and other equipment were almost impossible to come by. Practically every Jewish DP camp and many political parties published their own newspapers. Thus, some camps had more than one newspaper: Feldafing, for example, published *Dos Fraye Vort* (*The Free Word*) and *Dos Yiddishe Vort* (*The Jewish Word*), the organ of the ultra-Orthodox Agudat Israel. Newspapers, general-interest magazines, and even sports magazines were written largely in Yiddish and Hebrew, although there were also Polish, Romanian, Hungarian, Italian, English, and German papers.[86] The publications varied in quality depending upon the editor and the staff.

Landsberg probably had the best and most well known camp newspaper, the Yiddish-language *Landsberger Lager Cajtung* (*Landsberger Lager Tsaytung* [*Landsberg Camp Newspaper*]). Published since 8 October 1945 by Dr. Samuel Gringauz, its founder and editor in chief, the paper changed its name a year later to *Jidisze Cajtung* (*Yidishe Tsaytung* [*Jewish Newspaper*]) to emphasize its character as a publication for Jews throughout occupied Germany. Gringauz, a lawyer from Kowno (Kaunas), was at the same time chairman of the Landsberg camp committee and the Council of the Central Committee of Liberated Jews for the U.S. Zone. At its peak, the newspaper had a circulation of 15,000.[87]

Most of these publications were camp papers in the strictest sense of the word, limiting themselves largely to camp news, reminiscences of camp inmates, and such items as lists of missing persons. Frequently they lifted material from other newspapers or books published inside and outside of Germany; for the most part, they ignored copyright laws and permission to reprint.[88]

Newspapers geared especially to life in the camps also appeared at Föhrenwald. Qualitatively, they were not particularly outstanding when compared with other DP publications. The Föhrenwald paper was called *Bamidbar: Wochncajtung fun di bafrajten Jidn* (*Bamidbar: Vochntsaytung fun di bafrayten Yidn* [*In the Desert: Weekly Newspaper of the Liberated Jews*]). Its motto alluded to the wanderings of the Israelites as described in the Bible: "In the desert. In the wilderness. On the way. / We will remain. / In the desert. In the wilderness. On the way. / We will not return. / One goal: Erets Yisrael."[89]

Starting on 12 December 1945, *Bamidbar* appeared weekly on Wednesdays; later it was published biweekly. The number of pages per issue ranged from six to sixteen; the editor in chief was Menachem Sztajer. Since the camp was unable to secure a set of Hebrew type at first, the Yiddish paper was published for nearly half a year in Roman characters. In fact, most of the Jewish DP camps in Germany resorted to publishing their newspapers and magazines in Roman type until a set of Yiddish type became available. Beginning on 4 June 1946, half of *Bamidbar* was issued in regular Yiddish type. Then, on 21 June 1946, the entire paper began to appear in Hebrew characters.

For the most part, the paper devoted little space to world events.

The staff reported mainly about life in the camp—elections, schools, sports, and cultural events. They also profiled and interviewed members of the camp administration for the paper. Political news was given prominence only when it directly affected the lives of the Jewish DPs. Thus, the paper provided in-depth coverage of British Palestine policy and everyday events in the Holy Land as well as the Nuremberg war-crimes trials and the crimes committed against the Jewish people by the Nazis. UNRRA and JDC placed public notices and announcements in *Bamidbar*. The newspaper also received unsolicited poems, short stories, reminiscences, and long articles on a variety of subjects—for example, on Jews in agriculture or the concept of "nation" and its bearing on Judaism. The list of missing family members that appeared at the end of every issue was a very important feature. Families could place notices in the paper as well.

So far as we can determine, the last issue of the Föhrenwald camp newspaper appeared on 4 September 1946. However, this did not mean that the camp residents had to do without a Jewish paper. In 1946 a kind of consolidation took place in the DP newspaper market; the papers that survived were mainly those that appealed to the DPs across zonal and regional boundaries, for example, *Unzer Veg (Our Way)*, the official organ of *She'erit Hapletah,* which was issued from October 1945 to December 1950. The smaller camp newspapers gradually ceased publication.

It is difficult to evaluate the entire spectrum of the Jewish DPs' cultural life. The historian Koppel S. Pinson, a JDC educational officer in the northern part of the U.S. Zone, was an expert on the subject. In his opinion, the institutional and cultural life of the surviving Jews was rather "primitive" and "raw" in character.[90] Pinson's judgment, however, did not do justice to the facts, for one should not apply such exacting standards to a case of this nature. The first few months after liberation in particular were extremely trying. Given the seemingly insurmountable obstacles and enormous complexities with which they were confronted, the Holocaust survivors' achievements were considerable. Their single greatest achievement, however, was the revival of Jewish cultural life. Equipped with woefully inadequate resources but possessing an indomitable will, they staged theatrical performances, played music, and produced publications. Even though their productions were not always the world-class presentations they strived to be, they nevertheless received positive reviews and praise for their efforts to rebuild Jewish cultural institutions.

Leisure Activities and Entertainment

In addition to the cultural amenities offered in the camp, there was a wide variety of organized entertainment. The Joint supported and financed tours by Jewish entertainers. In May 1948, for example, the well-known American dance team of Katja Delakova and Fred Berk performed at Föhrenwald. They had cofounded the Dance Institute of the Jewish Theological Seminary in New York.[91] Föhrenwald even held a ball in the camp theater in January 1948. The organizers used posters to promote the so-called Chamisza-Oser [Hamishah asar bi-Shevat] (New Year's Day of the Trees) Ball, with music provided by the Münchener Jidisze Stern-Orkester (Munich Jewish Star Orchestra). The camp cinema was also a popular attraction. There were three to five films shown per week at first; later, the theater screened a double feature every evening. The camp cinema came under the jurisdiction of the Jewish camp committee, which obtained the films directly from various distributors in Munich. The rental fees were covered by ticket sales.

Sports were the most popular leisure-time activity in practically all the Jewish DP camps.[92] On 22 November 1945 an "appeal to Jewish youth" went out "to establish a sports club on the grounds of Camp Föhrenwald under the name . . . 'Maccabi Jewish Gymnastics and Sports Club.'" The appeal went on to say that it was to be "a nonpolitical institution representing all the sports teams in the camp—without regard to young people's views of political Zionism. . . . The terrible hunger, the tortures, the deaths and the crematoria are still fresh in our minds. This is why we wish to revive our ancient traditions by raising our physical and moral strength to new heights. We, the remnant of European Jewry, wish to participate actively in establishing Jewish independence. Therefore we must strive to provide our people with strong and healthy human beings. And we wish the future generation to be physically and mentally strong as well."[93]

Dr. Landau immediately began organizing the youth in the Maccabi Club at Föhrenwald. He had been a sportsman and leader of the famous Maccabi Club in Warsaw before the war.[94] The Maccabi World Union is the international Jewish sports organization. According to a November 1947 list, 51 of the 146 Jewish sports clubs registered with the Central Committee for the U.S. Zone of Germany had adopted this renowned name as their own.

The office of the Central Committee's Health Department responsible for physical education issued instructional brochures such as *Lern zich szwimen* (*Lern zikh shvimn* [*Learn to Swim*]) and the biweekly *Jidisze Sportcajtung* (*Yidishe Sportsaytung* [*Jewish Sports Newspaper*]), which commenced publication in the spring of 1947 and had a readership of 4,000 to 5,000.[95] However, because of financial problems resulting from the reform of western Germany's currency in 1948, the paper was forced to cease publication in the middle of that year.[96]

Camp residents engaged in many different types of sports, including gymnastics, soccer, boxing, skiing, basketball, track and field events, table tennis, and eurythmics.[97] At first, however, the U.S. Army had to supply the necessary equipment; the camp was especially in need of table-tennis tables and paddles, boxing gloves, and soccer balls.[98] Maccabi trained its own athletic instructors so that it could make proper use of all its sports equipment.[99] Inevitably, the question arose as to whether the instructors and the athletes should be paid. Representatives of the camp administration passed the following resolution: "In view of the fact that we do not wish to encourage the development of professional sports, none of the athletes in the camps in the 5th district (Landsberg, Föhrenwald, Freimann, Feldafing, and Weilheim) will receive any form of payment. Only the following will receive payment for services (in the form of additional food and cigarette rations): one athletic instructor, two soccer coaches for the first and second teams, one track and field coach, one boxing trainer (if available), and one gymnastics teacher."[100]

Soccer was by far the most popular sport in which the DPs themselves participated and which they followed with great enthusiasm. A soccer match on 2 December 1945 between a team from one of the Bavarian camps for former political prisoners and a team from one of the Jewish camps, for example, attracted some 3,000 spectators. The Jewish team won 2 to 0.[101] Matches between teams from the various Jewish assembly centers were more common, however. By 1947 there was even a soccer league made up of twelve teams from the Jewish DP camps. The clubs from Landsberg, Feldafing, Leipheim, Föhrenwald, Munich, Regensburg, Neu-Freimann, Bad Reichenhall, Gabersee, Pocking, Eggenfelden, and Weinheim competed in two rounds to decide the championship. After each team had played the required twenty-two games, Landsberg emerged as number one. With seventeen wins, four ties, and only one loss, the team chalked up thirty-eight points, streaking past Feldafing for the top prize. Föhrenwald, with twenty-four points and eleven wins, came in fourth in the final standings. And Weinheim, with seventeen losses and just three wins, came in last.[102]

Soccer was governed by a set of strict rules. The Rules Committee of the Association of Jewish Gymnastic and Sport Clubs of the *She'erit Hapletah* in the U.S. Zone imposed harsh penalties for any violations. A player named Steiner on the second Föhrenwald team, for example, was suspended from 24 August to 24 October 1947 *far a klap gebn dem gegner* ("for striking his opponent").[103] Besides league matches, informal competition and minor soccer tournaments took place on a regular basis. In the spring of 1946 the Leipheim camp invited Maccabi Föhrenwald to play their teams on the camp's home turf. Föhrenwald won two important games, Maccabi Leipheim losing 8 to 2 and Dror Leipheim going down to defeat the following day with a score of 9 to 3.[104]

In April 1948 Föhrenwald hosted a championship boxing match and a table-tennis competition.[105] In May 1948 the camp also organized a sports festival in which a large number of people participated. Later, the Funkkaserne camp in Munich likewise sponsored a sports festival, from 11 to 14 September 1947, where competitions were held in several sports, including track and field, swimming, boxing (for men only), table tennis, tennis, volleyball, soccer, and handball (for both men and women).[106]

Religious Life

Leisure activities and the Orthodox Jewish way of life may seem at a far remove from each other, but they coexisted harmoniously at Föhrenwald. Some residents sought diversion from the tedium of camp life in sports, whereas others found that they could restore their spiritual balance only by devoting themselves to the study of the sacred writings of Judaism. At first one might assume that many of the surviving Jews had returned to traditional religious values. This was not the case, however. The majority of the Jewish DPs in Germany were only moderately religious or not religious at all. Rabbi Bernstein, the adviser on Jewish affairs, noted that although a somewhat larger percentage of Jews practiced the observance of their faith than would be found in a normal Jewish community, there was no universal religious revival.[107] Part of the reason may lie in the fact that the older, mainly Orthodox Jews had been almost completely annihilated by the Nazis and that those surviving were mainly the younger, more worldly, and more assimilated elements of the Jewish population.[108]

As a rule—and of course there are exceptions in this extremely sensitive and personal sphere of life—the experience of the concentration camps had little impact on the degree of a survivor's religious faith. Jews who were Orthodox believers before the camps in general continued to be so after their liberation; those who were mildly or conventionally religious quite frequently lost their faith as a result of the Holocaust. And Jews who had grown distant from their faith before the war rarely regained it after their experiences in the concentration camps.[109] Ultra-Orthodox Jews and zealous Zionists generally recovered most quickly from the consequences of the Holocaust; the moderately or indifferently religious suffered longer. The Orthodox and the Zionists looked toward the future. The Orthodox Jews dedicated themselves to rebuilding their religious institutions, educating the young, and living their lives according to the precepts of the Torah. The Zionists devoted their energies to the founding of a new Jewish state in Palestine. Those with less religious faith fell between two stools: they did not wish to devote their lives to God, so the Orthodox had little use for them; nor could they share the enthusiasm and idealism of the dedicated Zionists.[110]

With the influx of Eastern European Jews, who were stricter in their observance of biblical law than their Western European coreligionists, Orthodox Judaism became a more powerful force in the DP camps. In early 1947 there were more than 100 *talmudei torah* (children's schools teaching mainly religious subjects) and ten yeshivas in the camps. Still, the Orthodox remained in the minority and were often at odds with one another. For most of the Jewish DPs—that is, those who observed some Jewish customs but did not make their faith the center of their lives—religion was a private matter.[111] Thus, in no DP camp was it possible to experience the real feeling of the traditional Sabbath, the kind of spirit that had hovered over the small towns of Galicia, Poland, and Lithuania.[112]

Nevertheless, Föhrenwald, along with Feldafing, became a center of Eastern European Jewish Orthodoxy. In December 1945, just eight months after the war ended, there were 4,938 Jews living in Föhrenwald,[113] 1,400 of whom called themselves Orthodox.[114] The Hasidic Rabbi Yehezkiel Yehuda Halberstam was instrumental in determining the direction of religious life at Föhrenwald. Like Rabbi Friedmann, a highly respected and popular leader in the camp, Halberstam came from Hungary. From the time of liberation until the middle of 1946, almost all the rabbis active in the camp were from Hungary or Slovakia. Hungary and Slovakia were the last Jewish areas to be ravaged by the Nazis, and liquidation of Jews there did not begin until 1944. While most of the Polish and Lithuanian rabbis, therefore, had been exterminated, a larger number in Hungary and Slovakia survived.[115] It was only with the mass influx of Eastern European Jews that Polish rabbis finally reached the DP camps.

As was mentioned above, the establishment early on of a yeshiva, an Orthodox Beth Jacob school for girls, and a religious kindergarten can all be credited to Rabbi Halberstam's initiative.[116] Besides his interest in schooling, the rabbi was extremely concerned about traditional religious observance among the Jewish DPs. As a result, he contrived to bring the Hasidic movement to the very center of Föhrenwald, the area surrounding the camp theater.

Rabbi Halberstam and the other rabbis at Föhrenwald received assistance from Va'ad Hahatzalah and the Joint. JDC, in fact, provided a number of prayer books, tefillin (phylacteries), tallises (prayer shawls), candles, and candlesticks. During the Jewish High Holy Days in particular, the Joint increased its support. It also funded the annual celebration of Hanukkah in the Jewish DP camps.[117]

Two political parties were active at Föhrenwald—the ultra-Orthodox Agudat Israel, whose members strove to live their lives strictly according to the Bible and Jewish tradition, and Mizrachi, the religious Zionist party whose aim was to build Palestine in accordance with the Jewish religion. Both were well represented in the camp, and the Orthodox Jews regarded them as representative of their own political views. However, the two parties were constantly at odds with each other, since each considered that its way and its way alone was right. Each party had its own kibbutzim in the camp to prepare young people for life in Palestine.[118] Five hundred DPs belonged to one of the religious kibbutzim and 800 others were organized in collective settlements that had no political affiliation.

To lead a life according to Jewish law, it was essential that in addition to a synagogue (there were six at Föhrenwald, the main synagogue being situated in what is now the parish church) and a *mikvah*[119] there must be a kosher kitchen. The kitchen that was set up during the first week of November 1945 was the result of some hard lobbying by Rabbi Halberstam and JDC in particular.[120] Initially, the kosher kitchen occupied part of the large nonkosher kitchen, from which it was separated by a wooden partition; later, it received a room of its own. Unlike its nonkosher counterpart, only Jewish personnel were allowed to work in the kosher kitchen. Each kitchen prepared a different menu every day. On 14 February, for example, those who observed the Jewish dietary laws were served a breakfast consisting of a half-liter of coffee and 350 grams of bread; a lunch made up of 60 grams of meat, a half-liter of potato soup, and a quarter-liter of pea soup; and a dinner made up of two eggs and a quarter-liter of coffee.[121] Simon Rifkind, the adviser on Jewish affairs at the time, the Joint, and UNRRA had managed to persuade the American Military Government to lift its ban on the slaughter of animals in accordance with rabbinical law. The upshot was that by May 1946 about half the camp residents took their meals in the kosher kitchen.

The Black Market and Anti-Semitism

Fed by envy and ancient prejudices, rumors kept cropping up about the illegal wheelings and dealings allegedly engaged in by the Jewish DPs. To help counter these charges, the American Military Governor General Lucius D. Clay issued the following statement in 1947: "In view of the conditions under which [the Jewish DPs] have had to live in Germany, with their future unsettled and their past suffering clear at hand, their record for preserving law and order is to my mind one of the remarkable achievements I have witnessed during my more than two years in Germany."[122] If in fact the Jewish DPs were guilty of any crimes, they were mostly petty offenses such as "black marketeering," possession of foreign currency, entering the U.S. Zone without permission, or possession of false identification papers. Holocaust survivors rarely if ever committed robberies or capital crimes.

The alleged involvement of Jewish DPs in black market activities and racketeering was a constant source of conflict between the displaced persons on the one hand and the American Military Government and the German authorities on the other. Anti-Semitism was often the ulterior motive behind accusations that Jews were more deeply involved in black marketeering than others and were amassing fortunes as a result. The *Landrat*[123] of the county of Wolfratshausen (of which Föhrenwald was a part), for example, wrote to the *Regierungspräsident*[124] in Munich that "residents of the camp, in particular, [who are] predominantly Eastern European Jews, . . . are engaged in black marketeering and smuggling on an unimaginable scale. In the case of some of the above-mentioned [Jews], their wealth can be measured in the thousands."[125] Preposterous allegations such as these, especially with regard to the sums involved, were utterly without foundation, as General Clay confirmed: "[T]he unsettled economic conditions in Germany have made barter trading and black-market operations a common problem. Even in this field, the Jewish DPs have not been conspicuous in their activities as compared to the other displaced persons groups, or, in fact, as compared to the German population itself."[126]

Jews were neither more nor less involved in black market activities than Germans or members of the American Military Government. Black marketeering was, of course, rampant in Germany after the war, and there is no question that it was against the law. However, one has to make some important distinctions with regard to the buying and selling that was going on. First, there was a so-called gray market in which practically everyone in Germany engaged and without which the German economy would not have been able to function. This involved mainly bartering rationed items for things one personally needed. If everyone who was engaged in this kind of trading had been arrested, one would have had to turn all of Germany into a prison. Most of the so-called black marketeering operations undertaken by

Jews fell into the "gray" category. Then there was real black marketeering: large-scale trading in rationed or forbidden goods. But here,
too, as was the case with the Germans and the Military Government,
only a few "bad eggs" among the Jewish population were actually involved.[127]

Accusations of black marketeering contributed greatly to reviving
the ancient stereotypes of the Jew as a trader and haggler who was
incapable of pursuing a real occupation. These prejudices were fos-
tered, on the one hand, by the traditional aversion that many Germans felt toward Eastern European Jews, whom they regarded as
quintessentially alien, and, on the other, by their desire for the material goods the Jews were able to offer for sale on the gray market. The
Jewish DPs often received items from the U.S. Army and UNRRA
that as a rule were unavailable to the German population. Needless
to say, it was impossible to make much of a profit from these goods—
not to mention the fact there were many fewer of them in circulation
than the Germans assumed. Nevertheless, cigarettes (the main me-
dium of exchange in postwar Germany), coffee, and chocolate could
be readily exchanged for urgently needed articles of clothing, essential commodities, or theater and cinema tickets.

Voices were raised on the Jewish side warning the DPs not to become involved in the black market. They were concerned about the
effect Jewish black market activities might have on the morale of the
DPs. The mood in the Jewish camps was becoming noticeably more
hopeless as the DPs were obliged to wait longer and longer for a
chance to emigrate. Those who had no occupation or did not attend
school often became involved in the black market out of sheer idleness.[128] Since school attendance was compulsory for young people in
the camps, they were rarely if ever engaged in large-scale black market operations. Many Jews were worried that the DPs who were en-
gaging in these illicit activities might undermine the social structure
of the DP camps.[129] Even more, fighting the black market was motivated by a belief that the criminal activities of a few might reflect
negatively on the Jewish community as a whole.[130] Moreover, many
Jews who traded on the black market felt they were being unfairly
treated by the American authorities. They realized, of course, that
they were engaged in illegal activities. However, given what the Jews
had suffered at the hands of the Germans, they could not understand

why they should be so severely punished for simply bartering and exchanging goods, illicit practices in which Germans also engaged but for which they were usually never apprehended. Nor did the Jewish DPs have any sympathy for the argument that the black market interfered with the rebuilding of the German economy. They reacted with a mixture of bitterness and despondency to the raids conducted by the U.S. Military Police, especially since the MPs often carried out these operations while Germans stood by watching the spectacle. One resident of Föhrenwald gave the following account:

> I myself was once a victim of a raid. We were in the railroad station at Nürnberg, having arrived from a small town named Fürth after a two-day teachers' conference. . . . Inside the railroad station at Nürnberg, we were suddenly surrounded by a group of MPs. They searched our briefcases and found some cans of food we had put aside for our journey home. The officer then announced: "You are under arrest!" There were roughly a hundred Jewish men and women in the station. The many Germans sitting around the station on built-in benches were having fun pointing to each other and saying, *"Judenschmuggler"* (Jewish smugglers). At first the military police herded us into the center of the station; then they ordered us onto a train. At two in the morning they finally let us go, after UNRRA and JOINT officials in Nürnberg had discovered what had happened and had intervened.[131]

The American Military Government's order in early April 1946 suspending the right of German police to enter the Jewish DP camps caused a great deal of bitterness on the German side. The order was prompted by frequent Jewish complaints of brutal treatment by the German police, especially as the result of an incident that occurred in Stuttgart. On 29 March 1946, 180 armed German policemen, accompanied by their dogs, and eight noncommissioned American MPs, raided a Jewish assembly center on Reinsburgstraße in search of black market goods. After one person was arrested, the residents of the center tried to expel the German policemen. The police fired their guns, killing one DP, a concentration camp survivor who had recently been reunited with his wife and two children, and wounding three others. Twenty-eight German policemen were also wounded. The raid netted a few illegally acquired chicken eggs. The adverse publicity created by this incident resulted in the removal of the Jewish DP camps from German jurisdiction.[132]

The DP Police and the Camp Courts

The Jewish DP police were in charge of policing the Jewish DP camps. As a rule, they were responsible for maintaining law and order in the camp as well as guarding the camp's perimeter; that is, they kept their own house in order. The Jewish camp police were impressive proof of the success of self-government.[133] An ordinance issued by the camp administration laid out the rights and responsibilities of the camp police. The police department was defined as the division of the camp administration responsible for safety and order. It consisted of a criminal investigation section, a constabulary, an emergency medical team, and a fire-fighting brigade. All branches of the department reported to the commander or chief of police. The police were permitted to detain for twenty-four hours anyone charged with the commission of a crime or whom the police believed guilty of having committed a crime. To keep a suspect in custody for longer than twenty-four hours, the police had to seek authorization from the camp court. The police could also obtain a warrant to search a house or other place for stolen goods and then confiscate those goods. Further, the camp police were responsible for enforcing the camp's administrative regulations, UNRRA's directives, and the camp court's decisions. In addition, the police guarded the outside of the camp in order to prevent unauthorized persons from gaining entry.[134]

One of the most important and complicated tasks facing the Jewish police in the camps—a task that had also confronted the German police—was fighting the black market. To deal with the situation, the police chiefs of the camps at Föhrenwald, Landsberg, Neu-Freimann, and Feldafing met on 18 November 1946 and passed the following resolutions: "(1) convene a meeting of all the senior residents from each block of houses in the camp to explain the possible consequences of continued black market activity; (2) make announcements to all camp residents by posting notices on walls and distributing circulars; (3) have the police chiefs subpoena all major black market operators; (4) have the camp police carry out a trial raid on the 24th of the month for UNRRA and the camp administrators; (5) have the UNRRA Safety Officer visit all camps for the purpose of determining the extent to which measures have been carried out; and (6) have UNRRA improve food supplies for the camp police."[135]

Apparently these measures were successful, for at the next meeting of the police chiefs on 29 November 1946 the Föhrenwald representative reported "that the black market in the camp has been brought completely to a standstill, and . . . black market activities are nonexistent. . . . From the reports of all the police chiefs, it appears that they have done everything in their power to bring every possible means to bear in fighting the black market."[136] American sources, too, indicated that the camp police were very cooperative in combating black market trading. To prepare them for conducting "search and seizure" operations, members of the camp police force were even sent for special training to the DP Police Training School run by the Third Army at Schleißheim. Ten policemen from the Föhrenwald, Landsberg, Neu-Freimann, and Feldafing camps attended the school on 2 December 1946.[137] Even the Wolfratshausen *Landratsamt*[138] commented positively on the help received from the camp police in fighting the black market.[139] However, it is difficult to judge how rigorous the camp police really were in dealing with the large-scale trading in rationed and forbidden goods.

One person who was steadfastly opposed to the black market was Henry Cohen, the director of UNRRA's team at Föhrenwald. In addition to ordering the confiscation of illegally acquired goods, he regularly sent black marketeers to prison and threatened them with expulsion from the camp. Ordering a resident to leave the camp was in keeping with an old Jewish ghetto tradition that had been used to enforce conformity with the rules of those confined within the ghetto's walls.[140] After the reform of western Germany's currency in 1948, black market activity declined significantly at Föhrenwald—and everywhere else in Germany.

Aside from a few offenses in connection with black market trading, the crime rate among the Jewish DPs was extremely low. During all of 1947, only seven Jewish DPs in the county of Wolfratshausen were charged with and convicted of a crime. All the cases concerned either the illegal slaughtering of animals, petty larceny, embezzlement, or bodily injury, four involved black marketeering as well, and three also involved various other offenses.[141] The reason for the low crime rate lay not so much in the fear of being sentenced to a term in prison—after having often spent years in Nazi concentration camps, the DPs were no longer afraid of incarceration—but rather in social control.[142] And here the camp courts played an important role. Strictly speaking, the Jews were subject to the military law of the United States. However, in the tradition of the *bet din* (Jewish court), the Jewish DPs had established their own camp courts, which helped maintain discipline among the residents. The job of these courts was to settle civil disputes between camp residents, investigate criminal offenses committed by Jews in the DP camps, and deal with cases in which former *Kapos* (prisoners in charge of a group of inmates in Nazi concentration camps and work-squad foremen—Trans.) and ghetto policemen were accused of having mistreated their fellow Jews. In questions involving civil law, the alternative to the camp courts would have been the German courts. But that was clearly not an option at the time. It would also have been inconceivable to indict former *Kapos* in a German court of law. In any event, criminal cases would have been tried in a United States military court. This is purely hypothetical, however, because a Jewish DP would never have violated the traditional Eastern European Jewish rule prohibiting Jews from making accusations to Gentiles about their fellow Jews or testifying against their coreligionists.[143]

The Föhrenwald internal court began its work on 1 November 1945. It was charged with "maintaining order," safeguarding the camp's "social and educational interests," and "prosecuting all violations of the camp's current administrative and disciplinary regulations," that is, "settling all disputes that arise in the camp."[144] Residents of the camp chose the members of the court in secret balloting. In payment for their services, the judges received the same food and cigarette rations as did members of the camp administration.[145] In June 1946 a secret election was held; all camp residents eighteen years and older were eligible to vote. After the ballots were counted, the following five persons were assigned to the court: Nosn-Cwi Horaw Fridmann (1,139 votes), Adam Wilk (1,106), Arje Zlotykamien (1,083), Josef Schawinski (1,018), and Isroel Mandelbaum (1,014).[146] At least one of the members of the court had to be a lawyer. The court could impose fines, order defendants to perform work in the camp for several days, take away certain privileges such as the cigarette ration, and impose short prison sentences that convicts had to serve in the camp prison, which had been operational since 1945. Both the camp police and camp residents could bring a case before the internal court. There was also a public prosecutor attached to the court.[147] The court's "investigation office" could depose former concentration camp inmates in cases involving *Kapos* who were not resident in the DP camp. The court then recorded their sworn statements and sent them to the proper authorities.[148]

The camp courts followed strict guidelines and were not known as a rule to make arbitrary decisions. A number of the judges on the court had been graduated from a law school before the war. Two of the future chairmen of the Föhrenwald court, Adam Wilk and Dr. Zygmunt Herzig, for instance, were graduates of the Lemberg (L'viv) University and Kraków University faculty of law, respectively.[149] The court appointed a public prosecutor; plaintiffs and defendants were to be questioned in detail regarding any matter before the court; and as many sworn witnesses as possible were to be allowed to testify. The court was to keep a written record of its proceedings. In certain cases the court could close its hearings to the public. Youthful offenders and defendants who had suffered greatly as a result of their past history could claim mitigating circumstances. Only DPs came within the jurisdiction of the internal camp courts; they had no authority over UNRRA or IRO workers.

The Föhrenwald court became a recognized authority in the camp and ensured that residents observed the rules of community life. The record of its proceedings and decisions bears witness to its huge case load, suggesting that the pressure of work referred to time and again in the sources was consistent with the facts.[150]

The camp court also did important work in recovering DPs' personal papers. Most of the camp residents had lost their birth certificates, marriage licenses, and so forth while they were on the run from the Germans. To be issued new papers, individuals had to appear in court with their DP cards and photographs, plus two witnesses who could swear under oath as to their identity.[151] Reissuing lost DP registration cards also came within the court's authority.[152] The court was obliged to render decisions even in basically trivial cases. A young woman, for example, had received a parcel from a relative in America that was addressed to her under her maiden name. On the basis of the evidence—she was able to produce a Soviet marriage license dated 18 April 1945 that had been issued after her civil wedding in Kivertsy (Kiwerce)—the court granted her the right to take delivery of the parcel.[153]

Life inside the camp also called for a regulatory authority. The past weighed heavily on residents, giving rise to social pressures that often had adverse consequences. Residents frequently resorted to the court to settle personal disputes. In August 1947, for example, religious Jews staged a protest in the camp theater, causing the policeman on duty to fly into a rage. He pulled out a knife and threatened one of the demonstrators, saying, *"Ven du gayst nisht avek, dan stekh ikh dikh"* ("If you don't get out, I'll shiv you"). After the incident, some of the religious Jews petitioned the court to have him removed from the police force. In his role as policeman, they maintained, he was supposed to set an example for the community and not let himself be carried away by his emotions.[154]

In another case a woman resident of the camp instituted a suit for eviction. She had permitted a young woman and subsequently the young woman's fiancé to occupy part of her residence on condition that the couple would move out when her husband returned. When her husband did return, however, the young people refused to vacate the room in which they were living, alleging that they had in fact occupied the residence before the woman had.[155]

Frequently the court had to handle complaints lodged with the employment office by persons who had been terminated from a job, at the post office or in the camp kitchen for instance, because dismissal entailed the elimination of the supplementary rations provided to those with steady employment. Even the loss of a book borrowed from the library or the failure to return a book became an issue for the court to decide. In one case the head librarian refused to accept a defendant's offer to reimburse the library for a lost book, since the librarian was unable to find a similar replacement title in a bookstore. He insisted that the patron reorder a book published in Yiddish. The court agreed with the librarian. So the defendant was ordered to "replace the missing title with another book in the Yiddish language." Moreover, the defendant was prohibited from leaving the camp for seven days.[156] In July 1947 a resident of the camp was sentenced to ten days of "forced labor" for rowdiness and disturbing the peace.[157] In addition, the court often had to hear cases involving "insults to one's honor." In issuing an amnesty during the celebration of Rosh Hashanah in 1946 and releasing all the inmates in the camp prison (except the *Kapos*), the court was in effect laying claim to both executive and judicial power.[158]

The internal camp courts were continually coming into conflict with the U.S. Military Government, which was unwilling to invest them with the full authority of law. However, since the institution existed in nearly all DP camps, the Americans recognized its importance in helping to keep the camps running smoothly. Still, they only permitted the courts to resolve minor internal disputes—despite the fact that in deciding even these questions they did not always conform to the American idea of the rule of law. After Germany's unconditional surrender in 1945, the Allies took over the government of Germany—her executive, legislative, and judicial powers. Therefore, it is not surprising that they regarded the existence of law courts in the Jewish DP camps, unauthorized as they were by the American Military Government, as illegal.[159]

In addition to the regular camp courts, there was also a so-called Court of Honor attached to the Central Committee of Liberated Jews in the U.S. Zone. This court was essentially responsible for looking into the activities of ZK members during the Nazi period and resolving disputes between the DPs on the one hand and the Central Committee and its various departments on the other. On 23 October 1947, for example, a hearing took place before the Court of Honor presided over by Chairman N. Markowski and Judges Feingold and Sygower. Josef Schawinski, who had been elected to the Föhrenwald court in June 1946, sued Dr. Henry Tulczyn, director of the ZK's legal department at the time, for compensatory and punitive damages. Prior to this action, in October 1946, the Föhrenwald camp court had rendered a judgment in the case of a *Kapo* who had tortured Jewish inmates in the concentration camp at Görlitz (Gorlice) in Silesia. Following a fair and impartial trial, the five judges found the defendant guilty as charged and sentenced him to six months in jail. However, the U.S. Military Government disagreed with their decision. The American authorities considered that in making its judgment the court had exceeded its authority, and they therefore ordered the camp court either to release the convicted *Kapo* from jail or hand him over to the American military court at Dachau. Schawinski, who had been assigned the task of gathering evidence on the *Kapo*'s wartime activities, immediately contacted Dr. Tulczyn. Tulczyn told him that the *Kapo*'s sentence was in fact too light, that the Jewish courts would soon be recognized by the U.S. authorities, and that therefore the Föhrenwald camp court should in no circumstances surrender the convict in question to the Military Government. The U.S. Military Government, however, disagreed with Tulczyn's contentions, and a protracted investigation into the lawfulness of the camp court's authority ensued, which ended with Schawinski being sentenced to nine months in jail, only five of which he actually served. It was after his release that Schawinski sued the ZK for damages. He claimed that Dr. Tulczyn, acting in the name of the Central Committee as head of its legal department, had given him and the Föhrenwald camp court false and misleading information and that this had ultimately led to his, Schawinski's, conviction. The Central Committee's Court of Honor agreed with Schawinski and upheld his complaint. The ZK, it stated, was responsible for having provided a misleading statement of the case to the Föhrenwald camp court. Therefore, the Court of Honor determined that the defendant Josef Schawinski, a member of the camp court, was entitled to payment of compensatory and punitive damages.[160]

The Americans were leery of the entire Jewish judicial system in the DP camps and tried once again, in the summer of 1948, to bring the camp courts more firmly under their control. All the camp directors received a letter instructing them to set up disciplinary investigation commissions that would act in their behalf and in lieu of the camp courts. The commissions were categorically prohibited from imposing penalties on camp residents. Only the IRO regional director or his authorized representative could do so. And the only person allowed to occupy the position of representative was the camp director, who was precluded from transferring the function to the camp court or any other institution. If a crime did not come within the purview of the American military court system or the German courts, however—that is, minor offenses such as "insults to one's honor," brawls, or infractions of the rules by camp employees—the camp director was responsible for assigning someone to investigate the case. After receiving the final investigative report together with a recommendation regarding possible punishment, the director had to decide whether or not to act on the recommendation. He was allowed to select from among the following penalties: giving the offender a warning or a stricter warning than had already been given; shutting off the offender's electricity for a period of one to two weeks; excluding the offender from participation in the camp's social activities for a maximum of one month; banning the offender from leaving the camp for two weeks and requiring him or her to report several times a day to the camp police; canceling the cigarette allowance or another type of ration; assigning the offender some task in the camp for a period of up to thirty days; moving the offender to poorer quarters; imposing several different penalties at the same time; handing the offender over to the Military Government; or officially expelling the offender from the camp.[161]

In practice, though, the camp courts continued their work as usual. The camp court settled minor disputes on its own; only in difficult cases did it have to call upon IRO for support. The degree to which UNRRA or IRO interfered in the work of the camp courts depended on who happened to be UNRRA's or IRO's camp director at the time and how that person viewed the system of Jewish self-government. Edouard Frum, who succeeded Henry Cohen as UNRRA's director at Föhrenwald in the fall of 1946, had a particularly high regard for the work of the court in maintaining law and order. In fact, he encouraged the court to expand its activities. He even referred a number of cases to the court in an effort to promote Jewish self-government.[162]

Underground Military Organizations

Jewish underground organizations were active at Föhrenwald as well as in the other DP camps in the U.S. Zone of Occupation. They spent most of their time organizing illegal immigration to Erets Yisrael and training young Jews for paramilitary activity in Palestine. In the British Zone, IZL (Irgun Tsva'i Le'umi [National Military Organiza-

tion]) and the Haganah (Hebrew, "defense") not only conducted illegal military training; they also carried out a number of attacks to
protest London's restrictions on Jewish immigration to Palestine. In
the U.S. Zone, by contrast, the two Jewish military groups limited
themselves largely to smuggling Jews into Palestine, although here
and there they did set up programs to instruct Jews in the use of
firearms. They directed their efforts toward winning support for the
cause of Erets Yisrael rather than attracting attention through acts of
terrorism. Their activities in the U.S. Zone were aimed at inducing
the Americans to exert influence over the British. And this, the underground organizations were convinced, would happen only if the
Americans came under pressure from the Jewish side.

The IZL operated a small cell at Föhrenwald. The Irgun was
founded in Jerusalem in 1931. It developed into a radical anti-British
underground military organization in the 1940s and was active both
inside and outside of Palestine. Until 1941 it worked closely with the
Revisionist Party and its leader, Vladimir Jabotinsky, after which it
broke off relations with the Revisionists. The Revisionists were maxi-
malist political Zionists who sought to establish a Jewish state "on
both sides of the Jordan." The Irgun achieved rather unfortunate notoriety when an IZL bomb exploded at the King David Hotel in Jerusalem on 22 July 1948, killing ninety-one people.[163]

The small Irgun cell at Föhrenwald consisted of five men. They
spent most of their time distributing anti-British leaflets and the Irgun newspaper, *Nor Azoy* (Yiddish for "only in this way"), which was
published in Paris. After the U.S. Third Army threatened in August
1946 to arrest and bring to trial anyone caught disseminating this
kind of propaganda, the Irgun conducted its campaigns covertly,
principally at night. Rumors kept cropping up that the Irgun was
conducting military training in the Jewish DP camps; however, the
Americans were unable—or unwilling—to expose the IZL's operations.[164] At any rate, the Brit Trumpeldor (Betar for short), a radical
Revisionist splinter group within the Irgun, kept training young
people at Föhrenwald.[165] Even the Maccabi Sports Club occasionally
trained camp residents to march, maintain military discipline, read
maps, and so forth. However, the sports clubs' activities in this area
do not appear to have been very extensive.[166]

The Haganah, the much more moderate underground organization run by the Jewish Agency for Palestine, was active in the U.S. Zone as well. After the founding of the state of Israel, it was to become the Israeli Army. Beginning in 1945, the Haganah was involved in training men and women in the U.S. Zone for paramilitary activity and then smuggling them to Palestine. In the camp at Königsdorf, which was administered by Föhrenwald, military training had been taking place since 1946; however, it had to be kept secret until the establishment of the state of Israel in May 1948, because the Jews were not permitted to set up an army for a country that did not yet exist. On 15 April 1946 there was actually a military parade in the Königsdorf camp.[167] The fledgling Jewish state was in urgent need of young people who could fight for the country's independence and then defend it. By March 1948 the Haganah demanded that childless young people, both men and women, be sent to Palestine as quickly as possible. A Haganah delegation headed by Nahum Shadmi was sent to Germany to find recruits between the ages of seventeen and thirty-five in the DP camps. Though the U.S. Army could not, of course, officially approve the process of recruitment, it tolerated the activities of the recruiters and passed over them in silence.[168]

Enthusiasm for Palestine

Nearly all the Jewish DPs agreed that after the Holocaust, Zionism was the only political movement that held any meaning for them. After liberation they differed only over details in the Zionist program. These differences were reflected in the various political parties. However, nearly all shared a fundamental belief in Zionism. There are several reasons for this. The Zionists were the only group to become politically active immediately after liberation. They conducted a propaganda campaign in the camps that was directed at a highly receptive audience, for Zionism gave new hope to the desperate Jewish survivors of Nazism. Further, the majority of Jews in the DP camps came from Eastern Europe, where Zionism had been much more influential than among the assimilated Jews of Central and Western Europe, who viewed the Zionist movement as a threat to the social emancipation they had recently achieved. Nor did the Eastern European Jews have any sympathy for the desire of some German Jews to build a new life in their former homeland after the war.

Zionism looked to the future and offered a ray of hope to those living in the depressing surroundings of the DP camps. The selfless help given by the Jewish Brigade had aroused a new fervor for Palestine among some DPs and reinforced the existing Palestine-centered attitude in others. These Jewish volunteers from Palestine serving in the British Army arrived in the camps before any of the Jewish service organizations appeared on the scene. They symbolized a vigorous, vibrant Palestine and a self-confident Jewish community.

In the meantime, David Ben-Gurion's visit to Germany showed how important the Zionist way of seeing things had become among *She'erit Hapletah.* For Ben-Gurion, there was only one answer to the problems facing the Jewish DPs, namely, immediate immigration to Palestine and the building of a Jewish state. The enormous enthusiasm he encountered during his visit in the fall of 1945 demonstrates the extent to which he met the survivors' expectations. "To the people of the camp, he is God," Major Irving Heymont wrote on the occasion of Ben-Gurion's visit to Landsberg on 22 October 1945. "It seems that he represents all of their hopes of getting to Palestine. . . . The first I knew of his coming was when we noticed the people streaming out to line the street leading from Munich. They were carrying flowers and hastily improvised banners and signs. The camp itself blossomed out with decorations of all sorts. Never had we seen such energy displayed in the camp. I don't think that a visit by President Truman could cause as much excitement."[169]

Zionism in the DP camps was not a theory of Jewish life but an active expression of the DPs' desire to immigrate to Palestine. Ernest Landau, a Jewish journalist and editor of *Neue Welt* (*New World*), for a long time the only German-language Jewish newspaper in the U.S. Zone, got to the heart of the matter when he wrote: "No more does anyone say: emigration at all costs. Now the slogan is: immigration to Palestine, to the land that has been solemnly promised as the National Home of the Jewish people."[170]

Koppel S. Pinson wrote that this euphoric attitude toward emigration was colored by "Palestinocentrism."[171] In a survey conducted by the American authorities at Dachau in early May 1945, shortly after liberation, the overwhelming majority of the 2,190 Jewish survivors stated that they wanted to return to their home countries; 491 chose immigration to the United States or elsewhere overseas; and only 236 opted to settle in Erets Yisrael. The results of the survey, however, were not based on a representative sample. On one hand, the survey reflected the respondents' psychological state and their uncertainty with their situation at the time. On the other, it mirrored a natural desire to return home and discover who and what had survived.[172] Bitterly disappointed after searching for relatives and traces of Jewish life in Eastern Europe, the DPs returned to Germany to find a changed situation. Jewish Brigade activists and Zionist leaders of *She'erit Hapletah* had strengthened the Zionist leanings of the survivors to prepare them for the establishment of a Jewish homeland in Erets Yisrael.

New surveys conducted in the summer and fall of 1945 showed results different from those obtained earlier: 80 percent of young people between the ages of twelve and twenty-five stated that they wished to live in Palestine.[173] At the Landsberg camp, 3,112 of the 4,976 polled chose immigration to Palestine; 884 opted for the United States; and the rest wished to go to England, Argentina, Brazil, Australia, Hungary, or Romania, mainly because they had relatives living in those countries.[174] These responses are probably a more accurate representation of the situation than those in the earlier survey, even though Rabbi Bernstein, adviser on Jewish affairs, estimated in October 1947 that, given the chance, 90 percent of all Jewish DPs would immigrate immediately to Palestine. If America were to open its gates to the DPs, Bernstein said, about 25 percent would choose to immigrate to the United States and about 75 percent would continue to prefer Palestine.[175]

Even if many DPs did not choose Erets Yisrael as the land in which they wished to settle, the majority still agreed on the need for the Jews to have a state of their own. It was common to hear people say things such as: "If the gates of Palestine stay closed, it would've been better if Hitler had killed us all." Or: "The dream of Palestine is the only thing that kept me from losing my mind in the concentration camp. That's the only reason I could endure all the torture. But if it remains a dream, I have no desire to go on living."[176] The survivors could not understand how the world could deny them their own state after the disaster that had befallen the Jewish people. Was not this the least that they could expect? Miriam Warburg, a JDC social worker at Föhrenwald, time and again heard people ask such desperate questions. There was a young nurse from Poland who looked very "Aryan" and had survived the war by passing as a Gentile. She had witnessed the Warsaw ghetto uprising, with all its horrors. Her only brother had been shot to death by the Nazis for failing to obey an order. She ended her tale by saying: "And all I want now is to go to Palestine and start a new life there. We ask for nothing but this tiny little country; why don't they give it to us?" "What can I answer?" Miriam Warburg noted sadly.[177]

In some cases people so yearned to go to Palestine that they were willing to give up close personal relationships in order to do so. Chaplain George Vida met a young girl named Carole, whose tragic history left only Palestine as the answer to her problems. "My father was a Polish Jew," she told him. "He came to Munich in 1918 to make his home *there*. When he found that the people hated him, he married a gentile woman so the world should forgive him for being a Jew. My father was killed at Dachau. My mother told me she does not want a Jewess as a daughter. I lost my mother, too. My real mother is Palestine. I am going home to her." "But how," her friend Joe interrupted. "They won't let you." Carole answered with tears in her eyes: "I don't know anything about politics. I don't understand what oil and all the other things have to do with it. I want to go home and I shall! No matter how." A few weeks later the rabbi met Carole again. "I have not seen your boyfriend the last few days. How is he?" he asked. Carole smiled sadly and said, "We decided to call it quits. For him there is only one place in this world where life is worth living. The Bronx! For me, I must go to Palestine." "Look, Carole," said the rabbi, trying to make his words sound casual, "I have been a Zionist as long as I can remember. I can understand your yearning. But I cannot help wondering. Are you yearning for Palestine or for a normal life with freedom and self-respect? Because you can find such a normal life in America, too." Carole blushed deeply. "All right, Chaplain! Call it an obsession; perhaps I am crazy. But if I knew for certain today that I will never be able to go to Palestine, I would not want to live another day. Who was the American who said, 'Give me liberty or give me death!' I will give up everything; my mother, my boyfriend, everything I have, for just a chance to go to Palestine."[178]

To the frequently asked question "But why Palestine?"—when Jews were living happily and in dignity in the United States and Great Britain—the answer was: "Yes, we know Jews live happily in many lands. But they lived happily in Germany, too. We do not say that what took place in Germany will take place in the United States or in Great Britain. But we do say we are too weary to go further. We have suffered too much to take another chance. The end of our road is Palestine—a Jewish land with Jewish people who are simply Jews and nothing else."[179] Even those who had no desire to go to Palestine had no doubt about the necessity of creating a Jewish state.

So when David Ben-Gurion declared Israel's independence on 14 May 1948 in Tel Aviv, the announcement was greeted with wild enthusiasm in the Jewish DP camps. After all the years of waiting marked by hopelessness and despair, the survivors suddenly had a new homeland. Even those who did not intend to immigrate to Israel were fired up by the enthusiasm. Now if their plans fell through, there was another option open to them.

On 18 May a large and impressive demonstration took place in Munich to show support for Israel; in the following weeks, 70 percent of the Jewish DPs registered to immigrate to the Jewish state.[180] The emigration departments of the Joint and the Hebrew Sheltering and Immigrant Aid Society (HIAS), which had unofficially promoted illegal immigration to Palestine before May 1948, now openly offered every possible assistance to those wishing to move to the new state of Israel. It should be noted, by the way, that until May 1948, some 69,000 Jews had risked their lives on ships bringing illegal immigrants to Palestine,[181] most of whom were arrested by the British before the ships landed, only to be deported to Cyprus. Despite the British position, however, the U.S. Army refused to prevent illegal emigration from the DP camps to Palestine. In compliance with a UN resolution passed because of the Arab-Israeli war, the army issued a directive in August 1948 prohibiting DPs of draft age from leaving the camps to fight in Israel's War of Independence, but it never actually implemented the policy.[182] Despite the intense fighting associated with Israel's first war with the Arabs, 28,224 Jews left Germany for the Holy Land between 15 May and 31 December 1948; in 1949 the number rose to 35,476 and in 1950 it plummeted to 1,938. In all, 65,638 DPs immigrated to Israel after the founding of the Jewish state.[183] At the same time, the United States, Canada, and Australia relaxed their restrictions on immigration.

Föhrenwald: The Camp for "Those Left Behind"

With the mass exodus from Germany, the number of Jewish DPs diminished so rapidly that one camp after another was shut down. By June 1950 anyone who wanted to emigrate and was physically able to do so had left the country.[184] In January 1949, there were 64,269 Jews in forty-eight camps in the U.S. Zone; by November that number had shrunk to 15,000 in nine camps.[185] Those who stayed behind were the sick and the weak; with the emigration of the physically and mentally able displaced persons, whose idealism and optimism had so profoundly influenced and sustained life in the camps, the internal structure of the DP camps changed radically. Virtually all the teachers in the camp schools and vocational training centers, most of the cultural elite, and a number of the "politicians" who had served on the Central Committee and in the camp administration—that is, the active segment of the DP population—had achieved their goal of leaving Germany.

Föhrenwald, too, was scheduled to be shut down, on 18 July 1949. However, since 3,623 Jewish DPs were still living in the camp, there was no real chance of putting the plan into effect.[186] A rumor in early December 1949 that the camp was to be evacuated by the twentieth of the month caused quite a stir and several protests. When it turned out that no moves had actually been made in that direction, conditions returned to normal.[187]

After the mass emigration of 1948 to 1949, the authorities began concentrating the remaining residents in a smaller number of DP camps and closing the others. In the process, they made a distinction between the acutely ill, or so-called hard-core cases, and Jews who had not indicated a country in which they wished to resettle, that is, the "undecided" DPs. The undecided were temporarily housed at Föhrenwald, Landsberg, and Lechfeld near Augsburg, and the acutely ill in Feldafing and at Gabersee near Wasserburg.[188] Then, in 1952, the authorities transferred to Föhrenwald all the displaced persons who for one reason or another had not yet emigrated. At that point most of the Jewish DPs still living in the camps were either too old or too feeble to rebuild their lives elsewhere or were unable because of illness to find a country that would admit them. Many simply were unprepared to deal with the problems posed by the Israeli climate. Their courage to face life had reached a low point. In past years the camp had radiated a sense of hope and become a center of postwar Jewish culture. Now it seemed dreary if not grim. Clearly, the camp was going downhill. Nonetheless, the longer Föhrenwald continued to function, the more difficult it became to dissolve the camp. After having grown accustomed to the relative security of camp life over so many years, the residents found it impossible to imagine living on their own.

The Transfer to German Administration

In the meantime, a major change had taken place—on 1 December 1951 Föhrenwald came under German administration. From then on it was called Regierungsdurchgangslager für heimatlose Ausländer (Government Transit Camp for Stateless Foreigners). The new arrangement made the camp residents feel nervous and insecure; it revived anxieties that recalled their traumatic experiences during the period of Nazi rule. Was it possible for Jews to live under German administration? JDC was well aware of the problems, so before IRO terminated its operations, the Joint made several requests to which the German authorities acceded. First, JDC asked that the Föhrenwald camp continue to be an exclusively Jewish camp. In other words, Jewish DPs could not be transferred against their will to a non-Jewish facility and Gentiles could not be sent to Föhrenwald, even if there were a sharp reduction in the size of the camp population. Second, German administrative personnel should be highly qualified professionals without a Nazi past. Apart from a small number of German officials, the camp administration would remain in Jewish hands, and only Jewish DPs from Föhrenwald could be employed there. Third, the Jewish character of the camp, with its cultural and religious institutions, its observance of the Sabbath and other Jewish days of worship, had to be preserved. Finally, JDC was to retain the special status it had enjoyed under IRO administration.[189]

Nonetheless, there was a public meeting in the camp during which the residents unanimously passed a protest resolution. "We declare publicly the intention of all the residents of the Föhrenwald camp, the sick and the disabled, not to submit themselves to German administration. We have no desire to be under either the political or legal protection of those who murdered our parents, children, sisters, and brothers." It was bad enough, the resolution stated, that as late as 1951 Jewish DPs still had to live on German soil, and they were not willing now to come under German administration.[190]

Resistance stiffened when, on 31 October 1951, the Germans began to register the residents of the camp. This procedure evoked horrible memories in the minds of Holocaust survivors, because it had been used by the Nazis to prepare for the deportation of the Jews. During the eight to ten days it took to register the camp residents, their anxieties subsided somewhat; after being bombarded with leaflets and attending meetings organized by IRO and JDC, they apparently realized that there was nothing they could do to prevent the transfer of authority.[191] Moreover, the Germans seemed to have taken to heart the instructions issued by the Bavarian State Ministry of the Interior and the Wolfratshausen *Landratsamt,* which stated that "the work required to transfer authority should be carried out with the greatest possible tact and empathy."[192] In the end, the business of transferring authority proceeded without any major problems, and the DPs gained confidence in the directors Dockal, Gareis, and Weigand of the German camp administration. The proof of their trust came when Dockal was slated for replacement in 1952, and the Jewish camp committee requested that "Mr. Dockal continue to be entrusted with the management of the Government Camp at Föhrenwald." "Mr. Dockal," the letter from the camp committee went on to say, "has succeeded in eliminating the distrust we felt when the camp came under German administration and has convinced us that making amends is not just a phrase; it stands for action as well. By the same token, Mr. Dockal showed us that measures taken by the [German] Government, which we felt were unjustified, were necessary and proper and should be implemented."[193] Hans Weigand, who succeeded Dockal as camp administrator, had been an opponent of the Nazis and a concentration camp inmate himself. Both he and Dockal adhered to the system of Jewish self-government that had proved so effective in the past. Thus, elections to the Jewish camp committee continued to be held under German administration.

Eighty-five percent of the cost of maintaining the German administration of the camp was borne by the German federal government and the remaining 15 percent by the state of Bavaria.[194] Now, for the first time, camp residents were subject to German laws; the German administration, however, showed special consideration to Jewish camp residents in interpreting and applying them. Under German administration, for example, there could continue to be a market on Sundays—which was ordinarily prohibited by German law—so long as "outsiders were prohibited from visiting the camp on Sundays and non-camp residents were thereby precluded from purchasing goods." Before permission was granted, however, extensive discussions took place. Residents argued they had been promised that the camp would retain its exclusively Jewish character, that the Sabbath took the place of Sunday for the Jews, and that the German law pertaining to Sunday as the day of rest therefore did not apply to them. The German administration countered by maintaining that most of the goods sold at the Sunday market were foodstuffs, semiluxury foods and tobacco, textiles, and shoes, that there were German as well as Jewish buyers, and that therefore it was impossible to speak of a purely Jewish market.[195]

The German administration did not inherit an easy task. It was obvious that caring for the residents of Föhrenwald—the old, the weak, and the sick who had been brought together in one place from all the DP camps that had been shut down—presented special problems. Yet, the German authorities sometimes showed little understanding for the desperate situation of the camp residents who had been "left behind" after the emigration of the able-bodied Jewish DPs. On 28 May 1952, an incident occurred that caused all the accumulated fear and rage to boil over. That morning 115 members of the Bavarian customs police and revenue service, accompanied by thirty-three armed members of the Bavarian state police, carried out a surprise raid on this last remaining displaced persons' camp in Germany. They blared out orders for an immediate search of the small businesses operating in the camp. The sudden appearance of a large number of government officials descending on the camp (Samuel Haber from the JDC went so far as to compare the raid to the actions of the

Nazi *Einsatzgruppen*)[196] brought a number of residents into the arena. They threw stones at the policemen's trucks to prevent them from driving on. Angered, the policemen yelled insults such as "The crematoria are still there" and "The gas chambers are waiting for you."[197] The situation threatened to escalate further when a shot was fired. Frustrated, the police officer in charge ordered a withdrawal without a search ever taking place.[198] The incident left both sides embittered.

Later, the police were careful to avoid carrying out such raids so as not to imperil the declared goal of the German administration—the rapid dissolution of the camp in a relatively orderly fashion. However, almost five more years would pass before the camp was actually closed in February 1957. During this period the Jewish camp committee and the Joint concentrated their energies on finding a country or countries that would accept these the last remaining Jewish DPs. At the same time, they tried to maintain a certain level of normalcy in the daily life of the camp residents. Cultural work was limited almost exclusively to the children who had remained at Föhrenwald with their ailing parents. For this reason JDC and the Jewish camp committee urged the German administration to renovate the camp's elementary school. On 10 June 1952, the refurbished facility was dedicated in an impressive ceremony. The building consisted of three attractive classrooms fitted out with modern school furniture, an assembly hall, and a teachers' room. The West German government had approved DM 33,000 for the expansion and an additional DM 18,000 for furniture and teaching aids.[199] In 1952 the rebuilt school had one Jewish and four German teachers who instructed 130 children using the standard German curriculum with added courses in Hebrew.

The new administration did not make any changes in the well-run kindergarten on Michigan Street. In addition to the seven workers who were already employed at the facility to care for the approximately 160 children, in December 1951 the administration approved the hiring of a state-certified female youth worker, four state-certified female kindergarten teachers, and a female kindergarten assistant. JDC expressed its willingness to provide a female cook and sufficient food to feed the children on a regular basis.[200] Starting on 1 April 1952, the government of Bavaria approved a quarterly subsidy of DM 0.60 to provide toys for each child.[201]

JDC had not only urged the German administration to renovate the camp school, but together with the Young Men's Christian Association (YMCA) it began, on 1 July 1952, to work directly with the young people in the camp through the Haus der offenen Tür (Open Door House) at Föhrenwald. The American service organizations' plan was to prepare some 200 young people for emigration or, if they wished to remain in Germany (which was rarely the case), to help them overcome their hostilities toward the country and its inhabitants. Following protracted negotiations, the Bavarian State Ministry of Education gave both organizations a subsidy of DM 1,000 per month to hire three youth services workers. Since many German government officials regarded YMCA staff as ideally suited for the assignment at Föhrenwald, the Federal Ministry of the Interior declared its willingness to expend DM 850 per month, initially for the period from 1 July 1952 through 31 March 1953, to hire two additional YMCA youth workers.[202] The only proviso was that there had to be at least 200 young people in the program.[203]

In the summer of 1953, the program comprised 230 young people aged ten to twenty-five. Classes in foreign languages, mathematics, and history were extremely popular, as were the film showings, the library, and the reading room. Thus, JDC and the YMCA rated the program a success.[204] The German authorities apparently thought so, too, since they extended the subsidy to 31 March 1954, even though the number of young people in the program had declined to about 140. However, instead of the original DM 850, the German government, beginning on 1 February 1954, reduced the monthly payment to DM 480.[205] Since there were still 149 young people living in Föhrenwald as of July 1954, the Germans extended their subvention to 30 September 1954.[206]

ORT, too, scaled down its training programs because of the decrease in the number of students. Although the Wolfratshausen *Landrat* gave the organization a positive evaluation because of the number of graduates who had passed the completion examinations in the various trades, the German camp administration cut back its subsidy to ORT, referring to an employment office report that gave the organization a much more negative rating.[207]

As the date for closing the camp approached, ORT terminated its program at Föhrenwald; the classes in watch repair, tailoring, and radio that were still being offered in the camp as of March 1956 were transferred to the ORT school at No. 39 Schwere-Reiter-Straße in Munich.[208] Apart from the camp residents working as apprentices in ORT trade schools, only about 10 percent of Föhrenwald's population were employed in regular jobs. The majority of the residents lived on small pensions, unemployment insurance, and—for the most part— welfare. The DPs remaining at Föhrenwald were simply unable to work; they were either too old, too sick, or too disabled physically and psychologically as a result of their experiences during the Nazi period.

The involvement of the DPs in cultural pursuits diminished in proportion to the decline of other activities in the camp. The last play presented at Föhrenwald—Abraham Prowantiner's *King Solomon and Shulamith* in three acts and four scenes—was performed on 14 April 1952. It was staged with the support of the Joint and ORT. The production reflected just how much the population profile of the camp had changed: the ensemble had more children than adults. Nevertheless, there was general praise for the performance.[209]

Children had become the symbols of what little cultural life was still left in the camp; they even gave performances for Jews living outside Föhrenwald. In March 1954, for example, forty schoolchildren from Föhrenwald performed for elderly "stateless" Jews in the banquet hall of Caritas House on Biedersteinstraße in Munich. They delighted their audience with dances and choral renditions of Israeli folk songs and poems. The inclusion in their repertoire of *Schuhplattler,* or Bavarian folk dancing, showed just how much the children had adapted themselves to their Bavarian environment.[210] That same month children from the camp school, together with members of the Open Door House, performed in Munich's *Amerikahaus*[211] to celebrate Brotherhood Week. The fact that the evening had been organized by Munich's Jewish community attests to the rapprochement that had taken place between the German Jewish survivors and the DPs. Soon the future of Jewish life in Germany would come to depend on these local Jewish communities alone.[212]

The first indication of future developments was the fact that the cultural dynamism that had been the hallmark of the Föhrenwald camp was largely a thing of the past; culture became something that the camp residents received passively. Famous artists continued to make guest appearances in the camp as part of their tours. JDC often helped make the arrangements, as, for example, when Dan Platkin, the famous American singer, performed in the camp before an audience of 1,200.[213] Various people regularly gave talks followed by discussions in the reading rooms. In March 1952, for instance, Föhrenwalders could hear a lecture on "Heinrich Heine's Attitude toward the Jews, Based on the Facts, on His Letters and Poems."[214] Even more popular than lectures, though, were the double features shown every evening at the camp cinema.[215]

The German authorities gave the Föhrenwald residents free rein when it came to cultural questions; however, they continually clashed with the Jewish DPs over the camp hospital. Since it was first established, Föhrenwald had had its own 120- to 150-bed hospital. Initially, the facility was run by a team of non-Jewish Hungarian doctors who were as dedicated to their work as they were capable. UNRRA appointed a non-Jewish Australian physician to assist them. At the time, Jewish physicians were in short supply, since only very few had survived the concentration camps. However, the situation improved when some doctors arrived in the U.S. Zone as part of the mass exodus of Jews from Poland. At first the nursing staff was made up mostly of German women and German girls; again, there were very few Jewish nurses. The situation quickly changed, though, when the camp administration arranged for Jewish girls to be trained as nurses in ORT schools.[216] The Joint had provided the relatively well equipped hospital with most of the necessary drugs and medical equipment.[217] In addition to the hospital proper and the JDC pharmacy that had been transferred to Föhrenwald from Munich in 1951, there was an outpatient clinic with its own dental department. Three physicians, one dentist, one dental technician, and four nurses were responsible for the outpatient treatment of between eighty and a hundred camp residents per day.

The outpatient clinic and the hospital had become a permanent feature of the camp. Before Föhrenwald came under German administration, the residents had been promised that the hospital would be kept open until the camp itself was closed. Consequently, the announcement by Bavarian authorities that the hospital was to be shut down on 1 December 1953 provoked bitter opposition from patients. A specially convened camp committee tried to counter the authorities' plan with the following arguments. First, it maintained that the costs of treating camp residents at the Wolfratshausen hospital or another facility outside the camp would be higher than at the Föhrenwald hospital. Second, it pointed out that the Jewish DPs did not wish to be put in a hospital together with German patients. Third, the committee contended that since Orthodox Jews could not obtain kosher food in a treatment facility outside Föhrenwald, it was imperative to have a hospital and outpatient clinic located in the camp. Finally, the committee claimed that a camp that still had 1,400 residents suffering from a variety of illnesses resulting from their persecution under the Nazis should for that reason alone have its own hospital. Tuberculosis, cardiovascular diseases, mental disorders, sciatica, rheumatoid arthritis, gastritis, vertigo, headaches, low back pain, and respiratory infections were commonplace in the camp.[218] The Bavarian authorities responded that the personnel and material costs of maintaining the camp hospital were simply too high. They pointed out that in the present circumstances it was impossible to perform surgical procedures in the hospital. If need be, they argued, a few beds could be set up in the outpatient clinic. Finally, they maintained that only a small percentage of patients actually requested kosher food.[219]

As a result of patients' protests, the closing of the hospital scheduled for 1 December 1953 was postponed. After several further attempts to shut it down failed, the German authorities finally set a deadline of 31 March 1955 for the facility's closing. They gave notice to both the doctors and the nursing staff. The nurses, however, were to be transferred to the Wolfratshausen county hospital along with some of the patients. In January 1955, as a result of JDC's plan to send camp patients to various hospitals in the area, the last fourteen patients at the Föhrenwald hospital went on a hunger strike, raising tensions to the boiling point. It is understandable, of course, that these patients were afraid of being separated from one another. The discussions that followed dragged on until 1 September 1955, when the camp hospital finally shut its doors and the last patients were transferred as a group to a rest home in Switzerland.[220]

Essentially, the camp hospital had treated adult patients for physical ailments. The camp's children, however, were in need mainly of psychotherapy and a stable environment. Therapists realized that they could frequently provide the latter simply by taking youngsters away from the grim reality of the camp. Therefore, in 1953, they began to organize vacations for the children. Föhrenwald's director and welfare department wrote to several summer camps, including Cohrs' in Nieblum on the North Sea island of Föhr, Frisch's in the county of Fischbachau, and Miesbach's and Bonnschlössl's in Bernau am Chiemsee, to find out whether and under what conditions they would be willing to accept Jewish children. The answers in most cases were positive; the camps could accommodate the children for between DM 4.50 and DM 5.50 per day, including medical care and the cost of the camps' recreation programs. The vacations were financed by the welfare section of the Bavarian Aid Society for Those Affected by the Nuremberg Laws (Hilfswerk, for short) and the *Allgemeine Ortskrankenkasse* [compulsory medical insurance for workers, the elderly, etc.—Trans.]. The camp's medical director, Dr. Ortenau, issued the required health certificates on the basis of the periodic physical examinations given to the students of the Föhrenwald school. Parents were also required to provide written permission for their children to attend the camps. If they refused, which did not happen often, their children were not allowed to go.

The program was successful on the whole; there were no complaints from parents. On the contrary, many of them reported that when their children returned it was as if they had been transformed. They had fewer problems in school. Generally when children were sent away now, it was not because of their physical or mental health but because a parent had fallen ill. For example, four siblings from one family were sent to a child-care center in Schlederloh because their mother had been in a Munich hospital for some time, their father was facing surgery, and there was no proper care facility inside the camp.[221]

These kinds of programs, however, were only a temporary solution; the various problems confronting Föhrenwald could be solved in the end only by closing the camp itself. Hence, JDC's Emigration Department devoted its efforts to finding countries that would admit the residents of the camp. Enthusiasm for Israel among the Föhrenwalders had waned after the first reports arrived about the harsh living conditions in the fledgling nation; Föhrenwald was populated mainly by Jews who could not deal with the problems posed by the Israeli climate or were not up to the physical strain of living in a developing country. Moreover, many of them suffered from tuberculosis, preventing immigration to other countries most able to accept refugees—the United States, Canada, and Australia.[222] The Kohn family, for example, saw no way out. "You see," Erica Kohn said, "my father had TB. His X rays still show deep scars in the lung. With X rays like that, he cannot go to the United States. The climate in Israel is such that if he goes there, within half a year, his TB will be reactivated and he will be a patient in a sanitarium for the rest of his life. Where will he go? Switzerland is a good place for TB patients, but they won't let us in. Of course, the best place for all the TB patients would be the Denver Jewish Hospital, but it is impossible to get there."[223]

Sweden and Norway admitted a number of DP families whose members were suffering from tuberculosis. The Norwegian authorities, in fact, admitted them virtually without any conditions attached: sixty-five Föhrenwalders—regardless of whether they had TB—found a new home in Norway. Social workers and employment officials in Oslo helped the refugees find accommodations and jobs. Health officials placed DPs with active TB in sanitariums. And the government granted them Norwegian citizenship. Finally, the refugees were assured that they could rely on the active support of the local Jewish community.[224] To prevent any disappointment or misunderstandings on the part of the DPs, the Norwegian refugee committee distributed a leaflet prior to their immigration in order to "orient them to the situation of refugees in Norway." The country had strict regulations regarding tuberculosis in order to prevent the spread of the disease. All DPs with TB "together with Norwegian patients will be sent to various treatment facilities. . . . Patients should not expect family members to find a residence close enough to these facilities to visit them [on a regular basis]. Patients must accept the fact that they will have to remain hospitalized for as long as the doctors consider it necessary." The leaflet mentioned the difficulty of finding housing and a job in Norway and also noted the country's high cost of living. Finally, the Norwegian refugee committee felt it was important to emphasize that "Norway desires to admit people [as immigrants] who will become happy and good citizens of our country and who wish to participate in building the nation and protecting the social benefits we have fought so hard to acquire. . . . Welcome to Norway."[225] Incidentally, this was the second resettlement of refugees in Norway; the first had been carried out in 1953.[226] Argentine president Juan D.

Peron, by the way, also granted visas to twenty-nine Föhrenwald families in 1955.[227]

Calling upon the technical assistance of United HIAS Service, the German authorities and JDC encouraged emigration through the use of financial incentives. Any adult DP who left Germany by 31 December 1954 received DM 100 and any child DM 50. The Joint, for its part, provided DM 200 per person or a maximum of DM 500 per family. After arriving in their new homelands, adults received an additional DM 2,000 plus DM 500 for each child from the West German government. JDC calculated its subsidy according to the country of resettlement and paid it in that country's currency—30,000 cruzeiros per person in Brazil, 12,000 pesos in Argentina, and 1,800 Uruguay dollars in Uruguay. The Joint provided no financial assistance for immigrants to the United States, Canada, and Australia, since it expected the local Jewish communities in those countries to assist refugees in the job of resettlement.[228] The emigrant subsidies were extended after the first deadline had passed at the end of 1954.

During the 1950s the residents of Föhrenwald migrated to many countries. In addition to the United States, Canada, and Norway, the new homelands for the Jewish DPs included Bolivia, Brazil, Argentina, Uruguay, and Australia.

The Returnees

While the voluntary relief organizations were dealing with the problem of emigration at Föhrenwald, a new phenomenon emerged that was to become the most contentious issue during the final years of the camp's existence—returning emigrants. Most were Jews who had immigrated to Israel but found it impossible to become part of Israeli society because of the difficult housing and employment situation there.[229] Problems with the language and the climate were further obstacles to integration. Some DPs had been euphoric about moving to the new Jewish nation but simply could not cope psychologically with the harsh day-to-day realities of life in a country under siege.

The American Jewish chaplain George Vida, for instance, ran into a young man whom he had first met at the Zeilsheim Displaced Persons Camp near Frankfurt. His name was Yossel, and he had lost his entire family to the Nazis. In 1946 he had only one wish—to go home to his mother, that is, the land of Israel. Seven years later, this same young man was back in Germany. "Well," he began in answer to the chaplain's question as to why he had returned, "it is hard to explain. You'll think I'm crazy. Maybe I am. But from the time I was 21 until now, the past 14 years I have spent my life in camps. First, I was sent from one concentration camp to another. Then, after liberation, I had lived in a Displaced Person's [sic] Camp. When I finally arrived in Israel, I was sent to a British detention camp. After a year there, I volunteered for the Israeli Army. Oh, I did quite well. I fought in the Negev and on the hills of Gallil. Then, in 1951, I was permitted to take off my uniform and to try to become what I always wanted to be, a normal human being. By then, I was 33 years old. Too old to learn anything and too young to retire. I had jobs and could not keep them. I had a room and I felt lonely in it."[230]

"You see, my dear Chaplain," a civilian rabbi in Munich tried to explain to Vida, "the tragedy of these people lies in the fact that they are healthy in body and of normal mind—only emotionally unstable. This kind of sickness is not at all apparent. The unbiased layman would think these people were just plain lazy. I saw people who had returned to Germany from five different countries already. They go to America, to South America, all the way to Australia or just over here to Sweden. They go with a great deal of enthusiasm, all set and eager to start a new life. But after a few months, their vigor wanes and they come back here, asking for a new chance—for a new life. What they need, however, is a new soul."[231]

The decision to return to Germany was not an easy one for emigrants. They felt as though they had failed and often did not tell even their close friends and relatives that they intended to go back. On top of everything else, the returnees encountered rejection, a lack of understanding, and even contempt from other Jews. A *Special Report from Germany* published in Israel stated:

> One of the most painful experiences for Jewish visitors to Germany is seeing the Jewish returnees from Israel. . . . They are the source of most of the horror stories about Israel making the rounds in Germany today. Many Germans who deeply detest Nazism and greatly admire what has been achieved in Israel are quite confused when they see these former

Israelis painting our country in the blackest of colors as a land marked largely by hunger and incompetence. . . . The most shameful chapter of the movement to return to Germany, however, is entitled "Föhrenwald." . . . As incredible as it may sound, former DPs began returning last year to the camp at Föhrenwald. . . . There they are again, just as they were after the collapse of the Third Reich, in a camp in Germany living off the generosity of Jewish welfare organizations. It does not take much to imagine a get-together at Föhrenwald of those shady characters who always seem to end up on the wrong side of the law. . . . The story of Föhrenwald is unpleasant and doubtless complicated. However, it is totally incomprehensible that the Joint did not bring this development to a timely conclusion that would have been acceptable to us Jews.[232]

Viewing the situation as a whole, one should not give undue emphasis to the problem of returnees. Nevertheless, for Föhrenwald the issue *was* one of major importance, because the only option for returnees who did not become part of a Jewish community was to move into this last existing DP camp. It is estimated that some 3,500 returnees from Israel arrived at Föhrenwald between 1949 and 1953.[233] Although the movement back to Germany had begun as early as August 1949, it was a trickle at first, reaching a peak in 1953.[234]

Initially, the German authorities did not pay much attention to the returnees. The law on "the legal status of stateless foreigners" of 25 April 1951 gave stateless persons, including many Jews, the right to return to Germany within two years of having left the country. In October 1952 camp administrators noted an increase in the population of Föhrenwald in spite of ongoing efforts to find countries of resettlement for the camp residents. As a consequence, they decided to prohibit any more newcomers from moving into the camp, though they actually did nothing to prevent them from coming. However, when Föhrenwald registered some 200 newcomers in December 1952 alone, camp authorities sounded the alarm. Most of the returnees had Israeli passports stamped "not valid for Germany." So German government officials notified their embassies in Rome and Paris, where most of the returnees obtained visas to enter Germany, to require anyone holding an Israeli passport with the "not valid for Germany" stamp to leave a deposit of $300. If the person holding the passport could not come up with the money, he or she was to be denied a visa. Although this measure resulted in a slight decline in the official number of emigrants returning to Germany, many now crossed the so-called green border and entered the country unobserved, at night. Thus, they were in Germany "illegally," which could have negative consequences when it came to issuing a new request to find countries of resettlement for them.

On 9 August 1953, a meeting to discuss the problem took place in Geneva among emissaries of the government of Israel, a representative of the West German government, and representatives of Jewish relief organizations. The German officials promised that "illegals" who agreed to be registered would be allowed to reside at Föhrenwald for six months, and the German government would pay the costs of feeding them. The agreement, however, applied only to those who arrived on or before the registration deadline. All other returnees would be treated as having illegally crossed the border. For their part, the Jewish service organizations promised to make every effort during these six months to resettle the "illegals" outside of Germany. The Bavarian authorities completed the process of registration between 14 and 17 August 1953; they counted 693 persons. At the same time, they set up a police station in the camp to guard against any movement by illegals into the camp. According to the instructions given to the police, "the admission of further illegals is absolutely forbidden." The Bavarian authorities felt it was important to continue making a distinction between "legal" and "illegal" camp residents and refused to grant the two groups equal status. In practice this meant, for example, that illegals had no claim to the supplementary rations given to TB patients and had no right to vote for members of the camp committee.[235] Further, the Bavarians made sure that the registered illegals in the camp did not receive residence permits, which were required in order to marry, accept employment, and obtain a passport.[236]

After the six-month period had expired in March, the German government extended the deadline to 1 July 1954 to acknowledge the "tremendous efforts" undertaken by the Jewish relief organizations in helping to solve the problem of the illegals. HIAS and JDC had managed to persuade 500 "illegals" to immigrate, mostly to South America.[237] Still, the problem could not be completely resolved. Although the bulk of the returnees had departed, some stayed behind either because they would not or could not leave. Disputes often arose between the "illegal" and the "legal" residents, because the latter were afraid they might have to give up some of their privileges.[238] Thus, the sick and disabled in the camp requested in October 1953 that Interior Minister Wilhelm Hoegner press for the removal of the "illegals."[239] The "illegals" were a particular problem when the camp was dissolved. Since they did not have any legal status, they could not be part of the Föhrenwald resettlement program. "The question of what will become of them," said Camp Director Weigand in December 1955, "is my single biggest worry."[240]

Closing the Camp

All those in positions of responsibility nevertheless agreed that the camp had to be shut down. Föhrenwald had apparently become a hopeless welfare problem. All plans by the German authorities and the Jewish relief organizations to close the camp had fallen through. The Bundesgrenzschutz (Federal Border Guard) had hoped to use Föhrenwald as a training camp in March 1953 after increasing its force to 20,000 men. Consequently, it wanted the camp to be evacuated as soon as possible.[241] But its plans, too, came to naught. After prolonged discussions it was decided in March 1954 to close the camp by 1 April 1955.[242] Meanwhile, the German authorities agreed with the Joint and HIAS that the problem could not be solved by emigration alone and that some of the residents would have to be integrated into German society. The West German government assumed the cost of building residences for the DPs who—because they suffered from tuberculosis, for instance—were unable to find a country to admit them or simply no longer wished to immigrate; Jewish service organizations provided the funds for their initial allowances.[243] The Germans were interested in the rapid success of the program, not least because of financial considerations. For the period from 1 December 1951 to 31 March 1956, Föhrenwald had cost the German government DM 10,957,246, of which DM 6,500,000 had been for payment in kind and administrative expenses and DM 4,457,246 for welfare expenditures. One should not infer from these figures that the camp residents were leading lives of luxury; based on the total outlay,

the average expenditure per resident was DM 124 a month.[244] From
a financial standpoint, it was actually more cost effective to house the
DPs in apartments. The German government paid 85 percent of the
DM 3.6 million cost of building the flats and the state of Bavaria paid
the remainder.[245]

Even though Jewish organizations were eager to close Föhrenwald,
they could not meet the new deadline for shutting down the camp in
spring 1955. However, in April and May 1954 residents had been
surveyed as to their future plans—that is, whether they intended to
emigrate or remain in Germany.[246] The 145 DPs who had indicated
neither a country in which they wished to resettle nor a place in Germany where they wished to stay were sent to one of three refugee
camps in Munich or to a camp in Ingolstadt.[247] The remaining 789
displaced persons were given accommodations in various German
cities, mainly in Munich (492) and Frankfurt (125), but also in Düsseldorf (73), Cologne (25), Wiesbaden (23), Stuttgart (19), Hamburg
(18), Nuremberg (10), and Kaiserslautern (4).[248] The transfer of camp
residents, however, did not always proceed smoothly. There were often psychological reasons for their resistance to being moved. Many
suffered from separation anxiety and were afraid to take responsibility
for their own lives in a strange country whose citizens they still dis-
trusted.[249] This is quite understandable when one considers how long
many of these people had already spent living in camps and the fact
that most of them were ill.

Some residents tried to take legal action to prevent their resettlement. Before being moved, the DPs received a notice informing them
that they had been assigned flats and giving them the exact address
of their new residences and the day on which they were to move in. If
they refused to avail themselves of the government's offer, they would
receive an "order to accept accommodations,"[250] which stated that in
the event of a second refusal "the *Land* police of the Wolfratshausen
Landratsamt have been instructed . . . to enforce the order by taking
you and your family into custody and moving them together with all
your household goods to your assigned residence." Residents had two
weeks after receipt of the notification in which to appeal the order.[251]

One camp resident did appeal. He hired an attorney who explained
that the flat in the Munich suburb of Pasing that had been assigned
to him and his wife was too small, consisting of just one room and a

kitchen, and that since his wife suffered from tuberculosis, she had a right to have her own bedroom. Further, the lawyer stated, the newly built flat was damp and detrimental to the woman's health. The law on "the legal status of stateless foreigners" of 25 April 1951, he argued, guaranteed stateless persons the same constitutional rights enjoyed by the citizens of West Germany in choosing a place to live and moving freely within the Federal Republic. Assigning the couple a flat in which they could not reasonably expect to live violated their right of free movement as guaranteed in the West German constitution. Stateless persons, he added, also enjoyed freedom of religion. And since the defendant was an Orthodox Jew, the lawyer added, he could only live in a flat that was located in close proximity to an Orthodox synagogue.[252] The defendant, however, never had a chance. The government of Upper Bavaria dismissed the case on its merits. The offer of a flat in Pasing, the Bavarian authorities argued, was nothing more than a suggestion, not a government order and not an administrative act subject to judicial review. Even "threatening to use the police to compel compliance with the order to accept accommodations . . . was nothing more than giving advance notice; it was not an administrative act that warranted a legal complaint."[253]

The problems encountered in closing the camp gave rise to fears that it would be difficult to integrate the former residents of Föhrenwald into their new surroundings. Fortunately, however, this did not turn out to be the case. A study conducted in the summer of 1959 concluded that, with the exception of the seriously ill and the very old, the former DPs had been integrated into West German society. Most had settled into their flats, and their children had made friends.[254] After the long years in concentration camps and/or at Föhrenwald, many felt happy to be living in real homes again that they could call their own.[255] When questioned about social contacts on the job or with neighbors and friends, fifty-one responded that they were on good terms with everyone, twenty-nine said they had some social interaction, seven reported they had none and felt isolated, and thirteen were hostile to or at odds with those around them.[256] All the same, at least a third of those surveyed still wanted to immigrate to the United States.[257]

The last Jewish DPs left Camp Föhrenwald on 28 February 1957,[258] some twelve years after it had been established. In late 1955, the archdiocese of Munich-Freising had purchased the Föhrenwald complex. The houses in the camp were renovated with the support of the German government and the Katholisches Siedlungs- und Wohnungsbauwerk (Catholic Society for Planned Community and Housing Construction). Just a few months later, families in Wolfratshausen could purchase a small house for a reasonable price in the new Waldram section of town. A 600- to 800-square-meter (6,456- to 8,608-square-foot) home cost DM 22,000. Buyers put DM 2,500 to 5,000 down and paid off the balance at DM 75 a month. These low-interest loans were still being offered in 1976 when the local *Isar-Loisachbote* newspaper noted with pride how in twenty years "the tidy planned community of Altwaldram had evolved from the notorious run-down Föhrenwald camp of post–World War II days."[259] This statement— no doubt subconsciously—provides a deep insight into the lack of sympathy and understanding with which Föhrenwald's German neighbors had responded to the problems facing the Jewish DPs.

Belsen

The Liberation of Bergen-Belsen

The name Bergen-Belsen will forever be associated with the concentration camp that existed in the area of Hanover near the town of Celle from April 1943 to 15 April 1945. What has generally been forgotten, however, is that until 1951 Belsen was the largest DP camp in Germany. SS chief Heinrich Himmler had ordered the construction of Belsen in April 1943 on the site of an underutilized Wehrmacht POW camp (Stalag 311) that had been built in 1940. The Nazis created Belsen as a "residence camp" (*Aufenthaltslager*) for Jews who had some special relationship to influential persons in countries hostile to Germany and could be used either as "exchange Jews" to recover German citizens interned abroad or as hostages. In actual fact, very few of the mostly Dutch Jews in the camp were ever "exchanged"; the vast majority were eventually murdered in the extermination camps. Until March 1944, conditions in Belsen were "better" than in other concentration camps. Then Belsen became a dumping ground for prisoners classified as "unfit to work," that is, for the weak and acutely ill survivors of the other camps.

Bergen-Belsen officially became a concentration camp when Josef Kramer succeeded Adolf Haas as camp commandant on 2 December 1944. Thereafter, conditions in what had been a camp for "privileged" Jews deteriorated dramatically. In the wake of the evacuation of the extermination and concentration camps located near the front lines, tens of thousands of survivors of the so-called death marches arrived in Belsen. In spite of the bitter cold, the camp administration provided no protection from the elements and practically no food or water. Then a typhus epidemic hit the camp. Some survivors explained later that when they arrived in Belsen, the conditions there were worse than in many of the camps they had passed through on their way. In spite of the high death rate, the population of Belsen increased from some 22,000 to 43,042 between 1 February and 1 April 1945. Yet the camp did not have any more latrines or water than in the spring of 1944, when just 2,000 prisoners were housed there. In one part of the camp, where some 8,000 to 10,000 human beings had been crammed together, there was not a single toilet or water faucet. Shortly before liberation, the camp's entire water supply system broke down after a bomb destroyed the main power station in Hanover and the electrically operated water pump failed. One can imagine the consequences this had for the inmates of Belsen.

Because of the spreading typhus epidemic, German and British army commanders reached an unprecedented local armistice agreement. The camp and part of the surrounding countryside, an area of 48 square kilometers (18.5 square miles), were not evacuated but declared a neutral zone and transferred to the British on 15 April 1945.[1] British troops were stunned by what they saw on the day of liberation. Brigadier General Hugh Llewelyn Glyn Hughes, deputy director of medical services for the Second Army, wrote down his impressions: "No description nor photograph could really bring home the horror that was outside the huts, and the frightful scenes inside were much worse. There were various sizes of piles of corpses lying all over the camp. . . . The compounds themselves had bodies lying about in them. The gutters were full and within the huts there were uncountable numbers of bodies, some even in the same bunks as the living."[2]

British war reporters attached to the Military Government's Eighth Corps reported in their weekly survey: "There were no sanitation facilities whatsoever; men and women were packed together and forced to relieve themselves however and wherever they could. The general impression of filth and neglect was reinforced by the presence of thousands of scraps of cloth which at first looked like mere rags but on closer inspection turned out to be pieces of clothing that had been torn off the bodies of the dead. An incredible stench permeated the entire area."[3]

On 15 April 1945, the British found some 10,000 unburied dead throughout the camp. They managed to free about 60,000 prisoners of fourteen nationalities, most of whom were more dead than alive. These figures are only estimates, however, because the Nazis had stopped keeping records on the flood of new prisoners dumped into

Belsen and had destroyed the camp's index-card file. Given the chaotic conditions that existed in the days immediately following liberation, it is no wonder that the British found it impossible to carry out an exact count of the survivors. It was even difficult to tally the number of dead. Because of the danger of epidemics, the British were primarily concerned with burying the dead as quickly as possible.

The liberated prisoners were in such poor health that, despite the best efforts of British Army troops, the mass dying continued. By late April some 9,000 human beings had died as a result of the appalling conditions, and by June 1945 another 4,500 had expired.[4] In the following months, still more internees died. Some Western European survivors were repatriated, and the Swedish Red Cross organized a relief action to transport 6,000 sick and helpless inmates to Sweden. As a result, the camp population stabilized in November 1945 at some 16,000, 11,000 of whom were mostly Polish, Hungarian, and Romanian Jews.[5]

From Concentration Camp to Displaced Persons' Camp

Bergen-Belsen was divided into four separate areas. Camp No. 1 was the former concentration camp; it was evacuated between 24 April and 21 May 1945. Immediately after the camp was cleared of all internees on 21 May, the contaminated huts were torn down and what remained of Camp No. 1 was burned.

Before liberation, Camp No. 2 had served as a backup when Camp No. 1 was filled beyond capacity. Together with Camp No. 3, it included the SS barracks to the south and north located in proximity to the SS Training School. Camp No. 4 consisted of the SS officers' compound. The "Bergen-Belsen D.P. Hohne Camp" was set up on the grounds of Camps No. 2, 3, and 4. The new accommodations for the survivors—unlike those in Camp No. 1—consisted of concrete barracks with beds, mattresses, running water, and electricity. Thus, outwardly the conditions were comparable to those at Föhrenwald and relatively well suited for a displaced persons' camp.

In contrast to Föhrenwald, however, hundreds continued to die every day for some time after liberation, even though Brigadier General Glyn Hughes had set up a hospital the day after the British had entered the camp. Further, Glyn Hughes had sent British medical units to the camp, together with a contingent of armed forces, including Military Government detachments. In addition, he had organized doctors and nurses from among the internees, who, despite their weakened condition, readily volunteered to render assistance. Glyn Hughes managed to transform Camp No. 2, once used by the Wehrmacht as an infirmary, into a huge hospital.[6] Patients were disinfected with DDT powder and sent to sixty blocks in Camp No. 2.

About a week after the camp was liberated, a contingent of the British Red Cross reached Belsen, followed shortly thereafter by a unit of the Swiss Red Cross. About two weeks later, 100 British medical students arrived. They took over the job of feeding and looking after the inmates. These students became very popular with patients. Their job was extremely important because the inmates' emaciated bodies were no longer used to taking in normal food. Consequently, they had to be fed a special diet prescribed for concentration camp inmates suffering from advanced states of starvation. When famine cases were not specially fed, they would die. Tragically, this happened quite often when food was first distributed in the liberated concentration camps.[7]

Despite the selfless efforts of Brigadier General Glyn Hughes and his team, the British found it necessary to employ German doctors and nurses, because even in June 1945 there were still 11,200 patients in the camp to care for, some of whom were acutely ill.[8] The patients were naturally terrified of being looked after by Germans, even under supervision. They remembered how inmates had been subjected to medical experiments, mistreated, even murdered. Many patients resisted when German doctors wanted to give them intravenous infusions. They often cried out, begging not to be taken to the crematorium. However, since the British had to care for so many patients, they found it impossible to dispense with the assistance of Germans, and little by little the DPs became accustomed to the presence of German personnel.[9]

Self-Help and Support from Abroad

Just a few days after liberation, members of the various nationalities in the camp began organizing themselves into self-help committees to represent their various interests. It would not have been unreasonable to assume that the DPs were harking back to an already existing prisoners' committee of the type that had operated in most concentration camps. However, there had been no such prisoners' committee in the Bergen-Belsen camp. Admittedly, the establishment of a DP committee on the foundations of a concentration camp prisoners' organization would have been unprecedented in the history of the DPs, because, except for Belsen, no other DP camp in Germany had been set up on the grounds of a former concentration camp. What made the situation at Belsen truly unique, though, was that all the prisoners of the concentration camp became residents of a single DP camp.

The main goal of the various national-interest groups was to have the DPs repatriated to their home countries as quickly as possible. In this respect they were of one mind with the occupying powers, but at the same time they found themselves at odds with the Jewish displaced persons. This was the first manifestation of the struggle that would come to dominate relations between Britain and the Jews in the following years, the essence of which was the British refusal to recognize the Jews as a separate group.

British policy thus ran counter to the interests of the Jewish DPs. So Josef Rosensaft created a temporary committee at Belsen in April 1945, which functioned as a provisional representative Jewish body until September 1945, when the Central Committee of Liberated Jews in the British Zone was founded. The committee's most important objectives were the physical rehabilitation of the survivors; the search for relatives, if any; and the fight for the political rights and spiritual rehabilitation of the DPs.[10] Since it represented the largest group of displaced persons at Belsen, the committee soon occupied an important position inside the camp. Rosensaft was thus able to force the British to give the committee de facto recognition. However, the British never granted the official recognition that the Americans had accorded to the Central Committee for the U.S. Zone of Germany.

Under pressure from the Americans—more fallout from the Harrison Report—and Rosensaft's committee at Belsen, the British Government issued a confidential directive on 30 November 1945 permitting Jews to be housed in separate accommodations reserved exclusively for them. However, the British continued to prohibit the establishment of separate, exclusively Jewish camps.[11] Belsen at that time contained 60 percent of the Jewish DPs in the British Zone. The Jewish blocks were set up in Camp No. 4 and in the recently opened Camp No. 5. French, Belgian, and Dutch internees, as well as most of the Soviet citizens, had already departed Belsen; apart from the Jewish DPs, the only remaining displaced persons were Poles and Hungarians.[12]

Having secured separate barracks, the Central Committee had achieved its first success and made an important contribution to the spiritual rehabilitation of the Jews in the camp. In addition, the Jews received support from the representatives of the major Jewish relief organizations, who arrived at Belsen in the summer of 1945. Of the Jewish clergymen who accompanied the British troops into the camp, Leslie H. Hardman was the one rabbi who probably developed the closest relationship to the DPs.[13] Rabbis Baumgarten and Wilensky from the Chief Rabbi's Religious Emergency Council soon arrived in Belsen as well. Operating under the auspices of the Jewish Relief Unit (JRU), they were primarily interested in looking after the Orthodox Jews.

On 29 July 1945, a Joint team under Maurice Eigen began working at Belsen. The members of the team were JDC's first officially recognized representatives in occupied Germany; the Joint did not arrive in the U.S. Zone until 4 August 1945. JDC was unable at first to meet the many needs and wants of the Jewish DPs. Eigen stayed at Belsen until November 1945. There was little food he could offer the residents of the camp. On the other hand, he managed to organize a mail service.[14] In August 1945 Josef Rosensaft vented his anger at Jacob L. Trobe, JDC director for Germany, asking why JDC had arrived so late. After hearing Trobe's response, he said: "Listen, if you can't give us things, give us some Yiddish typewriters so we can criticize the JDC to the Jews of the world."[15] Rosensaft's reproach, however, was misplaced. The chaotic conditions in postwar Germany and the dependence of the nongovernmental relief organizations upon the army, which resented any civilian interference, worked against the rapid provision of effective assistance. Moreover, relief supplies had to be acquired in the United States, Sweden, Denmark, France, or Switzerland first and then imported into Germany. There was no efficient way to supply the DP camps with everything they needed—

food, medicine, clothing, shoes, paper, school books, machinery, writing materials, and so on; so operations perforce started off slowly.

In early August 1945, JDC's Belsen team received support from twelve members of the Jewish Relief Unit. The major Jewish organizations in Britain, under the overall control of the Central British Fund, had established the Jewish Committee for Relief Abroad, which in turn had created the Jewish Relief Unit, that is, groups of volunteers to assist the DPs. Compared to the Joint, the JRU was a relatively new organization. Though it had little experience in the field of welfare work and a small staff, it made up in enthusiasm what it lacked in years and size.

The first JRU team reached Germany on 21 June 1945. Led by Shalom Markovich, it was sent to the DP camp at Diepholz, where some 1,200 Jews had been living since August 1945.[16] Lady Rose Henriques and Leonard Cohen, together with their assistants, arrived a short time after the Diepholz team to direct the work of the JRU in Germany from the town of Celle. During the second half of 1945, the JRU moved its headquarters to the small village of Eilshausen near Herford in Westphalia. In April 1946 there were sixty-eight members of the JRU working in Germany. The number rose to ninety-two by the summer of 1946, some of whom were active in the U.S. Zone as well. Many of the workers were British and had committed themselves to serve in Germany for at least a year; others, however, were themselves refugees, including a high percentage of German Jews who had escaped to Britain during the Nazi period.[17] In late 1949 the organization's headquarters, now responsible for all of Europe, were moved to Hanover, where they remained until the JRU completed its work in Germany in the summer of 1950 and in the rest of Europe in September of the same year.

The twelve members of the JRU team at Diepholz who had worked in Holland and Belgium before coming to Germany were posted to Belsen in August 1945, where they soon received additional volunteers. Sara Eckstein was head of the JRU's Belsen team from 1947 to 1950.[18] Among the first Jewish Relief workers to reach Belsen was Jane Leverson. She returned to Belsen with the team from Diepholz and reported on her experiences in November 1945: "They need security—security and affection. They need to live a normal life, among normal people. This can never be achieved for the majority of them in occupied Germany. Some may be saved, if they can get into a friendly, normal environment soon. Some but not all, but all should have the opportunity."[19]

Hence, the JRU volunteers were basically concerned with the psychological rehabilitation of the Jewish survivors. They tried to make it possible for them to lead halfway normal lives. In addition, they helped care for patients at the Belsen hospital.

The JRU was in competition, as it were, with the Joint's representatives in the British Zone. Problems seemed to emerge whenever the two organizations tried to cooperate. The JRU took the view that as a British organization it was responsible for the British Zone and the Joint should therefore limit its assistance to the U.S. Zone. The two organizations were able to settle their differences only as a result of high-level talks between British Army representatives and Directors Trobe (JDC) and Cohen (JRU).[20] The agreement they worked out stipulated that the JRU was to carry out its activities under the auspices of JDC and that its contacts with the British military also had to be channeled through the Joint. One factor that may have contributed to the beginning of a cooperative relationship between JDC and the JRU was that the American relief organization was no longer made up principally of Americans. The Joint now employed Canadians, Britons, French, and a number of DPs.[21]

In the wake of negotiations among the British military, JDC, and the JRU, the various tasks were allocated as outlined below. The Jewish Relief Unit was made responsible for welfare work in the broader sense of the term; for example, it provided food for babies, small children, and pregnant women and assisted in setting up a camp police force. The Joint initially focused on organizing a camp postal service. Adrienne Schwerner, the director of the post office and a Belgian, made a special contribution in this regard. The reason a postal service was so important for the DPs was that the German postal service had been shut down by the occupation authorities, and the only way displaced persons could give friends or relatives a sign that they had survived was by finding someone in the army who was willing to send a message for them.

In December 1945 David B. Wodlinger succeeded Maurice Eigen as JDC's director in the British Zone. In an effort to determine more precisely the actual food-ration requirements in the camp, Wodlinger tried to register the residents of Belsen. However, despite his and others' attempts, no one was ever able to come up with an exact figure for the number of residents in the camp. Because of their experiences during the years of Nazi oppression, the DPs still had a deep-seated fear of any kind of exact reporting of population statistics. Of course, on the other hand, it was in the camp residents' interest to be as well fed as possible. And the more people who were "officially" on the camp rolls, the more rations everyone would receive.[22] Supplementing rations by continuing to use the names of people who had left or died was practiced in many DP camps, but it seems to have been a real success only at Belsen, because we have relatively reliable statistics on the other camps. Contemporary witnesses credit the influence and skill of Josef Rosensaft for the perpetuation of this kind of inaccurate reporting, which ultimately redounded to the benefit of the camp residents.

In addition to establishing the camp's postal service and registering camp residents, the Joint helped draw up lists of survivors and search for missing family members. Further, it paved the way for the emigration program that was about to be inaugurated and assisted in organizing the ration distribution system.[23]

After August 1945, conditions at Belsen deteriorated markedly. With the arrival of several thousand Russian ex-POWs and Poles who had volunteered to work in Germany before the war, the camp was once again filled beyond capacity. The Russian DPs were repatriated in late September, but the Poles remained in the camp for quite some time.[24] This change in the composition of the camp's population resulted in a reduction in the percentage of Jewish residents and caused problems for the Jewish service organizations in their effort to provide relief for the DPs. At first they intended to send supplies to the non-Jewish DPs as well. But because of the increase in the size of the camp's population, they did not have the resources to do so. Beginning on 17 September, the minimum daily ration was continually reduced; by November, camp residents were receiving only 1,800 calories per day.[25] The nutritional value of the food rations was minimal; fresh fruits and vegetables were virtually unobtainable.

It was not until October 1945 that larger shipments of supplies began to arrive at Belsen. They came mostly from the Joint's warehouses in Denmark. By the early summer of 1946, JDC was sending

Belsen all the supplies destined for the British Zone; from there Rosensaft's committee distributed them to the Jews in the camp as well
as to those in the other camps and to German Jews living outside the
DP camps. To correct irregularities in the distribution system, Wodlinger moved the central warehouse from Belsen to Bremen in May
1945 and put Jacques de Gorter in charge of managing the facility.[26]
This massive intervention in the system of Jewish self-government
caused a great deal of friction between Rosensaft and Wodlinger.

Belsen under UNRRA Administration

UNRRA began its work in the British Zone in November 1945, although it did not actually take over responsibility for administering
Belsen from the British Army until early March 1946.[27] Earlier, on
26 November 1945, Field Marshal Sir Bernard Law Montgomery,
commander in chief of the British forces of occupation in Germany,
and Lieutenant General Sir Frederick E. Morgan, chief of UNRRA
operations for Germany, had signed an agreement arranging for the
transfer to UNRRA of administrative responsibility for the DP camps
in the British Zone.[28] The months-long delay in implementing the
agreement may be attributed to UNRRA's poor organizational structure in the British Zone as well as to its lack of equipment and
trained personnel.

For these reasons, the British Army hesitated to entrust UNRRA
with the responsibility for administering the largest DP camp in Germany. Indeed, when UNRRA finally began its work at Belsen in
March 1946, during the first few months a number of incidents arose
between the Jewish refugees and the UN authorities, some of which
were quite serious. In spring 1946 UNRRA gave the Jews at Belsen
an ultimatum: they were to evacuate their accommodations in Camp
No. 3 for the benefit of the military and move into Nissen huts. Michael Gelber, the representative of the JDC director for Germany at
Belsen, tried to convince the local UNRRA director, David Wheatman, of the absurdity of the idea. Wheatman flew into a rage, arguing
that many Englishmen would consider themselves lucky to be allowed to live in Nissen huts and that he himself had lived in one
during the war. In principle, Gelber was not opposed to the idea of

housing the Jews in Nissen huts; rather, he could not understand why the survivors of the Holocaust should move once again after having had to endure such unbearable living conditions for so many years in the camps. Wheatman shot back that he had heard the concentration camp argument once too often and that he did not have any sympathy for it anymore. If the DPs refused to move, he said, he would use force to remove them. Gelber then threatened to report the incident to the press and make it appear as though Wheatman was mainly to blame for the conflict, since UNRRA had made no effort to find adequate replacement housing for the DPs.[29]

The reasons why UNRRA gave in for the time being have not come down to us. Presumably Gelber's objections and threats decided the issue. Nevertheless, Camp No. 3 was evacuated during the second half of 1946. From then on, Belsen consisted of Camps No. 2, 4, and 5, which the residents dubbed the "Russian," "British," and "American" Zones, respectively. They had not given them these names arbitrarily. The names reflected the varying quality of the accommodations. The barracks in the "American" Zone were occupied by "old-established" DPs, that is, internees who had been liberated in Belsen; the barracks in the "Russian" and "British" Zones were inhabited largely by Jewish refugees from Eastern Europe who had not arrived in Belsen until 1946.[30]

The next major incident occurred just a few weeks after the crisis over Camp No. 3. Without giving any reason, UNRRA director Wheatman imposed a twenty-four-hour curfew on Belsen. No one could enter or leave the camp without his express permission. Only later did residents learn the real reason for his action. Riots had taken place in the camp, yet the military had been unable to find and arrest the guilty parties. It was thought that a collective punishment would force the DPs to hand over the perpetrators. A subsequent investigation showed that all punishable acts had been committed by non-Jewish Poles and that the Jews were therefore being penalized for crimes committed by Gentiles. When this became known, the Central Committee expressed its outrage in the form of a protest letter. The Jewish residents did not stop there, however. They held a spontaneous protest demonstration to which the British clearly overreacted. The British authorities brought up fire engines and drove the demonstrators back with water cannons; at the same time, Polish guards in the camp threw stones into the crowd, while uninvited German onlookers applauded. The situation escalated when demonstrators broke through the locked gates of the camp. The British threatened to use their weapons, but the Jews were not to be deterred and shouted jeers and taunts at them: "Go ahead and shoot, if you dare!" The British guards remained calm and would not be provoked. Incensed, the Jews returned to the camp. The curfew was lifted, but the incident left a deep sense of unease on both sides.[31]

Calm returned to Belsen, but only after the rapid removal of the non-Jewish DPs; the Jewish residents had finally attained their objective—to make Bergen-Belsen an exclusively Jewish camp.[32] Thus, in May 1946, they had achieved in the British Zone what the Americans had implemented in their zone after Eisenhower had issued his directives of 22 August 1945 in response to the Harrison Report.

The situation improved further with a change of UNRRA directors in the summer of 1946: on 8 July 1946 Simon Bloomberg replaced Wheatman.[33] Bloomberg had been an officer in the British Colonial Service. He knew the official mind and could talk on equal terms with the military and civil authorities. There was soon a different atmosphere at Belsen. The change was manifested in concrete terms in the distribution of clothes and other goods in quantities previously unseen in the camp. The newly appointed supply officer was soon a very popular person with camp residents.[34] Bloomberg identified so closely with the Belsen DPs that he resigned his position as UNRRA director of the camp in protest against the authorities' refusal to recognize the Jewish refugees from Eastern Europe as displaced persons and grant them rations. However, he continued to serve the interests of the survivors, for he was soon appointed field director for Europe of the Jewish Committee for Relief Abroad.[35]

Medical Care

After the first few weeks, conditions in the camp stabilized and the Jewish DPs gradually began to organize administrative, occupational, cultural, and religious facilities. But medical care was still of primary importance. The makeshift infirmary set up in Camp No. 2 by the British Army was expanded into a provisional hospital adapted to the day-to-day needs of the Jewish DPs. As patients recovered and the Red Cross began to participate directly in the medical rehabilitation of the ex-prisoners, the number of sick persons declined and the DPs were gradually able to convert hospital rooms back into regular living quarters. A general hospital built by the Germans in 1937 (the so-called German hospital), located just over a kilometer (0.62 miles) from the concentration camp, became the regular DP camp hospital. Twelve hundred German patients were removed from this hospital in early June 1945 to permit admission of patients from the camp. One wing was used for the treatment of orderlies and other health personnel who had themselves contracted typhus in the course of their duties.[36]

Until 21 August 1945, the 700-bed hospital was administered by the British Army's Sanitary Service. It was then taken over by UNRRA, which was already sending medical personnel to the British Zone, even though it did not have administrative responsibility for Belsen at the time.[37] As a token of their gratitude to Brigadier General Glyn Hughes, who had selflessly directed the work of transforming a death trap into a hospital, the DPs named the new facility the Glyn Hughes Hospital. When UNRRA left Germany in the summer of 1947, responsibility for administering the hospital fell to the Jewish Relief Unit. For some time the Joint had been financing the operation of this hospital, which was the only Jewish hospital in the British Zone. Ultimately, JDC assumed the job of administration and installed its own personnel.[38]

Four JDC doctors worked at Belsen until the middle of May 1947. They reported to the Joint's chief medical officer for the British Zone, Dr. Fritz Spanier, a Dutchman. Dr. Spanier employed two Jewish DP doctors—Dr. Leibel and Dr. Herz—four German general practitioners, and two medical specialists. In spite of great misgivings, the British authorities found it necessary to employ German physicians at Belsen after the liberation of the camp due to the army's and later UNRRA's lack of sufficient skilled medical personnel.[39] It is ironic that although they were forbidden to treat German patients because of their Nazi pasts, the German doctors were nevertheless allowed to practice in the DP camp.[40] In this connection we might mention Dr. A. Kurzke, a former SS doctor at the Dora/Nordhausen concentration camp in Thuringia, who, together with three other German physicians and one Polish woman doctor, treated patients in Camp No. 2 at Belsen. Dr. Kurzke and the other German doctors working in the camp were soon able to dispel the Jewish residents' initial misgivings when word spread through Belsen that Dr. Kurzke had treated patients humanely at Dora and that several hundred Jews owed their lives to his courageous efforts.[41] Kurzke worked at Belsen until the camp was shut down, probably in part because he had problems finding a job in civilian life, a fact confirmed by a request he submitted to JDC in October 1949 in which he asked the organization to help him find a country in which to resettle.[42]

Most of the nurses were German. The Jewish Relief Unit was responsible for hiring the nursing personnel at Belsen, including the ten nurses who came from the ranks of the DPs themselves.[43] Eva Minden was head of the nursing staff. Besides her work as head nurse, she trained Jewish nurses so as to enable them to find work in Palestine.[44]

The various departments in the Glyn Hughes Hospital were established to meet the special needs of the Jewish survivors. For example, there was a TB ward, where the many DPs who had contracted the disease could be treated. Those with particularly acute infections were sent to a special hospital in Gauting near Munich. The Joint made it possible for the DPs to stay at health spas in Switzerland and Merano in the South Tyrol. However, since it had taken so much time and negotiating skill to obtain a facility, the first group of twenty-four female and twenty-four male patients, aged twenty to thirty-five, were unable to leave for the JDC's sanitarium in Merano before 22 April 1947.[45]

The DPs were regularly given chest X rays at the Belsen hospital in order to diagnose new cases of pulmonary tuberculosis as quickly as possible. New cases of TB were also frequently detected during the routine medical examinations given to potential emigrants.[46]

The hospital had a separate ward for patients suffering from infectious diseases and an operating room for performing major surgery. It was also equipped to treat serious dental problems. Because of long years of poor nutrition, the DPs suffered from a variety of dental diseases, so many in fact that dentists found it advantageous to conduct part of their practices in the dental treatment facility of the ORT school as well as in a school administered by the Central Committee.

Beginning in the fall of 1945, the hospital had a department of obstetrics and gynecology. Because the department's nursing staff also cared for newborns, they were instrumental in helping reduce the high rate of infant mortality. At the same time, the birthrate in the camp was increasing at a phenomenal rate. In 1947 approximately fifteen babies a week were being born in the camp, so that by early February 1948 Belsen was able to celebrate the birth of its 1,000th child. Dr. Spanier, the camp's only pediatrician, was clearly overworked.[47] Consequently, the hospital urged the authorities to hire at least one more pediatrician as well as other medical specialists.

Great credit must be given to JDC in 1947 for eliminating the acute shortage of medical equipment and personnel that had characterized the previous year. With its 300 beds, 200 of which were occupied at any one time, the hospital became a place of refuge for the Jewish population outside the immediate perimeters of the camp. At the same time, the Jewish Relief Unit organized mobile outpatient and dental treatment facilities that traveled throughout the zone, providing medical care to Jews living outside the camp.[48] Patients obtained needed medicines from Otto Festing, a Pole who ran the camp pharmacy at Belsen. Since the Joint supplied pharmaceuticals to its facilities throughout the world, the Belsen pharmacy had ready access to drugs, such as penicillin, that were unavailable on the open market in postwar Germany. It filled some 3,000 prescriptions per month.

School and Educational System

As in the other Jewish DP camps, education and child care were the main focus of attention at Belsen. In July 1945 the camp authorities at Belsen opened a Jewish elementary school named in honor of Dr. Jacob Edelstein, the Czech Zionist and Elder of the Jews[49] in the Theresienstadt (Terezín) ghetto. Edelstein and his family had been killed at Auschwitz. In September 1945, the school was teaching ninety-two children Hebrew, reading, arithmetic, Jewish and world history, the history of Erets Yisrael, biology, and drawing. Sarah Lewkowicz was the principal. In the following months, the number of pupils increased to 220, peaking in March 1948 at 340. The figures for December 1948 show that only fifty pupils were enrolled. The first teachers were members of the Jewish Brigade. Later, they came from the ranks of the DPs themselves. The Jewish Agency recruited additional teachers in Palestine. Instruction during the five-hour school day was largely in Yiddish, although classes were also held in Polish and Hungarian, depending on the pupils' backgrounds. Suitable instructional materials such as books, maps, and so on were unavailable; however, writing materials and art supplies could be obtained locally.

The Central Committee made full-time education compulsory up to age eighteen. Consequently, the committee had to open a high school for youngsters over thirteen who had already completed elementary school. So on 17 December 1945 the camp authorities opened the Jewish Brigade Hebrew Secondary School. Its curriculum included modern Hebrew literature, Bible study, Latin, geometry, algebra, chemistry, and English. The languages of instruction were Hebrew and Yiddish. It was no accident that the school was named in honor of the Jewish Brigade. Soldiers from the unit had helped start the high school, just as earlier they had assisted in setting up the elementary school. Littmann, a kibbutznik from Palestine, was instrumental in founding the high school. Together with Helena Wrubell, its first principal and previously a geography teacher at the elementary school, he laid the groundwork for the school's rapid increase in enrollment to a total of 140 students—and ultimately to 198 in March 1948.

On 4 August 1947 Wilhelm Niebuhr, a German teacher from Bergen who gave private lessons "in algebra, geometry, etc. to young men aged 19 to 21" in the camp, spoke about his experiences at Belsen with Hanna Fueß, a local historian in Celle: "A high school was set up at Belsen by an international committee [the Jewish Brigade]. There were some outstanding teachers there, from France, Switzerland, and Canada. They expected a great deal from the students. I sometimes asked [the students] to show me their homework assignments. They were well designed and clearly explained. The high school had been set up in a barracks. Some 150 students attended school there. . . . I went to the camp to give my lessons. My students were planning for careers in business and engineering. I received DM 30 for providing instruction, plus coffee and cigarettes."[50]

The high school had a library, a small gymnasium, an infirmary, and recreation rooms. High school students and elementary school pupils were housed in their own barracks and ate breakfast and lunch together in the school cafeteria. The schools came under an education council of which both teachers and principals were members. Besides working out the schools' lesson plans, council members discussed teaching methodology and curriculum development with JDC. Once the schools had acquired books and instructional materials—mainly with the help of the Joint—new problems surfaced in 1947. There was a constant turnover in teachers due to emigration, and it was often very difficult to find replacements. Nonetheless, the schools at Belsen had a good reputation and served a unique purpose. Since the number of children in the other DP camps and the local Jewish communities was too small to warrant establishing a separate school system with its own curriculum, the Belsen schools emerged as the only institutions equipped to provide an education adapted to the special needs of Jewish children.[51]

Apart from the elementary school and the high school, Belsen also had a number of religious schools. These came under the authority of the camp rabbinate and received assistance from Va'ad Hahatzalah. Sixty-five boys aged five to fourteen attended the Belsen *talmud torah;* the principal was Rabbi Waschman. The She'erit Israel yeshiva, or Talmudic academy, had been opened shortly after the liberation of the camp. Four teachers taught 110 students at the yeshiva between September 1946 and September 1947.[52] Forty-six girls received religious instruction at the camp's two Beth Jacob schools during the first six months of 1947, one of which was designed for girls between the ages of eight and sixteen and the other for young women sixteen to twenty years of age. In addition to the schools for the children of Orthodox Jews, where Yiddish was the language of instruction, there was also a rabbinical seminary. Fifteen young men were enrolled in the seminary for the period from January to June 1947.[53]

The camp authorities finally set up a kindergarten in October 1946. The camp residents were particularly appreciative and supportive, because a school for young children was the most visible sign at Belsen of the revival of Jewish life. With the influx of the "infiltrees," it had become necessary to have a school for children six years and younger. In later years, children born at Belsen also attended the camp kindergarten. The school was administered by the Joint. Four kindergarten teachers and one representative each from JDC and the Jewish Agency met weekly to discuss educational and administrative issues. The children entrusted to their care were to learn personal hygiene and table manners as well as how to think for themselves and act responsibly. As part of their schooling, the children had to choose one of their own as a group leader responsible for maintaining order and discipline.

The kindergarten consisted of two playrooms (which also served as dining rooms), a kitchen, a cloakroom, an infirmary with a nurse always on duty, a playground, and a swimming pool. Some seventy children between the ages of three and six—and in special cases even children aged two—were picked up by bus every morning and driven to school. The school day began at 10:15 A.M. with morning exercises, followed by breakfast. The children played games until noon, at which time they ate their lunch, either inside or outside, depending on the weather. In the summer the younger children played in the swimming pool or in the sandbox. From 1 P.M. to 2:30 P.M. they took a nap, after which they spent time drawing or doing handicrafts. Before the bus came by at 4 P.M. to take them home, they were served tea and sandwiches. At least once a month a JDC doctor gave them a medical checkup.[54]

A nursery school was set up in Belsen at the same time as the kindergarten. It was designed to care for between ten and twelve children under five years of age whose mothers were ill or for some other reason were temporarily unable to look after them. The nursery was much less successful than the kindergarten, however, and was soon shut down. The children were sent to a Jewish children's home in Blankenese near Hamburg. However, in the summer of 1947, the limited capacity of the Blankenese facility made it necessary once again to consider opening a children's home at Belsen, especially since a new group of so-called unaccompanied children—orphans and children whose parents were missing—had to be cared for in the camp. By late June 1947, therefore, the camp authorities set aside a building and renovated it for that purpose. Equipped with sleeping quarters, playrooms, dining rooms, a kitchen, and medical facilities, it was soon ready for some fifty children to occupy. Five DP teachers and child-care workers, kitchen personnel, a JDC doctor, and a nurse were responsible for looking after the newcomers.[55]

At first Chana Holzmann was in charge of caring for the Jewish orphans at Belsen. Then, in January 1946, they were sent to a children's home in Blankenese that had been made available by the Warburg family. During the war the Wehrmacht had taken over the estate, but soon after liberation the British Military Government settled the question of ownership, and the Warburgs got their property back. The family subsequently leased a building on the grounds of the estate to JDC. The Joint then turned it into a home for Jewish orphans aged two to eighteen. JDC used the facility to prepare the youngsters for emigration to Palestine, which is why only Hebrew was spoken in the home. The first group left for Palestine in May 1946, and the empty rooms were then occupied by Jewish orphans from the British Zone. Betty Adler (JDC) and Reuma Schwarz (Jewish Agency for Palestine) were in charge of the children's home, the school, and the physical education department; a nurse named Tuschinska supervised the twenty-bed hospital.[56]

After the last large group of youngsters left Blankenese for Palestine in May 1947, the building was turned into a vacation home for undernourished and sickly children. Approximately 100 children at a time stayed in the home for a period of two months. In the morning, children received instruction in Hebrew, reading, arithmetic, geography, and Jewish history. The operators of the home were concerned mainly with restoring the children's health and therefore held a number of activities outdoors. A doctor regularly examined the children, making sure that they were gaining weight. The home permanently employed two nurses, and there was always a German Jewish doctor on call day and night. The kosher kitchen used plenty of butter, fat, eggs, fruits, and vegetables to help provide a nourishing diet and hasten the children's recovery. The natural beauty of the surroundings enhanced the children's convalescence and helped make their stay a complete success.[57]

At least as important as the children's programs—intramural as well as extramural—were the vocational training courses for young adults. They were specifically designed to give students the job skills needed to find employment in the countries in which they wished to resettle. It was therefore no accident that ORT set up its first vocational school at Belsen in early December 1945, just over half a year after the end of the war. Initially, of course, ORT offered just a few programs, but in time students could choose to be trained as tailors or dressmakers, knitters, carpenters, locksmiths, shoemakers, prosthesis makers, electricians, mechanics, or watch repairers. In June 1946 ORT even introduced a program for dental technicians. An instructor was brought over from America for the sole purpose of directing the program. Under his guidance the program acquired an outstanding reputation, attracting an average of eighty to a hundred students per semester.[58] After successfully completing the program, students had an opportunity to work in the camp's dental laboratory for six months.

The ORT training workshops were originally located in the camp school. Then, in the summer of 1946, they were given the opportunity to move into four barracks in Camp No. 2—with their own canteen. The relocation entailed an administrative reorganization, as a result of which the ORT school came under the supervision of the Central Committee. It was therefore administered independently of the other educational facilities in the camp. With assistance from the Joint and machines supplied by the Canadian Army, the school was able to upgrade its equipment and meet the standards of commercially operated vocational training programs. As a result of improving its organization and facilities, ORT expanded its programs to include courses in architecture, baking, and cooking.[59]

Depending on the program, ORT spent between two and six months training students ranging in age from seventeen to twenty-five. At the same time, students at the high school, the Beth Jacob school, and the yeshiva had a chance to attend vocational education courses in the afternoon. Josef Mack, the director of the ORT school at Bergen-Belsen until 6 February 1949, developed the so-called workshop system. Word of its success quickly spread beyond the limits of the camp and became a symbol in Belsen of the Jews' newly acquired self-esteem. The number of ORT graduates at Belsen attests to the important role the system played in the camp's vocational training courses. By mid-July 1947, 250 drivers, 77 tailors, 150 dressmakers, 15 locksmiths, 12 carpenters, 60 dental technicians, 45 electricians, 80 corset seamstresses, and 15 lingerie makers had received their diplomas. In other words, approximately half of those enrolled in courses had successfully completed the ORT programs.[60]

At this time there were 28 teachers providing specialized instruction in the various programs, whereas in spring of the same year there had been only 21 Jewish DP teachers and 2 non-Jewish German instructors teaching a total of 342 students. By 1948, however, the number of trainees and vocational courses steadily declined, even though the number of teachers remained the same. In the summer there were 189 apprentices—77 men and 112 women—attending 12 different courses in Belsen; by December the number at Belsen was just 89[61] out of a total of 365 ORT students in the British Zone.[62] On 2 January 1949, shortly before he completed his tenure at Belsen, Josef Mack awarded 110 diplomas to graduates of ORT vocational programs. Besides the instructors, those present at the graduation ceremony included Mark J. Lister, ORT director of the British Zone; Y. Baruchi, director of the Jewish Agency for the British Zone; Samuel Dallob of JDC; and Josef Rosensaft.

The graduation party was at the same time a way of saying farewell to the ORT schools at Belsen. In their addresses, the ORT representatives summarized the three years of ORT's activities in the camp, emphasizing the high level of cooperation among all the participating institutions. The only thing that remained for Mack's successor, Josef Krieger, the former deputy director, to do was to wind up a few of the lesser classes, such as the knitting courses. The other programs, including ORT's dental technician school, had already been shut down and the building in which they had been housed handed over to the British Military Government. The British put a few rooms at ORT's disposal for administrative purposes and to conduct its last classes. ORT personnel had been reduced to seven instructors, including the director and three administrative employees.[63]

In contrast to most of the camps in the U.S. Zone, adult education at Belsen was limited to a few courses in Hebrew, English, and housekeeping. Only the kibbutz groups offered a somewhat more diversified curriculum; however, their classes were reserved for kibbutz members only. The JDC's reports on educational work in the camp suggest that the small number of activities was due more to a lack of interest on the part of the camp residents than to any organizational problems.[64]

Cultural Life

The camp's cultural program, on the other hand, was extremely popular, especially performances by Belsen's two theater groups—Kazet-
Theater[65] (Katset-Teater [Concentration Camp Theater]) and Jidisze
Arbeter-Bine (Yidishe Arbeter-Bine [Yiddish Workers' Stage]). Samy
(Zami) Feder established the Kazet-Theater group in early July 1945,
just a few months after the end of war. Together with Sonia Baczkow-
ska, he was in charge of the Central Committee's Cultural Department. At the time the ensemble consisted of sixteen women and fourteen men. Feder had many years of experience as an actor. Before the
war he had been a member of a Jewish theater group in Poland, and
he had even put on plays in the concentration camps. On 6 September
1945 Feder directed his first production at Belsen—three short sa-
tiric plays. The actors had to perform on an improvised stage.[66] Many
years later Samy Feder still remembered that first production:

> Despite all the difficulties and improvisations, it was all right on the
> night, as it always is with good actors.
>
> Just before the curtain was to go up, there was an urgent summons for
> the producer. I came out and was faced with a score of Russian officers,
> who had come to the show and could not get in. I tried to explain to them
> that there was simply no room, but they would have none of it. One of
> them suddenly spoke to me in plain Yiddish: "Look here, comrade, we
> drove two hundred miles to see your show, are you going to turn us
> away?" I took them behind the stage and they watched the show from the
> wings. In the very last minute there arrived Chaplain Major Isaac Levy
> and Joe Wallhandler of the Joint who brought us from somewhere real
> make-up. I have never played to such a grateful audience. They clapped
> and laughed and cried. When we gave, as our last item, the famous song
> "Think not you travel to despair again," the thousand people in the hall
> rose to their feet and sang with us. Then Hatikvah. Never was Hatikvah
> rendered with such verve as on that first night.[67]

In the following weeks the group gave ten more performances of
the three plays. At the same time, Feder began rehearsals for Sholem
Aleichem's *Der Ferkishufter Shnayder* (*The Bewitched Tailor*). Meanwhile, various ORT programs had lent their support to the theater,

sewing costumes and building sets. The Kazet-Theater received special recognition for the productions it staged to celebrate the anniversary of Belsen's liberation.[68]

On 19 February 1947 the ensemble sent out invitations to the premiere of its production of Sholem Aleichem's *Dos Groyse Gevins* (*The Jackpot*) in the camp's tent theater. It, too, was directed by Samy Feder.[69] In the tradition of the Yiddish theater, the group took the show on tour, performing in various DP camps and hospitals in the British Zone. The group even had successful runs in Belgium and France. It was in no small measure because of its outstanding performances that on 27 June 1947 the Belgian government issued residence permits to the members of the Kazet-Theater group. Ultimately, most members of the company remained in Belgium until they immigrated to Palestine.[70]

Unlike the Kazet-Theater, the Jidisze Arbeter-Bine of the left-wing Poale Zion, or Labor Zionist Movement, used amateur actors. A. Zandman directed the company as well as the camp's six-man orchestra. The plays staged by the Jidisze Arbeter-Bine frequently dealt with the lives of Jewish laborers. They included David Pinski's *Der Oytser* (*The Treasure*)—one of the first dramas to pay tribute to the Jewish workingman and the coming of socialism to segments of the Jewish community—and *Der Toyber* (*The Dove*) by David Bergelson, a supporter of the Bund, the Jewish socialist party founded in Russia in 1897.[71] Like the Kazet-Theater, the Arbeter-Bine went on tour from time to time. The group gave two performances, for example, at the Landsberg camp in the U.S. Zone in October 1947.[72]

A year later, in December 1948, the most well known Jewish theater company in the U.S. Zone, MIKT, performed at Belsen.[73] The ZK's orchestra, under the direction of Michael Hofmekler, also visited the camp as part of a concert tour.[74]

The success of the Belsen theater groups underscored the importance of exposing the survivors to a wide array of the performing arts as a way to accelerate their spiritual rehabilitation. At the present time, there are many therapists who use music to help treat mental illness. Even though those who organized the musical events at Belsen were likely unaware at the time of scientific studies suggesting the therapeutic power of music, they continued to arrange concerts in the camp—almost as if they were responding intuitively to the audiences' needs. Interestingly, it was not the concerts put on by musicians from the camp but those given by performers from Germany and abroad that turned out to be the main attractions. Since the infrastructure of postwar Germany had largely been destroyed, camp residents rarely had a chance to attend a theater or listen to a concert outside the confines of Belsen. This is why the performers often had to come to them. At the same time, the guest artists had the benefit of learning firsthand about the life of *She'erit Hapletah*.

The first major event featuring guest performers from outside the camp was held on 5 and 6 June 1946 in the Belsen movie theater. The Hanover symphony orchestra brought fifty-five of its members to the DP camp, delighting an audience of more than 1,000.[75] An average of 1,500 DPs attended three concerts given at Belsen by Herman Yablokoff during August. The concerts were part of a tour of Germany that had begun in June and ended in September 1947. Born in Poland, Yablokoff had been living in the United States since 1924. He was an actor, director, and head of a theater company. During his presentations, which had been organized by the Joint, he performed his own compositions, which included folk songs and songs of the ghetto, and recited poems. Yablokoff refused to accept any payment for his work; he simply wanted his performances to provide *She'erit Hapletah* a few moments of diversion from their daily concerns.[76]

Just as the Kazet-Theater started staging plays, the first Jewish newspaper in postwar Germany commenced publication at Belsen. Even though the *DP Express,* published by UNRRA, had begun to appear in Munich at the same time, until fall 1945 Belsen's *Unzer Sztyme (Unzer Shtime [Our Voice])* was the only newspaper in occupied Germany written exclusively for the Jewish DPs. The *DP Express,* published weekly by UNRRA's DP Transient and Information Center located in the Deutsches Museum, provided information for all displaced persons, that is, Jews and non-Jews alike. Therefore, the articles were written not only in Yiddish but in Polish, Slovak, and German as well.[77] *Unzer Sztyme,* on the other hand, was published by the Centraler Idiszer Komitet Bergen Belsen (Tsentraler Yidisher Komitet Bergn Belzn [Central Jewish Committee of Bergen-Belsen]) and appeared entirely in Yiddish, starting with the first issue of 2 July 1945. The first four issues were handwritten and subsequently reproduced. Then plates were made and, beginning with issue 25 of 29 November

1945, the newspaper was printed from them. At the same time, *Unzer Sztyme* announced that it would appear twice monthly; however, it did not actually come out on a monthly basis until issue 24 of 30 October 1947. Nevertheless, it averaged as many as thirty-five pages per issue. When the paper began to be typeset in November 1945, two new sections were added—"Erets Yisrael and the Zionist Movement" and "The World of Literature and Art."

The first issue of the following year, issue 6 of 1 January 1946, appeared under an expanded name, *Unzer Sztyme Organ fun der Sheyres-Hapletye in der britisher Zone* (*Our Voice: Organ of She'erit Hapletah in the British Zone*). The First Congress of Liberated Jews in the British Zone was held from 25 to 27 September 1945 and elected a permanent Central Committee to replace the temporary Jewish Committee. At the same time it established a Cultural Department, to which responsibility for bringing out *Unzer Sztyme* was given. Rafael Olewski, Paul Trepman, and David Rosenthal, members of the editorial board, felt that the name of the paper should reflect the administrative reorganization as a result of which it had become the official organ of the Central Committee. So, starting with the 30 October 1947 issue, the paper once again adopted a new name: *Our Voice, Organ of the Liberated Jews in the British Zone, c/o Central Committee, Assembly Center Belsen.*[78] Unfortunately, it is impossible to provide any more details about the change in the masthead. Yet it may have been connected to the fact that shortly before the change, the British military authorities had finally granted the paper a license to publish. What is certain, however, is that it did not have a license prior to May 1947; that is, *Unzer Sztyme* was an "illegal" publication until that time.[79]

On 1 January 1946 the newspaper introduced yet another new section, called "We're Searching for Our Relatives." Along with news about Palestine and Zionism, this section became one of the most important parts of the paper. Besides the imminent prospect of emigration, what concerned the Jewish DPs most was searching for missing family members. As with the many DP newspapers in the U.S. Zone, one can use *Unzer Sztyme* to identify the issues that most concerned Belsen's Jewish DPs and to chart how those concerns changed over time. Generally, the articles dealt with the whole range of Jewish life as well as with Yiddish and Hebrew literature and various cultural events. Camp residents frequently contributed articles to the paper, and the editors reprinted reports from the international press. The first special edition, *Unzer Sztyme — Ayn Yor* (*Our Voice — One Year*), celebrated the anniversary of the paper's first full year of publication. The six-page supplement that came out on 15 July 1946 had been typeset and printed in the newspaper's own print shop in Camp No. 4, the so-called Roundhouse, which was the headquarters of the Central Committee. Even before then, however, issue 11 (12 July 1946) of *Unzer Sztyme* had been printed on equipment provided by JDC. The next issue, in August, contained photographs—part of another new section called "Our Life in Pictures." The jubilee edition celebrating *Unzer Sztyme*'s second year of publication featured a sixteen-page illustrated report that took up approximately one-fourth of the paper. The last special edition, on 14 September 1947, was dedicated to the "heroes" of *Exodus '47*, a ship that had brought illegal immigrants to Palestine and was then sent back to Germany by the British.[80]

Unzer Sztyme was superseded by the *Vokhnblat, Organ fun der Sheyres-Hapleyte in der britisher Zone* (*The Weekly, Organ of She'erit Hapletah in the British Zone*). The first issue appeared on 5 December 1947. The *Vokhnblat* was published in Yiddish and came out every Friday until 21 January 1949, when it began to appear every other week. Originally, the editorial board was made up of the three former editors of *Unzer Sztyme*. On 2 July 1949 the *Vokhnblat* hired two additional staff members, Dr. Michal Lubliner and B. Kosowski. Beginning in June 1948, page 8 appeared entirely in English. Later, the paper's name, too, appeared in English—*Jewish Weekly*.[81] The last issue was published on 18 August 1950.[82]

The Cultural Department of the Central Committee of Liberated Jews in the British Zone also published a periodical called *Das Monatsheft* (*The Monthly*) in German. The first issue appeared in December/January 1946/1947. Starting with issue 12, it was renamed *Jüdische Hefte, Ausgewählte Aufsätze* (*The Jewish Journal: Selected Essays*) and appeared on 1 January 1948 in a new format. It focused on the problems of the Jewish community in Germany and the Jewish community in general, mainly from the Zionist point of view. The magazine's first editor was B. Horowisz. He was followed somewhat later by A. Londner.[83]

Cojtn {Tsoytn}, Zamlheft far Literatur, Kritik un gezelshaftlekhe Fragn (*Times, Miscellany of Contemporary Literature, Criticism and Social Issues*), a literary journal edited by Meier Ber Gutman and A. Rozenfeld (from 1947 to 1948), as well as a number of other periodicals in both Hebrew and Yiddish were also published at Belsen. Increasingly, the various Jewish political movements began to publish their official organs in the camp, for example, the Yiddish-language *Unzer Front* (*Our Front*) of the United Zionist Revisionists that appeared from spring 1947 to February 1949. Earlier, in December 1946, the Revisionists had come out with a one-time Hanukkah publication entitled *Der Emes* (*The Truth*), which contained articles on the elections to the Second Zionist Congress as well as other political meetings and conferences. From 26 February 1947 to 11 February 1949, Poale Zion Histadrut issued an information bulletin in Belsen for the British Zone in both Hebrew and Yiddish called *Yedies* (sometimes referred to as *Yediot,* or *News*).[84]

Apart from the Jewish newspapers and magazines that appeared in the camp, Belsen had its own publishing house, which issued various books and brochures. Some of the brochures covered the lives of such well-known figures as Joseph Trumpeldor, the Russian-born Zionist-socialist leader, the Hebrew poet Chaim Nachman Bialik, and Theodor Herzl; these particular publications were financed by Keren Kayemet le-Yisrael (Jewish National Fund). The many books published at Belsen included a collection of songs from the concentration camps and ghettos edited by Samy Feder in collaboration with the directors of the Central Committee's Cultural Department, *Unser Churbon in Bild* (*Unzer Khurban in Bild* [*Our Catastrophe in Pictures*]), *Shtil vi in Rayvits* (*As Quiet as in Rajowiec Lubelski*) by Shemuel Drelikhman, *Farvolknte Teg* (*Cloudy Days*) by Meir Ber Gutman, and *Tsurik fun Gehenem* (*Back from Hell*) by Berl Friedler. Friedler also did drawings for *Unzer Sztyme* and worked as a set designer for the Kazet-Theater. The Belsen publishing house also reprinted a number of religious books and texts.[85]

The first and probably the most important book to appear in Belsen was the list of Jewish survivors in the camp, published on 7 September 1945. Issued under the title *Sharit ha-Platah Bergen-Belsen, vol. 1, 1945* by the First Temporary Committee at Belsen, the registry became an indispensable aid for those searching for lost relatives. The survivors were listed in alphabetical order according to surname. The list also included given names and dates and places of birth. Chaplain

Abraham J. Klausner and the Central Committee of Liberated Jews in Bavaria also compiled a list of some 60,000 Jewish survivors in camps in the American and British Zones of Germany and Austria, the first volume of which was published on 20 July 1945.[86]

At the beginning of 1946, JDC workers were still complaining about the lack of recreational facilities and reading rooms at Belsen.[87] So, in September 1946, the camp library—with the JDC's assistance—finally opened its doors to the public. It was the largest facility of its kind in the British Zone.[88] The Joint not only helped establish the lending library's operating procedures, but, together with the World Jewish Congress, the Jewish Labor Committee, and YIVO, it provided most of the books and magazines and set up the reading room. By the end of June 1947, the library had a collection of over 3,000 titles in English, Hebrew, Yiddish, French, Polish, Russian, and Hungarian. It soon circulated an average of about eighty books per day and had more than 500 patrons listed in its card file. Camp residents regularly used the reading room to study the newspapers and journals that were delivered to Belsen from other parts of Germany as well as from France, Poland, South Africa, the United States, Canada, and Palestine.[89] In an effort to serve the entire camp population, the patients in the Glyn Hughes Hospital were also supplied with reading material. In late January 1947, library workers began visiting the hospital on a regular basis, taking a selection of books along for patients to read.[90] Employees of the Joint and the Central Committee called the library the camp's crown jewel.

Entertainment and Sports

The library had been designed primarily for serious readers, but it also helped meet the leisure-time needs of camp residents. And although movies, by contrast, were primarily shown to entertain the DPs, they were also used to support adult education; British and American films, for example, could be valuable aids in giving English-language instruction. When the camp cinema was not being used for other cultural events, it screened four movies a week, including motion pictures in English, German, Yiddish, and sometimes even in

Russian. To give Jewish DPs living outside Belsen an opportunity to see a movie, JDC fitted out an old ambulance as a mobile cinema unit, complete with a team of projectionists, that traveled throughout the British Zone.[91]

Sports were the most important leisure-time activity, regardless of whether the DPs were active participants or merely spectators. In July 1947 the *Jüdisches Gemeindeblatt für die britische Zone* (*Jewish Community Newspaper for the British Zone*) reported that there were already eight sports clubs at Belsen. The camp offered residents the opportunity to box, engage in track and field events, play soccer, table tennis, tennis, handball, and so forth. The Joint, the JRU, and UNRRA together provided the necessary equipment.[92] The British military allowed Belsen residents to use the army's tennis court, which was located on the grounds of the camp.[93] The sports clubs did not limit themselves to playing in the camp or the zone, however; they held competitions and played soccer matches with clubs in the other camps and the other occupation zones. On 19 July 1946, for example, Belsen's soccer team Hatikva (Hope) played Ikhud (The One),[94] the Landsberg team. And about a month later, on 15 July 1946, there was a friendly match between Ikhud and Belsen's second team, Hagibor (Hero), which was made up exclusively of Hungarian Jews. Twenty-five hundred spectators watched the game in which Landsberg trounced Belsen 4 to 0.[95] The same day Belsen's Hagibor boxing team traveled to Landsberg to compete against Landsberg's Ikhud. Both teams had won the championship in their respective zones and were now pitted against each other in the finals, which Landsberg won 9 to 7.[96] In March 1948 Hatikva and Kokhav (Star), Belsen's two soccer clubs, invited the Munich team, Hapoel (The Worker), to play a match in the camp. The proceeds from the two games on 13 and 14 March—which the Belsen teams won, incidentally—were donated to a village in Palestine.[97] From 1 to 15 September 1946, the Landsberg camp became the site of *She'erit Hapletah*'s first chess tournament. Finkelstein from Belsen, the British Zone's chess champion, placed fourth and another player from Belsen eighth in the final round-robin. Sixteen players from throughout Germany took part in the tournament, which was won by Aleksandrov, the U.S. Zone's chess champion from the Jewish DP hospital at St. Ottilien near Landsberg.[98]

Religious Life

Immediately following liberation, Belsen's rabbis—Zvi Azaria (Hermann Helfgott; also spelled Zwi Asaria and Zvi Asaria), A. Goldfinger, Joel Halpern, Chaim Meisels, Israel Moses Olewski, and Israel Zelmanowitz—carried out the sad duty of burying thousands of dead. Soon afterward they began to teach young boys and girls in the camp's religious schools and the rabbinical seminary, conduct religious services, oversee the ritual slaughter of animals, and arrange for the circumcision of newborn males. They also lobbied for a kosher kitchen and a *mikvah*. The Joint and Va'ad Hahatzalah provided most of the required prayer books, prayer shawls, phylacteries, yarmulkes, and candles.

The rabbinate that had been established in Belsen to improve the coordination of religious responsibilities devoted much of its attention to the problem of the many *agunim* and *agunot,* that is, men and women who were unable to locate their missing spouses, most of whom had probably been murdered. Before remarrying, these men and women had to obtain permission from the rabbinate, a process that was preceded by a thorough investigation, including sworn statements by witnesses, into the whereabouts of their former spouses. To learn how to deal properly with the *agunim* and *agunot,* the Belsen rabbinate even communicated with the committee of the chief rabbinate in Jerusalem responsible for such matters. The camp rabbinate eventually granted 420 men and 350 women permission to remarry. Rabbi Halpern compiled a 320-page handbook for *agunim* and *agunot.* Published in 1948, it included a detailed history of the issue along with 1,000 depositions containing information on missing husbands and wives.[99] The many weddings at Belsen were always major events. Like the baby boom in the camp, they came to symbolize the continuity of Jewish life. By July 1947, the rabbis at Belsen had already performed 1,070 marriages.[100]

The "infiltration" of Jews from Eastern Europe bolstered the Orthodox movement in the camp. Even so, the Orthodox Jews remained a minority that was often at odds with the other residents of the camp, the camp committee, and its chairman, Josef Rosensaft. For example, the Orthodox rabbis tried to increase the number of their followers among the camp residents by limiting the distribution of aid packages sent to Belsen by Orthodox Jewish organizations abroad only to those who supported the Orthodox cause. The camp committee fought in vain against this policy, arguing that in Auschwitz there had been no such conflicts among the different religious groups.[101] Another point of contention between the Orthodox Jews and the camp committee was the supposed lack of religious education and the absence of religion in the daily life of the camp. For the moderately religious Jews, on the other hand, the Orthodox Jews' strict observance of the Sabbath had become a public nuisance. When the Sabbath began on Friday afternoon, they blocked the streets on which their residences and houses of worship were located to prevent vehicular traffic from passing through. It was only after a violent clash with the camp police that they reluctantly opened the streets to traffic again.[102]

In July 1947 Rabbi Zvi Azaria became the chief rabbi for all the local Jewish communities and camp committees in the British Zone. A former Yugoslav Army officer, he had been liberated by the British on 17 April 1945 in the vicinity of Hodenhagen and had worked as a rabbi at Belsen since 30 April of that year. He remained chief rabbi until immigrating to Israel in September 1948. In contrast to the camps in the U.S. Zone, those in the British Zone maintained much closer contact with the local Jewish communities. Since they did not have a sufficient number of their own rabbis to allow them to live strictly according to *halakha,* the religious law of the Jewish people, these communities were dependent on the services of the camp rabbi. The relationship was not without its problems, however.

The Jewish communities in Germany reacted with incomprehension to the uncompromising position of the traditionally oriented camp rabbis, in particular to their treatment of the non-Jewish spouses of Jews and the part-Jewish children who had remained steadfastly loyal to their families during the years of persecution. The non-Jewish spouses often asked to be accepted as members of the Jewish community; however, the *bet din* refused to recognize them as Jews.[103] The rabbis reacted angrily to attempts by the German Jewish communities to make decisions in such cases without first consulting a religious court. "We ask . . . the supreme authority in the British Zone [the ZK]," the rabbinate wrote in a letter to the Central Committee, "to announce to all the local Jewish communities and committees that no community shall be allowed to act upon a religious matter without first receiving a decision on that matter from a rabbi or the religious court. We cannot and will not recognize individuals [as Jews] who have been accepted by the Jewish community without the approval of a rabbi or a religious court."[104] The same rule applied to circumcisions that were not carried out in the presence of a rabbi. The rabbinate refused to recognize such circumcisions as having been part of a religious rite. In spite of these differences, the rabbinate nevertheless proved to be of great service to the German Jewish communities in helping them observe religious laws and traditions; without their support, Jewish religious life would never have developed outside the camps.

Political Involvement

When it came to matters of politics, two religiously oriented parties represented the Orthodox Jews at Belsen: the ultra-Orthodox Agudat Israel, which adhered to *halakha* as the principle governing Jewish life and society, and the religious Zionist Mizrachi. These and the other political parties established branches at Belsen in 1946 only when it became clear that the British were intent on keeping the gates of Palestine shut and that the Jews would therefore remain in the DP camps longer than had been anticipated. Despite their former differences and with the Holocaust still a vivid memory, the various political groups agreed during the first few months after liberation that only Zionism offered any real hope to the Jewish people. Thus, the politically active DPs joined to form the Histadrut Tsiyonit Akhida (Federation of Zionist Organizations). Although no one doubted the importance of Zionism in 1946, differences frequently arose over questions of detail and ultimately led to the federation's demise.

The Revisionists competed with the religious factions to win supporters for its program to establish a Jewish state in the entire territory of Palestine, "on both sides of the Jordan." The General Zionists traditionally turned for support to the Jewish middle class, while Mapai and Poale Zion addressed themselves to working-class Jews. Mapai, the moderate labor party, was founded in 1930 as a nonreligious Zionist-socialist party. One of the main reasons it became the dominant party in the Zionist movement and after 1948 in Israel was that

David Ben-Gurion, who led Mapai since 1944, was such a hugely influential figure. In fact, every Israeli prime minister until 1977 was a member of Mapai. The Zionist-socialist Poale Zion stood to the left of Mapai. Its most prominent representative at Belsen was doubtless the chairman of the Central Committee itself, Josef Rosensaft.[105] Hashomer Hatzair was also active at Belsen. A Zionist-socialist pioneering youth movement with its roots in Eastern Europe, Hashomer Hatzair took an active part in the organization of the "illegal" immigration to Erets Yisrael. Before the war, quite a few Jews had supported and identified with communism and anti-Zionist socialism. After 1945, however, both movements disappeared almost completely from the Jewish political scene.

The Administration of Justice and the Police

Apart from the camp administration, which was made up of the elected representatives of the various parties, Belsen, with its 10,000 residents, needed other institutions to regulate conduct within the camp. The camp court and the camp police played a key role in this regard. The Jewish police, commanded by S. Winnick,[106] were responsible for guarding the outside of the camp and maintaining order within. Until May 1946, when Belsen became an exclusively Jewish DP camp, non-Jewish policemen helped protect the camp's perimeter. As a quid pro quo, the Jewish police concentrated on patrolling the inside of the camp, for clashes and violent confrontations often arose between the Jewish and non-Jewish DPs.

The camp court dealt with actions considered harmful to the DP community at Belsen. Its structure, procedures, and problems were similar to those at Föhrenwald and many other camps. Even though there are no sources to document the British Military Government's response to the presence of the Jewish courts, the military authorities tolerated but never officially recognized them, just as the U.S. military authorities did in their zone of occupation. Among other things, the camp court ruled on cases involving larceny, counterfeiting, the receipt of stolen goods, embezzlement, and the abuse of one's position. Of particular importance were the investigations undertaken by the court into the cases of Jewish camp residents who had served as

Kapos in the Nazi concentration camps to save their own lives.[107] British courts-martial were responsible for trying persons accused of capital offenses such as armed robbery, murder, looting, and rape. However, since Jews were very rarely charged with such crimes, they were seldom dealt with by the British military justice system.

The crime rate among the Jewish DPs was very low compared with that of the non-Jewish displaced persons, and only a few actually had to answer to the courts for black market activities.[108] Many of the charges of black marketeering were obviously motivated by latent anti-Semitism. The views expressed by some of the residents of the nearby town of Bergen make patently clear that the end of the war had not brought an end to this kind of prejudice. An *Amtsgerichtsrat* (district court judge) noted: "I had no idea how heavily populated the camp was. I had always assumed that there were 1,500 to 2,000 persons living there. It was only about a week before Allied troops entered Bergen that I learned to my horror that there were over 50,000 there, most of whom were dangerous criminals. If the authorities had released them at that time, they would instantly have engaged in the worst kind of looting."[109] While confirming some of the judge's speculations, a farmer, also from Bergen, came closer to the actual facts: "The concentration camp inmates weren't the worst—they were just grateful to get some food—it was the Russian and Polish POWs who went on a rampage." It is apparent after examining the terminology the farmer carried over from the Nazi period, however, that he too was an anti-Semite: "The Jews in the camp got lots of support from members of their own race [*Rassegenossen*] around the world, especially in America. It wasn't long before they were enjoying things that the locals could only dream of. Then the wheeling and dealing began in earnest."[110]

As in the U.S. Zone, the Jewish DPs in Belsen were constantly under suspicion of trading in cigarettes, coffee, tea, and other foodstuffs. This revived the ancient anti-Semitic stereotype of the Jewish profiteer and huckster. The interior minister of Lower Saxony, for example, maintained in the summer of 1948 that 200 tons of coffee were being smuggled into Belsen every month in the form of gift parcels. This meant that every resident of the camp, including the children, would have had to receive sixty pounds of coffee. In actual fact, only 300 to 400 parcels reached Belsen every month. So each parcel would have had to contain at least 500 kilograms (1,102 pounds), a patently absurd allegation, as the British officer responsible for DP affairs noted.[111]

In February 1948 an incident took place that caused a major uproar in the camp. A German truck driver was caught on the autobahn near Hanover transporting 6 million cigarettes from Antwerp. When he was arrested, he claimed that the shipment was destined for Belsen and that he had earlier brought a truckload of 13 million cigarettes to the camp. On February 18, at 1:30 A.M., armed German police encircled Belsen. It was then decided that British soldiers would accompany the searchers to ensure their safety. Josef Rosensaft negotiated with the British in the early morning hours about how the search was to be conducted. Allowing German police or British soldiers to enter the camp was completely out of the question, Rosensaft argued, and the British military authorities finally agreed. The search then proceeded at 11:30 A.M. with 150 British officers from every part of the zone. A Jewish policeman accompanied each search party. Before the search began, the British had assured Rosensaft that German police would not enter the camp.

The British conducted a very thorough search, examining every corner of the camp. The officers were extremely considerate, and Rosensaft made a point of thanking them for their thoughtfulness. Apart from a cow, twenty-five men's sweaters, and a few cartons of cigarettes, the raid netted nothing. The British were surprised at how little black market activity there was at Belsen. An incident that had begun so disastrously with the deployment of armed German police ended peacefully with the agreement of both parties.[112]

Exodus '47

On 14 February 1947 the British government in London decided to hand over their mandate in Palestine to the United Nations. In April the UN appointed a Special Committee on Palestine (UNSCOP) to suggest a solution to the Palestine and Jewish refugee problems. After discussions in Europe and the United States, the members of UNSCOP traveled to Palestine in the summer of 1947 to learn about the situation firsthand. It was in the midst of UNSCOP's deliberations, in fact, while they were in Palestine, that the *Exodus* affair broke, bringing to the boiling point the already tense relations between Britain and the Jews.

Exodus '47 was one of sixty-five illegal ships that had been chartered during the period between the end of the war and the establishment of the state of Israel in May 1948 to carry Jews from Europe to Palestine. For most refugees, the journey on these often unseaworthy ships ended in internment camps set up by the British, some in Palestine but most on the island of Cyprus. The British used every means possible to prevent Jews from illegally entering Palestine by sea. When they seized these so-called Haganah[113] ships off the coast of Palestine, resistance by the refugees often resulted in violent clashes with British soldiers.

Exodus '47, which got her name while she was in transit, left the French port of Sète near Marseille on 10 July 1947 with 4,500 people on board. Originally called the *President Warfield,* the old Chesapeake Bay steamer had been bought by the Haganah in the United States in early 1947 for around $60,000. She was no longer up to sailing the high seas, however. While she was anchored in French waters, the British tried to prevent her from being repaired or taking on passengers. And as she headed for Palestine, the warships of the Royal Navy never left her side. On the evening of 17 July, *Exodus '47* had nearly reached her destination; she was just a few miles outside the territorial waters of Palestine and planning to disembark her passengers at dawn along a beach south of Tel Aviv, where the British warships would be unable to follow her because of their shallow draft. The Haganah had arranged to get the refugees on land quickly and block the channels before the British could intern the new arrivals.

That night, however, the British fleet attacked the ship, even though she was still in international waters. With their destination straight ahead, the passengers and crew of the *Exodus* defended themselves as best they could; however, armed with tin cans and the like, they never had a chance against the superior power of the British. The unequal fight cost the refugees three dead, twenty-eight seriously wounded, and scores of lightly wounded. Surrounded by British warships, the heavily damaged *Exodus '47* was towed into Haifa harbor. The passengers on board the *Exodus* were forcibly transferred to three British troop transports—*Runnymede Park, Ocean Vigour,* and *Empire*

Rival. While the transfer took place, they were prohibited from having any contact with the local population, the press, or even members of UNSCOP. Without telling the refugees where they were being taken, the ships set sail on 19 July. Since the internment camps on Cyprus were filled to capacity, the transport ships headed back to France, and on 29 July they docked in the harbor of Port-de-Bouc. The French government offered the passengers asylum but refused to let the British disembark them forcibly. A few refugees left the ships for reasons of health, but the others tried to resist the British by remaining on board, though without much hope of success.

After being incarcerated for more than three weeks in their cages on the deportation ships, in the sweltering heat of southern France and under totally inadequate sanitary conditions, the second act of the drama—Operation Oasis—began after the British ships weighed anchor for their journey to Hamburg on 22 August 1947.[114]

On 23 and 24 July demonstrations against the treatment of the *Exodus* refugees took place in Frankfurt, Munich, Stuttgart, Bamberg, and several other German cities.[115] A month later, on 23 August, thousands of Belsen camp residents protested against Britain's policies. The biggest demonstration at Belsen, however, took place on 7 September to express outrage at the British government's order to send the Jews back to Germany. The residents of Belsen demonstrated their solidarity with the refugees aboard the *Exodus* by carrying banners, some of which read "End the Bevin Terror in Palestine!" "*Exodus* in Hamburg—a Mark of Cain for England," and "Together with the *Exodus Mapilim* in the Struggle for a Free *Aliyah!*"

The Jewish DPs were not alone in their criticism. Worldwide protests against the insensitivity of Britain's actions followed. The disembarkation in Hamburg's harbor on 8 September was at least a propagandistic success for the refugees; they were supported by a press corps that was almost unanimously on their side. Nevertheless, the Jews realized more than ever that there was no real hope of immigrating to Palestine in the near future. The *Exodus* affair gave rise to a deep sense of despair among the survivors of the Holocaust. The opening of Leon Uris's novel *Exodus,* later made into a motion picture, was a dramatic tribute to these immigrants and one that moved millions of readers.

The British transferred the disappointed returnees to two temporary transit camps—Pöppendorf and Am Stau near Lübeck. The camps were surrounded by barbed-wire fences, and the refugees were initially kept under strict military guard. There were Nissen huts and tents, but the inclement weather made housing in tents impossible. The choice of quarters and the poor facilities in the camps suggest that the British were taking revenge on the hapless refugees for the resistance they had offered aboard ship. Nevertheless, the British granted them DP status, a move that was out of keeping with their usual practice.[116]

The Joint, the Central Committees for both the U.S. and British Zones, and various DP camps expressed their solidarity with the refugees in the form of food, clothing, and material assistance.[117] Fearing public reaction and political repercussions, the British authorities moved them in November 1947 to Sengwarden near Wilhelmshaven and to Emden.[118] For the majority of the refugees, these camps were only brief stopping-off places. Brichah managed to smuggle most of them into the U.S. Zone, and many reached Palestine before the establishment of the state of Israel. By April 1948 there were only 1,800 Jews still living in the two so-called *Exodus* camps.[119]

Emigration

A month earlier, the Haganah had begun to recruit and train volunteers to serve in the war against the Arabs in Palestine. Since 29 November 1947, when the United Nations approved of the partition of Palestine and agreed to the establishment of a Jewish state in part of it, the Haganah had been conducting paramilitary training in the DP camps. Although it still had to work underground, the organization nevertheless received unofficial support from the Jewish relief organizations and was more or less tolerated by the military governments in the occupied zones. The Haganah group at Belsen appointed Zvi Azaria head of Sherut Ha'am (National Service) to improve the coordination of its activities with the camp's operations. Azaria's position as chief rabbi put him above suspicion in the eyes of the British. Paramilitary training took place at night on the grounds of the camp cemetery, where Rabbi Azaria had buried thousands of dead after the liberation of Belsen.

In spite of the creation of a special propaganda unit under Rafael Kriman and Azriel Holzmann, there were not enough volunteers for service in Palestine. Consequently, the Haganah called on the Central Committee to put additional pressure on the DPs by reducing their food rations. On 23 May 1948, the *Vokhnblat, Organ fun der Sheyres-Hapleyte in der britisher Zone* published a mobilization order for all Jews in the British Zone: "The State of Israel calls upon all young men aged 17 to 35, including married men without children, to report immediately to the Jewish Army in Erets Israel. The central office of the National Service in the British Zone, which has been recognized by the Jewish Agency and all [other] Jewish organizations and institutions, hereby orders all Jewish men who fall within this age group to report at once at . . . in blocks. . . ."[120] The Haganah finally managed to get several thousand trained soldiers from the British Zone to Erets Yisrael via Marseille.

Even though not all able-bodied DPs were prepared to serve in the Haganah after the long years of persecution and privation, their enthusiasm for Palestine remained undiminished. According to a survey conducted in September 1945, 68.5 percent of the 10,783 Jewish residents of Belsen (7,317 persons) expressed the desire to immigrate to Erets Yisrael. The United States came in a distant second, with 9.4 percent.[121] From the reaction of the British and American Central Committees of Liberated Jews to a British offer to take 900 children from the DP camps and resettle them in England, one can gauge the degree to which Erets Yisrael ranked as the only possible country to which to immigrate. A resolution passed by the Central Committee under the chairmanship of Josef Rosensaft on 21 October 1945 stated: "(a) it [the Central Committee] cannot agree to the removal of the children to England; (b) it cannot permit the children, who were with us in the ghettos and concentration camps, to be moved from *galuth* [exile] to *galuth;* they must stay where they are until their *aliyah* [emigration]; (c) it [the Committee] demands that the first available *Aliyah* certificates [certificates of admission to Palestine] be allocated to the children, so that they can leave the camps as soon as possible."[122] One week earlier, the council of the Central Committee in Bavaria had explicitly rejected all attempts to settle Jewish children anywhere other than in Palestine.[123] In January 1945 both committees reaffirmed their stand on the issue.

David Ben-Gurion's visit to Belsen on 25 October 1945[124] underscored the importance of Palestine. As in his earlier sweep through the camps in the U.S. Zone, he embodied the innermost hopes of the Jewish survivors and struck fire with the masses at Belsen. Young people were particularly enthusiastic about the Zionists' ideas. Soon after liberation, they established a number of kibbutzim in the camp, which were affiliated with various political movements and helped prepare emigrants for agricultural work in Palestine.

There was great joy in Belsen when the Jewish Agency reported in spring 1946 that Colonel Robert Solomon, the British adviser on Jewish affairs, had managed to secure 200 immigration certificates for the camp's children. Shortly afterward, they were taken to Marseille by Hadassa Bimko and Rabbi Azaria. Together with 800 more children from other DP camps in Germany, they left Europe and headed for Palestine aboard the SS *Champollion*.[125]

However, the chance to immigrate remained the exception, not the rule. Most potential immigrants did not reach Israel until the end of 1948 or sometime during 1949. Finally, on 27 January 1949, the British secretary for foreign affairs granted the DPs the freedom to come and go as they pleased: "All Jewish refugees under British control have the freedom to move: . . . The ban on immigration to Israel from British occupied territories for Jews subject to military service has . . . been lifted."[126]

With the elimination of all barriers to immigration, the mass movement of Jews to Israel could begin. In mid-February, groups of refugees started leaving the British Zone on a regular basis, heading for the new Jewish state by sea and air.[127] The second transport left the camp on 21 March 1949: "Once again over 600 people were driven from the Bergen-Belsen camp to the infamous unloading platform in Bergen to board a train that had been decorated with Jewish flags. . . . The Central Committee and the American Joint Distribution Committee have done their best to make the trip as comfortable as possible. Representatives of all the major news agencies were present to see for themselves how happy the people were as they began the journey to their old-new homeland. . . . As the train moved away from the ramp at 4 P.M., over 600 people began singing "Hatikvah" [the Israeli national anthem], putting their whole heart and soul into it during their last moments on German soil, on the very spot where just a few years before thousands of condemned men and women, half naked, were dragged out of cattle cars to be led like animals to the death camp at Belsen."[128]

After 1945 various agencies and organizations regularly arranged for the emigration of small groups of refugees—usually some thirty-five DPs a month at Belsen—to a multitude of different countries. Sweden had already taken in thousands of Jews during and immediately after the end of the war. Starting in 1946, the Swedish government issued visas mainly to the family members of Jews who were already residing in the country.[129] JDC organized a project to reunite French Jewish families, the only stipulation being that the family member already living in France had to provide an affidavit of support. From June 1945 to September 1946, 984 Jewish DPs migrated from the British Zone to France, a large number of whom continued on to South America.[130] In February 1946 the British Home Office set up a special program in all three Western zones of occupation for persons suffering from emotional distress due to persecution under the Nazi regime—the so-called distressed persons' scheme. By September 1946 and with the help of the British Red Cross, JDC, and the Jewish Refugee Committee, seventy-three Jewish DPs had been taken by ship from the British Zone to England via Cuxhaven, where the British Red Cross had set up a special transit camp for the purpose.[131]

An emigration project proposed by the Canadian textile workers' union seemed to offer a promising future. Three hundred Jewish and 200 non-Jewish tailors in the British Zone were to be selected for immigration to Canada. To test the 625 candidates' aptitude for the job, JDC installed a number of sewing machines in the Buchholz emigrants' transit camp near Hanover in October 1947. The Joint had borrowed the machines from ORT. At the end of November, the first tailors, together with their families—forty DPs in all—left the British Zone. They were followed by more but not all the candidates.[132] Ultimately, former residents of Belsen spread out across the globe. Apart from the countries already mentioned, Paraguay, Venezuela, Bolivia, Brazil, Chile, Peru, Cuba, Mexico, Rhodesia (Zimbabwe), and Australia became new homes for the Jewish DPs.

Closing the Camp

On 10 July 1950 the last 1,000 DPs left Belsen and the camp permanently shut its gates. Among those departing was Josef Rosensaft, who went to America with his family.[133] The occupation authorities first considered the idea of shutting down the DP camp and handing the facility over to the British Army as early as spring 1946. It was only at the end of 1949, however, that the idea was put into concrete terms. Violent resistance by residents prevented the authorities from carrying out the evacuation that had been scheduled for 1 April 1950. Rosensaft explained the reason for their negative reaction: "Permit me to point out again that the end of the Belsen camp should coincide with an end to camp life for the Jewish DPs in the British Zone."[134]

Most of the DPs still living in Belsen were so-called hard-core cases, who, because of medical problems, had very limited opportunities for resettlement or who were loath to give up their familiar surroundings and the relationships they had established over the years. Others waited to obtain visas for the United States. There were delays, however, because the Americans gave the DPs in their occupation zone preferential treatment when it came to immigrating to the United States. The deliberations over the impending evacuation of the camp became so emotionally charged that in March 1950 the residents not only demonstrated against the decision, they went on a hunger strike.[135]

Despite their protests, the residents were first put into Camp No. 4, and then in July, together with patients from the Glyn Hughes Hospital, they were transferred to Jever near Wilhelmshaven. Even though the accommodations in Jever were good, the former residents of Belsen were once again obliged to adapt themselves to new conditions, and many were forced to spend yet another year living in a camp. For some, even this was not yet the end of their lives as displaced persons. On 13 August 1951, two days before Jever was closed, seven hard-core cases and seventy-six residents who had been accepted by Israel were taken to the DP camp at Föhrenwald.[136] The closing of Jever and its transfer to the British Army on 15 August 1951 ended the last chapter in the story of the Belsen DPs. Josef Rosensaft summed up the situation:

Since 1945 almost 23,000 Jews have left the British Zone. In the meantime, they have made new lives for themselves and live under normal
conditions in new homelands, especially in Israel. We are also pleased
to note that over 2,000 children were born during this time. This is a
considerable number, given the heavy spiritual burdens that our people
had to bear in the concentration camps. The work done in the medical
area deserves special mention. Thousands of sick and acutely ill patients
have been rehabilitated in these six and a half years. And more than 4,000
operations have been performed in our hospitals alone. . . . I cannot say
that I have always been right, but I assume the authorities now understand that I was merely fighting on behalf of people who needed help,
even though my efforts were not always in accord with the regulations or
the law.[137]

In 1950 Belsen survivors in Israel established the Irgun sheerit
hapleita me'haezor ha-Briti (Organization of Survivors from the British Zone). Under its first director, Zvi Azaria, the organization established its headquarters in the World Jewish Congress building in Tel
Aviv. Each year on 15 April, Belsen survivors gather at a hotel and
meet with those from many other places who lived through the mar-
tyrdom in order to commemorate the liberation. At the tenth anniversary celebration in 1955, the "Belsen Wood" was planted near Jerusalem.[138]

The survivors began to build monuments in their former place of
residence. On 25 November 1945, the Central Committee of Liberated Jews erected the first monument. Made of wood and meant to be
temporary, it was placed in the middle of the mass graves. On 15
April 1946, the first anniversary of the liberation, members of the
Central Committee unveiled a monument in stone, the Bergen-
Belsen Martyrs Monument, with inscriptions in Hebrew and English.
In October the British Military Government began to show an interest in preserving Belsen and erecting a monument in the center of the
camp. After lengthy deliberations, it was decided that a 24-meter-
high (79-foot-high) obelisk and a 50-meter-long (164-foot-long) wall
would be built opposite the obelisk with inscriptions in fourteen languages. Work was begun in the middle of 1947, but financial difficulties and problems in acquiring materials to build the monument

delayed the project. It was only after the reform of western Germany's currency in June 1948 that work on the monument could continue. Still, it took until the fall of 1949 to complete what eventually became known as the International Monument.

Then a serious dispute broke out with the Central Committee of Liberated Jews and other Jewish organizations over the fact that the builders had neglected to put Hebrew and Yiddish inscriptions on the wall.[139] So three more years passed before the official dedication finally took place on 30 November 1952. West Germany's president, Theodor Heuss, and the president of the World Jewish Congress, Nahum Goldmann, delivered addresses at the unveiling ceremony.

That same year, the state of Lower Saxony took over the facility and in 1966 opened a museum with a small exhibit on the history of the camp from 1943 to 1945. On the fortieth anniversary of the liberation, the *Landtag* (state parliament) of Lower Saxony passed a resolution to redesign the Belsen memorial and commissioned the Niedersächsische Landeszentrale für politische Bildung (Central Office of Political Education of Lower Saxony) to carry out the project. Today the Belsen memorial administration focuses its attention on working with visitors to the camp, particularly schoolchildren.[140]

❀

Final Reflections

With the closing of Föhrenwald, the story of the Jewish DPs in Germany had come to an end. Those who remained behind would shape the future of Jewish life in the Federal Republic.

The events of the Nazi period had a lasting effect not only on the survivors but on the Jewish people as a whole. Viewed from a historical perspective, the Holocaust was the greatest catastrophe to have befallen the Jewish people. It affected the Jews' religious views, their cohesiveness as a people, their integration into various nation states, their cultural life, and their relation to Western civilization. To the Jewish DPs, life in the diaspora was tantamount to being threatened with yet another catastrophe. Not only had they been persecuted by the Germans during the war, but they were subjected to pogroms in Poland after the war, outrages that had nothing to do with National Socialism. At the same time, they became the targets of restrictive immigration policies in the United States and Great Britain, especially after their liberation. Added to this was the latent anti-Semitism that still existed in a number of countries and broke out with particular vehemence in Eastern Europe. Nor was anti-Semitism a thing of the past in postwar Germany.

Just a few months after liberation, a letter from the representative of the Landsberg city council's housing office, Hermann Aumer, to the state commissioner in charge of caring for Jews in Bavaria clearly reflected the role that anti-Semitism played in the tense relations between the Jewish DPs and the surrounding German population:

The situation in the housing market here is a disaster. . . . The drive on the part of the Jews here to expand and the methods they use have become so blatant that sooner or later an incident may occur which we will never be able to put right. The most urgent task for all the responsible authorities is to prevent this from happening. . . . Based on my personal observations as well as those of others, furniture looted from homes has been taken to the barracks, smashed, and used for fuel. . . . At the same time I have noticed that some Jews have secured rooms for themselves by offering substantial amounts of money or promising payment in food. Others have obtained rooms using papers issued by the "housing office in the barracks," while another type [of Jew] has used sheer intimidation to force an anxious and frightened population to provide them with rooms. . . . The only way to remedy this situation is for the housing office to act with utmost ruthlessness, as it has in the past. Otherwise the outskirts of the city will quickly become one big ghetto.[1]

It is obvious that this particular city official—like broad segments of the West German public in subsequent years—had already buried the past, even though the actual dimensions of the Nazi persecution of the Jews had just become known. The assistance given to the Jewish DPs by the military, UNRRA (later IRO), and JDC caused envy among the Germans, who were living in a country destroyed by war and were not as well provided for. These sentiments resulted in the revival of old anti-Semitic prejudices and stereotypes. Instead of trying to understand what the few Jewish survivors had gone through, the Germans began to counterbalance Auschwitz with the bombing of Dresden and compare the expulsion of Germans from Eastern Europe to the persecution of the Jews.

Also typical was the attitude of the Bamberg Refugee Committee. In July 1950 it formally petitioned the city not to house German expellees[2] together with Jewish displaced persons, "since it is unreasonable to expect the expellees to live under one roof with people such as these, many of whom are criminals, have no regular jobs, no concern for morality, and no respect for the authority of the state." Even the mayor of the city, who, according to the Bamberg Jewish community, "regularly referred in his speeches to mutual understanding, the fear of God, and brotherly love," used the occasion of the Refugee Committee's petition to call the DPs the "chief carriers of lice" and suggest that they be housed "in unused stables."[3]

The closing of nearly all the DP camps in 1951 and the emigration of the majority of the Jewish survivors did not signal the end of anti-

Semitism in the new German democracy. A survey conducted by the Allensbach Institute for Demoscopy in 1949 found that 23 percent of the population was still "decidedly anti-Semitic" and had "negative feelings" toward Jews; three years later the number jumped to 34 percent.[4] Although the growth of anti-Semitism has diminished as new generations have taken their place in society, 12 to 15 percent of the German population surveyed in the 1980s and early 1990s still held anti-Semitic views; another 5 percent were radical anti-Semites who believed that Jews should be the targets of active discrimination.[5]

Even though there were only some 30,000 Jews living in Germany (until the emigration of Jews from the Soviet Union in the 1990s), they continued to be the victims of one wave of anti-Semitic outbreaks after another. The attack on the Cologne synagogue in December 1959 achieved a sad notoriety and was followed within the next four weeks by 470 other anti-Semitic and neo-Nazi acts.[6]

These kinds of incidents, particularly the desecration of cemeteries, have been part of the history of the Federal Republic down to the present day. In the face of the violent attacks on asylum seekers in the past few years, many Jews have wondered whether it would not be better to leave Germany for good. The majority, however—including the descendants of the displaced persons who remained in Germany after the end of the war—have pinned their hopes on the strength of German democracy to ward off these assaults. They now view what had once been a temporary "waiting room" for the Jewish DPs after the war as their new home—albeit with a certain ambivalence.

❖

Appendix: List of Camps

Camps in which a majority of the residents were non-Jewish are not listed here, nor are camps that were set up only for summer recreation or as transit facilities for emigrants. For the American and French Zones, the figures given for "number of Jewish camp residents" always represent the total population of the camp. This is not the case, however, for the British Zone.

The data and other information presented here were gathered from the following sources: YIVO DPG, New York (Yidisher Visnshaftlekher Institut [Yiddish Scientific Institute] displaced persons' archive) and YIVO's copy of the LWSP (Leo W. Schwarz Papers); IfZ, Munich (Institut für Zeitgeschichte, Munich) Fi 01.30–01.34; Yad Vashem, Jerusalem, RA (Rosensaft Archive of Bergen-Belsen); YIVO LWSP folder 244, Annual Report of Vaad Hatzala Activities, 15 June 1946–15 June 1947 (religious institutions); and Juliane Wetzel, *Jüdisches Leben in München, 1945–1951: Durchgangsstation oder Wiederaufbau?* (Munich, 1987).

The "districts" in the U.S. Zone referred to below correspond to the military districts activated by the U.S. Military Government on 28 September 1946: District I Stuttgart; District II Frankfurt; District III Bamberg; District IV Regensburg; District V Munich; and Berlin.

U.S. Zone

AGLASTERHAUSEN

Stuttgart District; children's home; number of Jewish camp residents 31 May 1946: 24, 30 June 1947: 43, 3 October 1947: 85, 18 October 1948: 38; closed: 23 November 1948.

AINRING (NEAR FREILASSING)

Munich District; transit and DP camp; number of Jewish camp residents 31 December 1945: 300, 31 May 1946: 325 (DP camp), 800 (transit), 19 October 1946: 3,613 (DP and transit camp), 3 October 1947: 375 (DP camp); closed: transit camp, end of September 1947; residents transferred to Lechfeld.

ALTÖTTING

Munich District; number of Jewish camp residents 19 October 1946: 207, 3 October 1947: 172; closed: 12 April 1948.

ANSBACH BLEIDORN KASERNE [BARRACK]

Regensburg District; number of Jewish camp residents 19 October 1946: no Jews, 8 February 1947: 1,287, 3 October 1947: 1,213, 18 October 1948: 953, 25 July 1949: 168; closed: 1 October 1949.

ANSBACH STRUTH

Bamberg District; children's camp; children's home; opened in January 1946; Dror[1] and Hashomer Hatzair[2] kibbutzim; school: *talmud torah* (director: J. Goldberger) 10 June 1947: 106 students; number of Jewish camp residents 31 May 1946: 385, 19 October 1946: 443, 3 October 1947: 100, 18 October 1948: 152; closed: 1 April 1949.

ARNIDOR

Regensburg District; number of Jewish camp residents 3 October 1947: 51.

ASCHAU

Munich District; children's home; Bnei Akiva[3] yeshiva (director: Dr. Winternitz) 10 June 1947: 180 students; number of Jewish camp residents 31 May 1946: 464, 19 October 1946: 522, 3 October 1947: 263, 18 October 1948: 342, 26 July 1949: 476; closed: 1 July 1949.

ASCHBACH (32 KILOMETERS [19.8 MILES] FROM BAMBERG)

Bamberg District; kibbutz housed in an old castle; 5 hectares [12.35 acres] each of farmland, vegetable gardens, pasturage, and 300 trees; number of Jewish camp residents 31 May 1946: 111, 3 October 1947: 47; closed: March 1948.

ATTEL (NEAR WASSERBURG)

Munich District; number of Jewish camp residents 3 October 1947: 413, 18 October 1948: 387, 25 July 1949: 330; closed: 15 January 1950.

AUERBACH (NEAR PASSAU)

Regensburg District; kibbutz; number of Jewish camp residents 30 July 1947: 67.

BABENHAUSEN (NEAR ASCHAFFENBURG)

Frankfurt District; former POW camp; reception camp for Eastern European migrants from Landshut; school: *talmud torah* (director: B. Truskiewicz) 10 June 1947: 77 students; number of Jewish camp residents 19 October 1946: 3,026, 25 July 1949: 191; closed: 6 September 1949.

BACKNANG

Stuttgart District; DP camp in a teacher training college; number of Jewish camp residents 31 May 1946: 533, 19 October 1946: 535, 3

October 1947: 314, 18 October 1948: 485, 25 April 1949: 262, 25 July 1949: no more Jewish residents; closed: 25 April 1950.

BAD AIBLING

Munich District; barracks camp; opened in September 1946 for 7,000 DPs to relieve pressure on Cham and Landshut; 1,100 DPs soon transferred to Neu-Ulm; closed: 30 April 1948.

BAD NAUHEIM

Frankfurt District; number of Jewish camp residents 1 June 1946: 319, 19 October 1946: 383, 3 October 1948: 394; closed: 1 March 1949.

BAD REICHENHALL

Munich District; schools: *talmud torah* (director: Ch. Rosnik) 10 June 1947: 236 students, November 1948: 85 students; Jawne [Yavneh] school November 1948: 180 students; newspaper: *Der Morgn (The Morning)*; number of Jewish camp residents 19 October 1946: 5,997, 3 October 1947: 5,153, 18 October 1948: 3,269; closed: 31 July 1951.

BAD SALZSCHLIRF (NEAR FULDA)

Frankfurt District; school: *talmud torah* (director: S. Reich) 10 June 1947: 38 students, fall 1948: 25 students; newspaper: *Zaltsshlirfer lebn (Salzschlirf Life)*; number of Jewish camp residents 9 August 1946: 832, 19 October 1946: 827, 3 October 1947: 726, 18 October 1948: 615; closed: 24 March 1949.

BAD WÖRISHOFEN

Munich District; kosher kitchen (director: R. Schneider) to feed 300 persons; number of Jewish camp residents 31 May 1946: 89, 3 October 1947: 258; closed: May 1948.

BAMBERG ULANENKASERNE [UHLAN BARRACKS]

Bamberg District; opened in January 1946; schools: *talmud torah* fall 1948: 44 students; Bet Meyer yeshiva (director: Rabbi Belfar) 10 June 1947: 45 students; *mikvah;* kosher kitchen (director: Rabbi Halberstadt) to feed 800 DPs in June 1947; newspaper: *Unzer Wort (Our Word)* (editor in chief: M. Jungsztajn [Yungshtayn]); number of Jewish camp residents 31 December 1945: 750, 31 March 1946: 1,608, 19 October 1946: 1,838, 3 October 1947: 1,459, 18 October 1948: 1,196; closed: 27 April 1949.

BAYREUTH

See Zettlitz (near Münchberg).

BAYREUTH VORKENHOF

Bamberg District; kibbutz; number of Jewish camp residents 31 May 1946: 42.

BAYRISCH GMAIN (NEAR TRAUNSTEIN)

Munich District; children's camp; Gurdenya kibbutz; number of Jewish camp residents 3 October 1947: 83, 18 October 1948: 25, 25 July 1949: 110.

BENSHEIM (50 KILOMETERS [31 MILES] FROM FRANKFURT)

Frankfurt District; camp director in August 1946: Mr. Balmelle; originally a camp for Polish non-Jewish DPs; from August 1946 for Jewish DPs; schools: elementary school April 1947: 76 students; *cheder*[4] April 1947: 41 students; *talmud torah* (director: N. Gemora) 10 June 1947: 38 students; Klausenburg [Cluj-Kolozsvar] yeshiva April 1947: 10 students; kindergarten April 1947: 35 students; 30-bed hospital (in a German clinic); theater group; sports group; synagogue; number of Jewish camp residents 9 August 1946: 468, 19 October 1946: 1,196, 3 October 1947: 1,124, 18 October 1948: 870; closed: 6 April 1949.

BERNSTEIN A. WALD

Bamberg District; kibbutz; number of Jewish camp residents 30 July 1946: 170, 30 July 1947: 114; closed: September 1947.

BINDLACH (NEAR BAYREUTH)

Bamberg District; opened in March 1948 for Jewish DPs from Romania; number of Jewish camp residents March 1948: 250 (previously in separate transit camps).

BOXDORF (NEAR FLOSS/WEIDEN)

Regensburg District; kibbutz; number of Jewish camp residents 3 June 1946: 28, 30 July 1947: 32.

BUCHBERG (ON THE SHORES OF THE TACHINGER SEE NEAR TRAUNREUT)

Munich District; former powder factory; barracks camp; number of Jewish camp residents June 1945: 1,000.

BUCHENWINKEL/DORFEN (NEAR WOLFRATSHAUSEN)

Munich District; sanitarium; administered by Föhrenwald; number of Jewish camp residents 31 May 1946: 67, 19 October 1946: 33, 29 January 1947: 30, 3 October 1947: 67, 18 October 1948: 64, 25 July 1949: 14, after December 1949 no more residents; closed: 1 September 1951.

CHAM

Regensburg District; tent camp; like Landshut, served as a transit camp during mass influx of refugees from Eastern Europe; many of the DPs set off on their own for other camps; an orderly transfer took place only in the case of orphans who were subsequently accommodated in Rosenheim and Ulm (Dornstadt); adult DPs were transferred, among other places, to Wetzlar; school: *talmud torah* (director:

Rabbi Rosenwald) 10 June 1947: 35 students; kosher kitchen (director: Rabbi Rosenwald) to feed 300 persons; number of Jewish camp residents 3 October 1947: 204.

Chofec Chaim[5] (near Creussen)
See Creußen Chofec Chaim.

Creussen B'nai Akiba (near Bayreuth)
Bamberg District; kibbutz; number of Jewish camp residents 31 May 1946: 30.

Creussen Chofec Chaim (near Bayreuth)
Bamberg District; kibbutz; number of Jewish camp residents 30 July 1946: 65, 3 October 1947: 45.

Dachau
Munich District; kibbutz; youth camp near Mühldorf; school: *talmud torah* (director: Rabbi Katan) 10 June 1947: 32 students; kosher kitchen (director: Rabbi Katan) to feed 350 persons; number of Jewish camp residents 31 May 1946: 135.

Deggendorf (Lower Bavaria–Upper Palatinate)
Bamberg and Regensburg Districts; schools: elementary school and kindergarten December 1946: 103 students; *talmud torah* fall 1948: 35 students; ORT school; library (1,700 books in December 1946); home for the elderly operated by Va'ad Hahatzalah June 1947: 80 persons; theater group; synagogue; *mikvah;* kosher kitchen; Negev kibbutz; newspaper: *Cum Ojfboj, Wochnszrift fun der "Histadrut Cijonit Achida" — snif Deggendorf [Tsum Oyfboy, Vokhnshrift fun der "Histadrut Tsiyonit Akhida" — snif Deggendorf (Reconstruction, Weekly of the Federation of Zionist Organizations — Deggendorf Branch)]*, printed in Roman letters with Polish spelling (first issue of November 1946: "Mit a szarfn blik" ["Mit a sharfn blik," ("With a Sharp Eye")], published until

February 1947, editor in chief: Menachem Sztajer [Shtayer] (formerly editor in chief of *Bamidbar* at Föhrenwald); *Deggendorf Center Review* in Yiddish (Roman letters) and in German, editor in chief: Alexander Gutfeld; camp currency: 5-, 10-, 25-, 50-cent pieces, 1-, 5-, 10-dollar bills (with the stamp "Jewish Committee—D.P. Camp 7 Deggendorf" and the initials of the camp treasurer "Ba"—Basch). Various examples can be found in the banknote collection of the HypoVereinsbank in Munich, Theatinerstr. 11; number of Jewish camp residents October 1945: 1,000, including 700 (of whom 330 were older than 60) liberated in Theresienstadt [Terezín] who arrived in Germany via Prague, and 300 Jews from Poland who arrived in September 1945, 31 December 1945: 1,350, 31 May 1946: 1,203, 19 October 1946: 1,537, 3 October 1947: 1,290, 18 October 1948: 1,965 (Old and New Barracks); closed: 15 June 1949.

DIEBURG

Frankfurt District; schools: elementary school April 1947: 89 students; *talmud torah* (director: W. Faskowitz) April 1947: 44 students, 10 June 1947: 90 students; Beth Jacob school April 1947: 47 students; kindergarten April 1947: 37 students; yeshiva (director: Rabbi Blut) 10 June 1947: 28 students; number of Jewish camp residents 3 October 1947: 832, 18 October 1948: 619; closed: 23 March 1949.

DIESSEN (ON THE SHORES OF THE AMMERSEE)

Munich District; Dror kibbutz in the Finster Inn; potters' school; number of Jewish camp residents 1946: 50, 30 July 1947: 97.

DORFEN

See Buchenwinkel (near Wolfratshausen).

DORFEN — VILLA BAUER (NEAR ERDING)

Munich District; kibbutz; summer camp organized by Agudat Israel and Mizrachi for religious children; supported by JDC, summer

1948: 600 children at a spa; number of Jewish camp residents 31 May 1946: 51.

Düppel Center Berlin[6]

Berlin District; barracks camp; schools: elementary school 31 December 1947: 385 students; also religious schools; kindergarten; Baderech (On the Way) theater group; sports club; synagogue; newspaper: *Undser Lebn (Our Life)*; number of Jewish camp residents 1 June 1946: 1,055, 4 September 1946: 5,130, 19 October 1946: 3,527, 30 July 1947: 3,327, 3 October 1947: 3,277; closed: at the end of July 1948 the camp was suddenly evacuated because of the Berlin blockade and the DPs were flown to Frankfurt.

Eggenfelden

Munich District; camp director: Military Government Officer Lt. Fuchs; AJDC representative: Mr. Levine; ORT school 1947: 92 students, 3 teachers.

Eichstätt Jäger-Kaserne [riflemen's barracks]

Bamberg District; the camp was subdivided into three sections (Jäger-Kaserne, Annex, BC); schools: *talmud torah* (director: G. Gottesmann) 10 June 1947: 90 students; *talmud torah* (director: M. Salomon) 10 June 1947: 35 students; *talmud torah* (director: Rabbi Goldberger) 10 June 1947: 45 students; Klausenburg [Cluj-Kolozsvar] yeshiva (director: A. Feldstein) 10 June 1947: 20 students; *mikvah* (built by JDC in 1948); number of Jewish camp residents 3 October 1947: 1,283, 18 October 1948: 1,222; closed: 1 October 1949.

Eisolzried (near Dachau)

Munich District; kibbutz; number of Jewish camp residents 30 July 1947: 60.

ELMAU

Munich District; sanitarium for inactive TB cases; Dr. Müller-Elmau, the former owner, had been categorized as a major offender [in a de-Nazification hearing] before the Garmisch *Spruchkammer* [tribunal of local, non-Nazi citizens] and as a consequence had to surrender his property; with the approval of the Bavarian Interior Ministry, JDC set up a facility for Jewish DPs in May 1947; administered by the Bayerisches Staatskommissariat für rassisch, religiös und politisch Verfolgte [Bavarian State Commissariat for the Racially, Religiously and Politically Persecuted]; comfortably furnished; library; reading room; camp capacity: 200 persons.

ERDING BLUMENGARTEN

Munich District; kibbutz; number of Jewish camp residents 31 May 1946: 50, 30 July 1947: 68.

ESCHENSTRUTH

See Rochelle Eschenstruth.

ESCHWEGE AIRBASE

Frankfurt District; opened in January 1946; schools: preschool April 1947: 30 students; elementary school April 1947: 148 students; *talmud torah* (director: M. Taub) 10 June 1947: 60 students; *cheder* and yeshiva 28 April 1947: 40 students; Beth Jacob (director: Miryam Krakauer) 19 March 1946: 30 Hungarian girls; kindergarten April 1947: 50 students; synagogue; *mikvah;* sports club with 100 members; camp cinema; theater for 550 persons, theater group; newspaper: *Unzer Hofenung (Our Hope)* (editor in chief: M. Duniec); number of Jewish camp residents: 1 June 1946: 1,764, 19 October 1946: 3,353, 3 October 1947: 3,114; 18 October 1948: 2,383; closed: 26 April 1949.

ESCHWEGE HOLZHAUSEN

Frankfurt District: Mosad Chinuchi[7] school: *talmud torah* (director: Silberberg) 10 June 1947: 28 students; number of Jewish camp residents 19 October 1946: 122, 30 July 1947: 94, 3 October 1947: 8; closed: October 1947.

ESCHWEGE SCHWEBDA CASTLE

Frankfurt District; children's home; number of Jewish camp residents 9 August 1946: 190, 19 October 1946: 1,945; closed: August 1947.

FELDAFING (ON THE SHORES OF THE STARNBERGERSEE, 35 KILOMETERS [21.7 MILES] SOUTHWEST OF MUNICH)

Munich District; former *Napola* (short for *Nationalpolitische Erziehungsanstalten,* or National Political Training Institutes, schools established by Hitler to train a Nazi elite); stone buildings and wooden barracks; first camp director (until October 1945): Lt. Irving J. Smith, who set up the camp on 1 May 1945 to accommodate 3,000 Hungarian Jewish women liberated at Tutzing on 29 April 1945; also housed non-Jewish Russian, Polish, Hungarian, and Yugoslav former concentration camp inmates until August 1945; in fall 1945 40 additional villas in the vicinity requisitioned and a 1,000-bed Jewish hospital opened at Elisabeth Hotel (director: Dr. Henri Heitan, JDC); first elected camp committee in the U.S. Zone; separate "children's block" for 450 children and young people; schools: elementary school (established November 1945) November 1946: 138 students; *talmud torah* (director: Schlapoberski) 10 June 1947: 30 students; kindergarten; evening school; ORT school June 1947: 170 apprentices, December 1947: 203 apprentices, February 1948: 50 apprentices; Bet Aron yeshiva (director: H. Rosenblatt) 10 June 1947: 46 students; nurses' training school; synagogue; *mikvah;* Chofec Chaim Ohel Sarah [Hebrew, literally "Sarah's tent"] religious kibbutzim; dressmaking course for Orthodox Jewish women; theater groups: Amcho,[8] Partisan, Habima;[9] newspapers: *Dos Fraye Vort* (*The Free Word*) (editor in chief: Meier Gawronski), *Dos Yiddishe Vort* (*The Jewish Word*) (editors in chief: Josef Friedenson and Awieser Bursztyn of Agudat Israel), *Unter-*

wegs (Untervegs [Underway]) (magazine); number of Jewish camp residents 16 September 1945: 4,900 (Elisabeth Hotel hospital: 250), 31 May 1946: 3,821, 19 October 1946: 3,999, 3 October 1947: 3,801, 18 October 1948: 2,809, 7 January 1949: 2,856, 25 July 1949: 2,672, 30 January 1950: 2,093, 19 July 1950: 2,482, 25 April 1951: 1,585, 19 October 1951: 32; closed: hospital 25 April 1950, Jewish camp 31 May 1951; from 1 December 1951 under German administration; finally closed in March 1953.

FIRSTBACH (NEAR MOOSEN, KREIS [DISTRICT] ERDING)

Munich District; number of Jewish camp residents 31 May 1946: 62, 30 July 1947: 72.

FLOSS

See Boxdorf.

FÖHRENWALD

See the corresponding chapter in this book, pp. 95–166.

Number of Jewish camp residents 31 May 1946: 4,030, 19 October 1946: 4,234, 3 October 1947: 4,296, 18 October 1948: 3,950, 25 July 1949: 3,477.

FORKENDORF (NEAR GESEES)

Bamberg District; kibbutz; number of Jewish camp residents 30 July 1946: 68, 30 July 1947: 57; closed: August 1947.

FRANZHEIM (NEAR ERDING)

Munich District; kibbutz; number of Jewish camp residents 31 May 1946: 70.

FRITZLAR

Frankfurt District; Watter-Kaserne [barracks]; schools: elementary school for girls April 1947: 62 students; Tarbut school April 1947:

47 boys; *talmud torah* (director: Rabbi Gortler) 10 June 1947: 160 students, fall 1948: 40 students; synagogue; theater group; soccer team; weekly film showings; number of Jewish camp residents 3 October 1947: 949, 18 October 1948: 839; the last camp residents were transferred to camps in the area of Stuttgart in January 1949; closed: 31 January 1949.

FÜRTH

Bamberg District; school: *talmud torah* fall 1948: 19 students; *mikvah;* kosher kitchen (director: Rabbi Spiro) for feeding 200 persons; number of Jewish camp residents 31 December 1945: 850, 31 May 1946: 750, 19 October 1946: 748, 3 October 1947: 684, 18 October 1948: 664, 25 July 1949: 76; closed: 15 July 1949.

GABERSEE (NEAR WASSERBURG)

Munich District; opened 29 March 1946; number of Jewish camp residents 31 May 1946: 1,557, 19 October 1946: 2,087, 3 October 1947: 1,920, 18 October 1948: 1,570, 25 July 1949: 1,591; closed: 30 June 1950.

GAUTING

Munich District; TB sanitarium; originally a barracks, during the war a TB sanitarium for the German Air Force; requisitioned by the U.S. Army for DPs on 30 April 1945; assisted by Chaplain Klausner, the first Jewish patients came from the Dachau concentration camp and made up half of all patients until the beginning of 1949; JDC warehouse for medications and medical equipment; Jewish patients' committee; kosher kitchen (supplied by Föhrenwald) for feeding 200 patients; guest performances by various theater groups; newspaper: *Unser Leben (Our Life)* of the patients' committee, *Biletyn, Ferband fyn Kielcer jidn yn die amerikaner zone Dajczhland (Byuletin, Ferband fun Kieltser yidn in die amerikaner zone Daytshland [Bulletin, Association of Kielce Jews in the U.S. Zone of Germany]);* number of Jewish camp residents: October 1945, 500, 31 May 1946: 688, 19 October 1946: 624 (total occupancy: 1,251), 3 October 1947: 519 (919), 18 October 1948:

441 (948), 25 July 1949: 377 (1,040), 30 January 1950: 273 (816), 19 July 1950: 206 (797), 24 April 1951: 170 (753); as of 1 May 1951 under German administration.

GERETSRIED

Munich District; former factory workers' housing owned by the Geretsried Arms Works; opened as a Jewish camp May 1947; originally set up for non-Jewish DPs, then empty for several months; camp director David Jakubowitz, who moved to Föhrenwald after Geretsried was shut down and headed the camp committee at Föhrenwald; kindergarten 12 June 1947: 27 children; school-age children (20) had to attend the Föhrenwald school; special school for deaf-mutes (May 1947–18 July 1948) and stutterers (May 1947–3 June 1948); library with reading room; number of Jewish camp residents 3 October 1947: 793, 18 October 1948: 607, 28 October 1949: 572; the 360 remaining camp residents were transferred to Föhrenwald in March 1950; closed: 15 March 1950.

GERINGSHOF (NEAR FULDA)

Frankfurt District; number of Jewish camp residents 27 September 1945: 80, 1 June 1946: 83, 19 October 1946: 92, 3 October 1947: 79; closed: September 1948.

GERSFELD (NEAR FULDA)

Frankfurt District; opened on 1 September 1945 to relieve Geringshof; agricultural training; vocational school for various branches of industry; number of Jewish camp residents October 1945: 80, 1 June 1946: 94, 19 October 1946: 115, 30 June 1947: 89, 3 October 1947: 78; closed: November 1947.

GIEBELSTADT (NEAR WÜRZBURG)

Frankfurt District; number of Jewish camp residents 18 October 1948: 1,417; closed: 22 June 1949.

GOLDCUP (NEAR HESSISCH LICHTENAU)

Frankfurt District; Mizrachi children's camp; Tarbut school for the first grade, all other grades completed school in Herzog; synagogue; *mikvah;* choir with 10 singers; maternity clinic that served all camps in the Hessisch Lichtenau complex; number of Jewish camp residents 9 August 1946: 706, 19 October 1946: 825, 3 October 1947: 656, 18 October 1948: 526; the last residents were transferred to Heidenheim in January 1949; closed: 6 January 1949.

GRASS

Munich District; kibbutz; number of Jewish camp residents 30 July 1947: 73.

GREIFENBERG (NEAR LANDSBERG)

Munich District; kibbutz; former Nazi school for girls; supplied by Landsberg; number of Jewish camp residents 31 May 1946: 196, 19 October 1946: 198, 3 October 1947: 135; closed: March 1948.

HASENECKE (NEAR KASSEL)

Frankfurt District; schools: Tarbut April 1947: 116 boys; religious school for girls 10 June 1947: 80 students; *talmud torah* (director: S. Blut) April 1947: 40 students; synagogue; religious camp committee: soccer, boxing, and chess teams; number of Jewish camp residents 19 October 1946: 2,099, 3 October 1947: 2,208, 18 October 1948: 1,846; closed: 8 March 1949.

HASENECKE MOSAD CHINUCHI

Frankfurt District; kibbutz; *talmud torah* (director: M. Freiheiter) 10 June 1947: 35 students.

HEIDENHEIM

Stuttgart District; school: *talmud torah* (director: A. Immerglick) 10 June 1947: 35 students; Klausenburg [Cluj-Kolozsvar] Rabbi Kook[10] yeshiva (director: A. Lichtenstein) 10 June 1947: 45 students; kosher kitchen (director: Rabbi Frankel) for feeding 250 persons; number of Jewish camp residents (Voith Settlement) 19 October 1946: 1,905, 3 October 1947: 2,091, 22 November 1948: 1,754, 25 July 1949: 2,328; number of Jewish camp residents (Jewish Home—in the former police academy) 19 October 1946: 579, 3 October 1947: 402, 22 November 1948: 273, 25 July 1949: 216; number of Jewish camp residents (rabbinical school) 3 October 1947: 40, merged with the Voith Jewish Home in December 1947; closed: 5 August 1949.

HERZOG (PART OF THE HESSISCH LICHTENAU COMPLEX)

Frankfurt District; workers' housing built during the Nazi period for an underground munitions factory; set up as a DP camp in June 1946; schools: Tarbut with eight grades for all camps in the Hessisch Lichtenau complex (Goldcup had an elementary school for the first grade only); *talmud torah* (director: Rabbi Freibuch) 10 June 1947: 50 students; kindergarten (also for the children at Teichhof); theater group; bookmobile that served the other camps in the Hessisch Lichtenau complex; number of Jewish camp residents 9 August 1946: 1,116, 19 October 1946: 1,222, 3 October 1947: 1,117, 18 October 1948: 932; the last residents were transferred to Heidenheim in January 1949; closed: 25 January 1949.

HESSISCH LICHTENAU CLUB HOUSE

Frankfurt District; each camp belonging to the Hessisch Lichtenau complex (see Goldcup, Herzog, Rochelle, Teichhof, and Velmeden) had its own camp committee, then all the committees were combined into one "supreme" committee until the beginning of 1947, when the individual committees resumed operations; school: *talmud torah* (director: Rabbi Rosen) 10 June 1947: 45 students; kindergarten; theater group; number of Jewish camp residents 9 August 1946: 49, 19 October 1946: 712; closed: February 1947, when Rochelle was opened.

HOCHLANDLAGER (NEAR WOLFRATSHAUSEN)

Munich District; kibbutz; number of Jewish camp residents 31 May 1946: 309, 19 October 1946: 360, 3 October 1947: 279, 18 October 1948: 233; merged with Föhrenwald in December 1948.

HOF

Bamberg District; former SS housing; mainly a camp for children; 250 children brought here from Rehau on 22 July 1946; school: *talmud torah* (director: Szafranowitz) 10 June 1947: 65 students; number of Jewish camp residents 19 October 1946: 1,104, 3 October 1947: 747; December 1947 no more residents.

HOFGEISMAR

Frankfurt District; schools: April 1947 one elementary school for 86 boys and one for 44 girls; Tarbut school April 1947: 42 boys and 88 girls; *talmud torah* (director: S. Gewurz) 10 June 1947: 220 students; kindergarten (director: S. Gewurz) 10 June 1947: 50 students; soccer, boxing, and gymnastics teams; theater group, drama circle; number of Jewish camp residents 19 October 1946: 2,103, 3 October 1947: 1,710, 18 October 1948: 1,291; closed: 20 February 1949.

HOLZHAUSEN (NEAR ESCHWEGE)

See Eschwege Holzhausen.

HOLZHAUSEN (NEAR LANDSBERG)

Munich District; "Chane Senesh"[11] Dror kibbutz supplied by Landsberg; formerly a school for educationally handicapped girls who were looked after on the top floor by nuns who also cared for the DPs;

newspaper: *Igeret* (Hebrew, "letter"); number of Jewish camp residents
31 May 1946: 154, 19 October 1946: 155.

INDERSDORF

Munich District; twelfth-century monastery; formerly a girls' board-
ing school; prior to the establishment of the Jewish children's camp in
August 1946 was an international children's home; children's camp—
Dror kibbutz; care continued to be provided in part by Catholic nuns;
director in the summer of 1946: Jean Henshaw, previously director
at Föhrenwald; newspaper: *Uj Elet* [Hungarian, "new life"] (editor in
chief: Jozsef Schwarz); number of Jewish camp residents 31 December
1945: 40, 31 May 1946: 67, 19 October 1946: 339, 3 October 1947:
177; closed: September 1948.

JÄGER-KASERNE [RIFLEMEN'S BARRACKS] (NEAR KASSEL)

Frankfurt District; a *mikvah* was installed in 1948; number of Jewish
camp residents 5 December 1947: 2,409, 18 October 1948: 2,282;
closed: 30 June 1949.

KÖNIGSDORF

Munich District; kibbutz; illegal Haganah paramilitary training; administered by the Föhrenwald camp.

KREUTH

Munich District; former hotel and two additional buildings, one served
a kibbutz with 30 members from the *Funkkaserne* [signal corps bar-
racks] in Munich; number of Jewish camp residents 25 July 1946:
147.

LAMPERTHEIM

Frankfurt District; opened in December 1945 to relieve Zeilsheim;
schools: elementary school April 1947: 20 boys, 28 girls; *talmud to-*

rab; kindergarten April 1947: 13 students; synagogue; kosher kitchen; newspaper: *Frayhayt* (*Freedom*), one-time Passover edition; number of Jewish camp residents 1 June 1946: 1,201, 19 October 1946: 1,062, 3 October 1947: 1,102, 18 October 1948: 1,080; closed: 24 May 1949.

LANDSBERG

Munich District; former Wehrmacht barracks; at first a general DP camp, from October 1945 exclusively Jewish and up to that point the largest camp in Bavaria; together with a group of other survivors, Samuel Gringauz was the first camp committee chairman to lay the foundation for Jewish self-government; the camp became known beyond its perimeters and was unable to accommodate the stream of newcomers; further movement of refugees to the camp halted and rerouted to Föhrenwald, including 1,000 DPs already residing at Landsberg; Jacob Oleiski inaugurated the first ORT vocational training courses in October 1945, other camps soon followed his example; first camp directors: Lt. Gerold J. Foley, Robert Craddock (UNRRA), then Major Irving Heymont (19 September–15 November 1945), from November 1945 Adolph Glassgold (UNRRA); hospital at St. Ottilien administered by the camp; schools: *talmud torah* fall 1948: 32 students; Klausenburg [Cluj-Kolozsvar] yeshiva spring 1946: 80 students; total of 8 kibbutzim, including those at Greifenberg and Holzhausen; kosher kitchen; first *mikvah* in the U.S. Zone; Hatzomir choir; Sholem Aleichem dance-café; cinema; 1,300-seat theater; 25-member theater group; own radio station; newspapers: *Landsberger Lager-Cajtung* (*Landzberger Lager-Tsaytung* [*Landsberg Camp Newspaper*]) (editor in chief: Samuel Gringauz, managing editor until 2 January 1946 Rudolf Volsonok, then Baruch Hermanowicz), renamed *Jidisze Cajtung* (*Yidishe Tsaytung* [*Jewish Newspaper*]) on 25 October 1946, *Deror* (Hebrew, "freedom") of *Merkaz Dror* (Hebrew, "freedom center"), *Biuletin* (UNRRA Team 1065, Landsberg); number of Jewish camp residents 16 September 1945: 5,079, 31 May 1946: 4,810, 19 October 1946: 4,983, 3 October 1947: 4,478, 18 October 1948: 3,506, 25 July 1949: 2,150.

LANDSHUT

Regensburg District; tent camp; like Cham, served as a transit camp for the mass influx from Eastern Europe; many DPs left on their own for other camps; only a group of orphans sent to Rosenheim and Ulm (Dornstadt) were part of an official transfer; in September 1945 2,800 persons were transferred to Babenhausen; later, an International Children's Camp was established in the vicinity; number of Jewish camp residents (children's camp) 19 October 1946: 75, 30 July 1947: 27.

LECHFELD (NEAR AUGSBURG)

Munich District; opened in August 1947 at an airfield formerly belonging to the Messerschmidt company; at the end of September 1947 arrival of residents from the Ainring camp, which had been closed; *talmud torah* fall 1948: 127 students; number of Jewish camp residents 3 October 1947: 2,973, 17 January 1949: 1,887, 25 July 1949: 1,840; closed: 31 March 1951.

LEIBACH

Bamberg District; kibbutz; number of Jewish camp residents 30 July 1946: 50.

LEIPHEIM

Munich District; opened in December 1945; schools: *talmud torah* (director: S. Perlmutter) 10 June 1947: 30 students, fall 1948: 28 students; Chofec Chaim [Hafets Hayim] yeshiva (director: M. Litzman) 10 June 1947: 45 students; *mikvah;* newspaper: *A Heim [A Haym (A Home)]* (editor in chief: Abraham Szulewicz); number of Jewish camp residents 31 December 1945: 1,196, 31 May 1946: 3,150, 19 October 1946: 3,060, 3 October 1947: 2,838, 18 October 1948: 1,864; DP camp closed: June 1950; converted into a reception camp for refugees.

LIEPHOF (NEAR DACHAU)

Munich District; kibbutz; number of Jewish camp residents 31 May 1946: 40, 30 July 1947: 49.

LINDENFELS LOSAU-MAPILIM

Frankfurt District; children's camp; Hashomer Hatzair kibbutz; hotels and houses; school: elementary school April 1947: 336 students; number of Jewish camp residents 9 August 1946: 279, 19 October 1946: 412, 3 October 1947: 222, 18 October 1948: 17; closed: 15 November 1948.

LOSAU

Bamberg District; kibbutz; number of Jewish camp residents 31 May 1946: 67, 3 October 1947: 68; closed: October 1947.

MAINKOFEN-NATTERNBERG (PART OF THE DEGGENDORF CAMP COMPLEX)

Regensburg District; kibbutz; number of Jewish camp residents 19 October 1946: 204, 3 October 1947: 117; closed: October 1948 (unoccupied since June 1948).

MARIENDORF (BERLIN)

Berlin District; opened in July 1946 because of the mass influx from Eastern Europe; schools: elementary school 31 December 1947: 407 students; yeshiva December 1946: 21 students; kindergarten 31 December 1947: 110 students; synagogue; *mikvah;* kosher kitchen for feeding 900 persons; number of Jewish camp residents 4 September 1946: 4,185, 19 October 1946: 3,605, 30 July 1947: 2,671, 3 October 1947: 2,614; residents evacuated to Frankfurt at the same time as residents of Düppel.

MARITIME SCHOOL KIBBUTZ (NEAR DEGGENDORF)

Regensburg District; kibbutz; number of Jewish camp residents 30 July 1947: 46; closed: 24 June 1948.

MARKTREDWITZ SCHWAN HOTEL

Regensburg District; number of Jewish camp residents 3 October 1947: 240.

MIETRACHING (NEAR DEGGENDORF)

Regensburg District; opened in August 1946 as a transit camp for the mass migration from Eastern Europe; number of Jewish camp residents 19 October 1946: 214, 3 October 1947: 169, 18 October 1948: 89; closed: October 1948.

MITTENWALD (KARWENDEL HOTEL)

Munich District; recreation center for Föhrenwald DPs; number of Jewish camp residents 3 October 1947: 135.

MÖNCHEHOF (NEAR KASSEL)

Frankfurt District; schools: Tarbut school April 1947: 49 boys, 54 girls; *talmud torah* (director: J. Rosanski) 10 June 1947: 60 students; number of Jewish camp residents 3 October 1947: 1,557, 18 October 1948: 1,512; closed: 29 March 1949.

MÜNCHBERG

Bamberg District; kibbutz; number of Jewish camp residents 31 May 1946: 35, 30 July 1946: 120; closed: 29 March 1949.

MUNICH DEUTSCHES MUSEUM

Munich District; transit camp for all DPs; number of Jewish camp residents 31 December 1945: 600, 19 October 1946: 6, 8 February 1947: 8; closed February 1947.

MUNICH NEU-FREIMANN (KALTHERBERGE)

Munich District; workers' housing with garden plots (220 units) requisitioned on 4 December 1945; 214 units were occupied by Polish Jewish DPs; school: *talmud torah* fall 1948: 28 students; dental treatment facility; number of Jewish camp residents 31 May 1946: 1,684, 19 October 1946: 3,011, 3 October 1947: 3,055, 18 October 1948: 2,537; closed: 15 June 1949.

MUNICH FUNKKASERNE [SIGNAL CORPS BARRACKS]

Munich District; transit and emigration camp for both Jewish and non-Jewish DPs, de facto DP camp; extremely poor living conditions due to overcrowding; director at the end of 1946: Bruriah Szapira; in late 1946 the Jewish DPs living in the transit facility were transferred to the Traunstein base hospital and the transit camp was temporarily closed; in April 1948 the DPs slated for resettlement were transferred by IRO to the SS barracks; camp capacity: 650; number of Jewish camp residents 31 May 1946: 962 (transit camp), 378 (emigration camp), 3 October 1947: 15 (transit camp), 547 (emigration camp); transit camp closed in March 1948, transfer of residents to the Warner-Kaserne; number of Jewish camp residents (emigration camp) 18 October 1948: 10, 25 July 1949: 3; closed: 22 April 1950.

MUNICH WARNER-KASERNE [WARNER BARRACKS]

Munich District; number of Jewish camp residents 9 April 1948: 475, 18 October 1948: 11, 25 July 1949: 8, 19 July 1950: 385.

NOCHAM-PREBITZ

See Prebitz Nocham.

NEU-FREIMANN

See Munich Neu-Freimann.

NEU-ULM (LUDENDORFF-KASERNE) [LUDENDORFF BARRACK]

Stuttgart District; set up in the summer of 1946 to relieve the over-crowding at Bad Aibling and the Munich Funkkaserne; 1,100 DPs arrived in August and September 1946 from Bad Aibling and 750 from the Munich Funkkaserne; school: *talmud torah* (director: A. Walowitz) 10 June 1947: 96 students; number of Jewish camp residents 19 October 1946: 1,732, 3 October 1947: 1,662, 18 October 1948: 1,332, 25 July 1949: 1,120; closed: evacuated in March 1951 but not officially closed.

NILI-PLEICHERSHOF (NEAR FÜRTH)[12]

Bamberg District; kibbutz; also known as Streicher's Farm and Cadolzburg; 80 hectares [197.6 acres] of agricultural land, 8 hectares [19.7 acres] of pasturage, 10 hectares [24.7 acres] of woods under the management of a trained agronomist; number of Jewish camp residents 31 May 1946: 100, 19 October 1946: 135, 3 October 1947: 150, 18 October 1948: 28; after December 1949 no more Jewish residents; closed: 28 February 1951.

OBERSCHWARZBACH (NEAR CREUSSEN)

Bamberg District; kibbutz; number of Jewish camp residents 31 May 1946: 31, 30 July 1946: 65.

PLEICHERSHOF

See Nili-Pleichershof (Streicher's Farm).

POCKING AIRPORT I

Regensburg District; number of Jewish camp residents 19 October 1946: 1,312.

POCKING PINE CITY (ALSO WALDSTADT)

Bamberg District; largest DP camp in the U.S. Zone, second largest camp in Germany after Belsen; opened in January 1946; schools: *talmud torah* (director: Ch. Chaikin) 10 June 1947: 45 students; *talmud torah* (director: Z. Brav) 10 June 1947: 200 students; Lubavitch yeshiva (director: Rabbi Plotkin) 10 June 1947: 300 students; Klausenburg (Cluj-Kolozsvar) yeshiva; kosher kitchen (director: Rabbi Meisels) for feeding 200 persons; cultural office under Jisrael Braun (1947); drama circle; theater; Hagibor [Hebrew, "hero"] sports club; number of Jewish camp residents 31 May 1946: 4,500, 19 October 1946: 7,645, 3 October 1947: 6,249, 18 October 1948: 4,404; closed: 16 February 1949.

PREBITZ DATAI (25 KILOMETERS [15.5 MILES] FROM BAYREUTH)

Bamberg District; kibbutz; number of Jewish camp residents 31 May 1946: 30, 30 July 1947: 62; merged with Prebitz Nocham kibbutz in August 1947; closed: October 1947.

PREBITZ NOCHAM[13]

Bamberg District; kibbutz; number of Jewish camp residents 31 May 1946: 92, 30 July 1947: 71; closed: October 1947.

Prien am Chiemsee

Munich District; children's camp; number of Jewish camp residents 19 October 1946: 172, 3 October 1947: 225, 18 October 1948: 73; converted into a YMCA training center (no more Jews); closed: 30 June 1949.

Pürten I (near Mühldorf am Inn)

Munich District; Ichud [Hebrew, literally "number one"] children's camp Noar Zioni;[14] number of Jewish camp residents 30 July 1947: 278; the Jewish residents were transferred to Aschau at the end of August 1947; closed: 24 April 1950.

Pürten II (near Mühldorf am Inn)

Munich District; kibbutz; number of Jewish camp residents 23 August 1947: 168; the Jewish residents were transferred to Rosenheim at the end of August 1947.

Rehau

Bamberg District; transit camp; opened in July 1946; number of Jewish camp residents 30 July 1946: 250, 19 October 1946: 172; closed: September 1948.

Reithofen (near Erding)

Munich District; kibbutz; number of Jewish camp residents 31 July 1946: 150, 30 July 1947: 83.

Rochelle Eschenstruth (near Eschwege, part of the Hessisch Lichtenau complex)

Frankfurt District; opened in February 1947 to replace the "club-house" in Hessisch Lichtenau, which was shut down; schools: *talmud torah* (director: S. Lobkin) 10 June 1947: 115 students; *talmud torah* (director: Ch. Koleman) 10 June 1947: 30 students; *talmud torah* (director: Ch. Klug) 10 June 1947: 35 students; Bet Yosef yeshiva (director: Rabbi Tribuch) 10 June 1947: 32 students; number of Jewish camp residents 3 October 1947: 1,630, 18 October 1948: 1,318; closed: 1 March 1949.

ROSENHEIM

Munich District; children's camp; beginning in September 1946 orphans from the transit camps Cham and Landshut were received, then at least three weeks later transferred to other camps; number of Jewish camp residents 19 October 1946: 1,376, 3 October 1947: 856, 18 October 1948: 594.

ROTSCHWEIGEN (NEAR DACHAU)

Munich District; kibbutz; number of Jewish camp residents 31 May 1946: 149, 30 July 1947: 124.

SCHAUENSTEIN

Bamberg District; children's camp; number of Jewish camp residents 30 June 1947: 104, 30 July 1947: 104.

SCHESSLITZ (16 KILOMETERS [10 MILES] FROM BAMBERG)

Bamberg District; kibbutz comprising 5 small formerly Jewish-owned farms; 20 hectares [49.4 acres] of agricultural land, 4 hectares [9.9 acres] of pasturage, 2 hectares [4.9 acres] of woods, managed by a trained agronomist; number of Jewish camp residents 31 May 1946; 32, 19 October 1946: 161, 3 October 1947: 81; closed: April 1948.

SCHLIERSEE

Munich District; number of Jewish camp residents 19 October 1946: 477, 28 June 1947: 387; closed: August 1947; residents transferred to Rosenheim.

SCHLUPFING

Regensburg District; opened September 1946; number of Jewish camp residents 19 October 1946: 641, 3 October 1947: 443; closed: November 1947.

SCHWÄBISCH HALL

Stuttgart District; DPs accommodated in a confiscated housing development: Galil (Galilee), Negev, and Yehuda (Judea) DP camps (until February 1947 the three sections of the development were called Łódź—Ziegeleiweg [brickworks way], Lwów—formerly the Kocherfeld [cookers' field] development), and Warszawa—formerly the Kriegsopfer [war victims] development); school: *talmud torah* (director: Rabbi Spalter) 10 June 1947: 39 students; number of Jewish camp residents December 1946: 1,334 (total), 3 October 1947: 691 (Lwów), 761 (Łódź), 18 October 1948: 1,376 (total); closed: August 1947 (Warszawa), 15 February 1950 (Łódź, Lwów).

SCHWABMÜNCHEN

Munich District; number of Jewish camp residents 18 October 1948: 2,513.

SCHWANDORF

Regensburg District; transit camp for DPs from Poland; kosher kitchen (director: A. Jacobson) for feeding 150 persons.

SCHWARZENBORN

Frankfurt District; schools: elementary school April 1947: 85 students; *talmud torah* (director: A. Orlick) April 1947: 41 students, 10 June 1947: 90 students; kindergarten April 1947: 25 students; synagogue; sports club; cinema; drama club; number of Jewish camp residents 28 June 1947: 550, 3 October 1947: 538; closed: November 1947.

SCHWEBDA CASTLE

See Eschwege Schwebda Castle.

ST. OTTILIEN

Munich District: Jewish hospital from April 1945; schools: elementary school; *talmud torah* (director: Rabbi Weiclowski) 10 June 1947: 20 students; kindergarten; library; theater with facilities for showing films; number of Jewish camp residents 15 September 1945: 785, 31 May 1946: 646, 19 October 1946: 557, 3 October 1947: 322; closed: November 1948.

STREICHER'S FARM

See Nili-Pleichershof.

STRUTH

See Ansbach.

STUTTGART DEGERLOCH

Stuttgart District; the former Katz Sanitarium (Hohenwaldau); number of Jewish camp residents 19 October 1946: 182, 3 October 1947: 172, 18 October 1948: 73; closed: 23 November 1948.

STUTTGART WEST

Stuttgart District; Obere Reinsburgstraße; school: *talmud torah* (director: M. Peterfreund) 10 June 1947: 45 students; kosher kitchen (director: Schwingelstein) for feeding 400 persons; newspapers: *Oyf der Fray (On the Way to Freedom)* (editor in chief: Sam Waks); *Shtutgarter byuletin (Stuttgart Bulletin)*; number of Jewish camp residents 19 October 1946: 1,393, 3 October 1947: 1,409, 18 October 1948: 1,310; the remaining DPs were transferred to Heidenheim, to the Voith Jewish Home; closed: 13 June 1949.

Teichhof (part of the Hessisch Lichtenau camp complex)

Frankfurt District; wooden barracks camp; opened at the beginning of July 1945; number of Jewish camp residents 9 August 1946: 476, 19 October 1946: 827, 3 October 1947: 12; closed: October 1947.

Teublitz

Regensburg District; castle grounds comprising 300 hectares [741 acres], acquired by JDC; Nocham [a nonparty Halutzim movement] kibbutz; opened in the middle of June 1946; number of Jewish camp residents 3 June 1946: 35, 19 October 1946: 95, 30 July 1947: 82.

Traunstein

Munich District; children's camp; number of Jewish camp residents 19 October 1946: 208.

Traunstein Military Hospital

Munich District; school: *talmud torah* (director: Rabbi Ehrlich) 10 June 1947: 65 students; kosher kitchen (director: M. Finkewski) for 300 persons; number of Jewish camp residents 3 October 1947: 1,634, 18 October 1948: 1,096; March 1950: no more Jewish residents; DP camp closed in September 1950; converted to a home for the elderly.

Türkheim

Munich District; besides Buchberg, the only exclusively Jewish camp in June 1945; number of Jewish camp residents June 1945: 450, 19 October 1946: 522, 3 October 1947: 473; closed: May 1948.

Ulm Bleidorn

Stuttgart District; Agudat Israel children's camp; number of Jewish camp residents 19 October 1946: 171, 30 June 1947: 169; closed: September 1948.

ULM BOELCKE KASERNE [BARRACKS]

Stuttgart District; school: *talmud torah* (director: M. Czarniewski) 10 June 1947: 75 students; number of Jewish camp residents 19 October 1946: 1,432, 3 October 1947: 1,200, 22 November 1948: 1,020, 25 July 1949: 1,010; from September 1949 only occasional Jewish residents; closed: June 1950.

ULM DONAU BASTION

Stuttgart District; school: *talmud torah* (director: J. Zimmermann) 10 June 1947: 30 students; number of Jewish camp residents 19 October 1946: 528, 3 October 1947: 489, 22 November 1948: 457, 25 July 1949: 541; closed: 15 October 1949.

ULM DORNSTADT

Stuttgart District; former military airfield; children's camp without any political affiliation; in September 1946 orphans were taken from the transit camp to Cham and Landshut; number of Jewish camp residents 19 October 1946: 257, 30 June 1947: 338; as of September 1949 no more Jewish residents; evacuated on 31 March 1950 and converted into a home for the elderly.

ULM HINDENBURG KASERNE [BARRACK]

Stuttgart District; school: *talmud torah* (director: N. Kornblum) 10 June 1947: 35 students; number of Jewish camp residents 19 October 1946: 1,406, 3 October 1947: 951, 22 November 1948: 810, 25 July 1949: 1,187; as of September 1949 no more Jewish residents; closed: 31 January 1951.

ULM Q. M. BAKERY

Stuttgart District; number of Jewish camp residents 8 February 1947: 1,357, 28 June 1947: 1,511; merged with the Ulm Sedan Kaserne [barracks] in August 1947; closed: August 1947.

ULM SEDAN KASERNE [BARRACKS]

Stuttgart District; accommodations in the barracks and in private homes; schools: *talmud torah* (director: Rabbi Ausibel) 10 June 1947: 57 students; Or Hameir yeshiva (director: Rabbi Fuhrer) 10 June 1947: 62 students; number of Jewish camp residents 19 October 1946: 1,484, 3 October 1947: 2,264, 22 November 1948: 1,895, 25 July 1949: 2,102; as of September 1949 no more Jewish residents; closed: June 1950.

VELMEDEN (PART OF THE HESSISCH LICHTENAU CAMP COMPLEX)

Frankfurt District; number of Jewish camp residents 9 August 1946: 104, 19 October 1946: 279; August 1947 no more residents.

VIESECK (NEAR AMBERG)

Regensburg District; opened in the summer of 1946; school: *talmud torah* (director: L. Korn) 10 June 1947: 48 students; number of Jewish camp residents 19 October 1946: 1,434, 3 October 1947: 1,708; closed: April 1948.

VOYTA (NEAR PEGNITZ)

Bamberg District; Negev kibbutz; number of Jewish camp residents 31 May 1946: 62, 3 October 1947: 47; closed: November 1947.

WALDTSTADT

See Pocking Pine City (also Waldstadt).

WARTENBERG

Munich District; children's camp; number of Jewish camp residents 30 July 1947: 4.

WASSERALFINGEN (KREIS [COUNTY] AALEN)

Stuttgart District; Steigäcker-Alfing housing development; camp director Jacques F. Palustre; schools: *talmud torah* (director: M. Rachowski) 10 June 1947: 100 students, fall 1948: 51 students; yeshiva (director: Nachum Rakowski): 85 students, 6 teachers; number of Jewish camp residents 7 December 1946: 1,964, 3 October 1947: 1,853, 22 November 1948: 1,663, 25 July 1949: 1,503; closed: 15 March 1950.

WASSERBURG

Munich District; schools: *talmud torah* (director: Rabbi Goldman) 10 June 1947: 60 students; *talmud torah* (director: B. Schiessel) 10 June 1947: 35 students; kosher kitchen (director: Rabbi Goldman) for 600 persons; Va'ad Hahatzalah children's home (director: F. Dichter) 10 June 1947: 75 children.

WAWEL (NEAR HOFGEISMAR)

Frankfurt District; number of Jewish camp residents 22 March 1947: 635, 3 October 1947: 561, 18 October 1948: 422; closed: 15 February 1949.

WEILHEIM (BRÄUWASTL AND NEIDHARDT HOTELS)

Munich District; school: *talmud torah* (director: Rabbi Rutner) 10 June 1947: 18 students; kosher kitchen (director: H. Bonchanoch) for 150 persons; number of Jewish camp residents 19 October 1946: 483, 3 October 1947: 529, 18 October 1948: 420.

WEILHEIM LANDWIRTSCHAFTSSCHULE [AGRICULTURAL SCHOOL]

Munich District; kibbutz (No. 10 Fischgasse); number of Jewish camp residents 3 October 1947: 41; closed: June 1948.

WETZLAR

Frankfurt District; former barracks; DP camp opened in September 1946; first DPs were transferred from Cham and Berlin; schools: elementary school April 1946: 456 students; *talmud torah* (director: R. Mandel) 10 June 1947: 180 students; *talmud torah* (director: Ch. Beticki) 10 June 1947: 80 students; Bet Yosef yeshiva (director J. Raimon) 10 June 1947: 32 students; Klausenburg [Cluj-Kolozsvar] yeshiva 25 August 1948: 7 students; kindergarten April 1947: 95 students; special children's program; number of Jewish camp residents 9 August 1946: 51, 19 October 1946: 4,203, 3 October 1947: 4,329, 18 October 1948: 3,717; closed: 31 March 1949.

WINDISCHBERGERDORF

Regensburg District; school: Le Arje [Hebrew, literally "for Aryeh"] yeshiva (director: S. Millert) 10 June 1947: 28 students; number of Jewish camp residents 19 October 1946: 608, 22 March 1947: 423; December 1947 no more Jewish residents; closed: 15 June 1949.

WINDISCHENLAIBACH

Bamberg District; kibbutz; number of Jewish camp residents 3 October 1947: 14.

WINDSHEIM (NEAR NEUSTADT IN CENTRAL FRANCONIA)

Bamberg District; schools: *talmud torah* fall 1948: 70 students; Lubavitch Merkaz *torah* [Hebrew, "learning center"] yeshiva (director: Rabbi Roshanski); Klausenburg [Cluj-Kolozsvar] yeshiva 10 June 1947: 200 students; Va'ad Hahatzalah children's home (director: Schneiderman) 10 June 1947: 75 children; kosher kitchen (director: Schneiderman) for 150 persons; number of Jewish camp residents 21 July 1946: 2,800, 3 October 1947: 2,431, 18 October 1948: 1,822, 25 July 1949: 149; closed: 15 July 1949.

ZECKENDORF (NEAR SCHESSLITZ)

Bamberg District; kibbutz; number of Jewish camp residents 3 October 1947: 59; closed: September 1948.

ZEILSHEIM (NEAR HÖCHST)

Frankfurt District; former camp for Russian forced laborers; wooden barracks, later workers' housing requisitioned from the Hoechst chemical company was added (brick barracks); until December 1945 the only camp in the district, then Lampertheim was opened to take the pressure off Zeilsheim; streets and buildings in the camp were named after cities and kibbutzim in Palestine; schools: elementary school 15 April 1946: 125 students, April 1947: 80 students; high school 15 April 1946: 40 students, April 1947: 25 students; Bet Yosef Navardok yeshiva (director: Gershon Libman) 10 June 1947: 90 students; nurse training school; kindergarten 15 April 1946: 30 students; theater group; Hashmonai (Hasmonean) sports club; jazz orchestra; cinema; library; *mikvah;* synagogue; newspapers: *Undzer Mut (Our Courage)* (editor in chief: Sauko Gittler), *Unterwegs (On the Way)*; number of Jewish camp residents 16 September 1945: 300, 10 October 1945: 1,585, 1 June 1946: 3,353, 19 October 1946: 3,563, 3 October 1947: 3,163, 18 October 1948: 2,617; closed: 15 November 1948.

ZETTLITZ (NEAR MÜNCHBERG)

Bamberg District; kibbutz; number of Jewish camp residents 31 December 1945: 60, 30 July 1946: 110, 3 October 1947: 49; closed: September 1948.

ZETTLITZ (NEAR SCHÖNBRUNN IN THE STEIGERWALD)

Bamberg District; kibbutz; number of Jewish camp residents 30 July 1946: 65, 30 July 1947: 46; closed: August 1947.

ZIEGENHAIN

Frankfurt District; schools: elementary school April 1947: 250 students; *talmud torah* (director: P. Lipiner) April 1947: 120 students, 10

June 1947: 180 students; kindergarten April 1947: 40 students; TB sanitarium 30 June 1947: 30 patients; synagogue; *mikvah;* kosher kitchen; number of Jewish camp residents 19 October 1946: 2,161, 3 October 1947: 1,880; closed: November 1947.

British Zone

AHLEM

Kibbutz sponsored by the Jewish Agency for Palestine; number of Jewish camp residents 28 February 1947: 58.

AM STAU (NEAR LÜBECK)

District IV Schleswig-Holstein; transit camp for *Exodus* refugees.

BAD HARZBURG

District III Braunschweig [Brunswick]; began operating on 17 September 1946 (officially opened on 19 January 1947); rest home for Jewish DPs; also for children; number of Jewish camp residents 28 February 1947: 112, September 1947: 120.

BELSEN

See the corresponding chapter in this book, pp. 167–210.

Number of Jewish camp residents January 1946: 9,000, 15 June 1946: 9,199, 17 August 1946: 11,139, 22 February 1947: 10,867, 15 August 1947: 8,810, 30 November 1947: 8,311, 31 December 1947: 7,877, 30 April 1948: 8,124, 28 October 1948, 6,870 (150 in Glyn Hughes Hospital), March 1949: 4,679 (115 in Glyn Hughes Hospital).

BERGEN-BELSEN

See Belsen.

BLANKENESE (HAMBURG)

Number of Jewish camp residents 28 February 1947: 111, September 1947: 105.

BLECKEDE

District I Hanover; number of Jewish camp residents 15 June 1946: 254.

BOCHOLT

District II Westfalen [Westphalia]; former prisoners' camp consisting of wooden barracks; transit camp for Palestine; not exclusively Jewish, also included Balts and Yugoslavs; number of Jewish camp residents 15 June 1946: no Jews at this point, 15 August 1947: 454, 31 December 1947: 45.

DIEPHOLZ

District I Hanover; number of Jewish camp residents June 1945: 1,000, 15 June 1946: 13; closed soon afterward, DPs transferred to Belsen.

EMDEN

Camp for *Exodus* refugees; number of Jewish camp residents (together with Sengwarden) April 1948: 1,800.

FRACK (NEAR CELLE)

District I Hanover; number of Jewish camp residents 28 February 1947: 32.

GOSLAR

District I Hanover; number of Jewish camp residents 15 June 1946: 117, 22 February 1947: 108, 15 August 1947: 94, 30 November 1947: 16.

HANOVER BOTHFELD

District I Hanover; number of Jewish camp residents 15 June 1946: 886.

HANOVER LINDEN

District I Hanover; number of Jewish camp residents 22 February 1947: 320.

HANOVER STÖCKEN

District I Hanover; number of Jewish camp residents 15 June 1946: 163.

HOHNE

See Belsen.

KAUNITZ

District I Westfalen [Westphalia]; number of Jewish camp residents 15 June 1946: 358, 28 February 1947: 279, September 1947: 300, 28 October 1948: 122.

LÜNEBURG

JDC children's home; number of Jewish camp residents March 1946: 34, 28 February 1947: 37, September 1947: 30.

NEUSTADT

District IV Schleswig-Holstein; barracks camp in a former submarine school belonging to the German Navy; housed many of the first survivors arriving from Stutthof and Neuengamme; initial medical treatment by an Oeuvre de secours aux enfants team that arrived on 1 August 1945; hospital, camp outpatient facility; ORT school for the entire British Zone; number of Jewish camp residents 15 June 1946: 505, 22 February 1947: 361, 15 August 1947: 322, 31 December 1947: 397, 30 April 1948: 281, 28 October 1948: 249, March 1949: 194.

PÖPPENDORF (NEAR LÜBECK)

District IV Schleswig-Holstein; former POW camp; transit camp for *Exodus* refugees.

RHEDA

North Rhine-Westphalia District; number of Jewish camp residents 22 February 1947: 313, 15 August 1947: 247, 31 December 1947: 231, 30 April 1948: 190.

SENGWARDEN (NEAR WILHELMSHAVEN)

Camp for *Exodus* refugees.

VECHELADE

District I Hanover; number of Jewish camp residents 28 February 1947: 4.

VINNHORST (NEAR HANOVER)

Number of Jewish camp residents spring 1946: 200; 28 February 1947: 148.

French Zone

BIBERACH JORDANBAD

Southern District; Hashomer Hatzair kibbutz; number of Jewish camp residents 18 December 1945: 250, 19 November 1946: 219, 28 February 1947: 130; in March 1947 all residents left the kibbutz without the permission of the French Military Government.

BIBERACH JORDANBAD AMERIKAHAUS [AMERICA HOUSE]

Southern District; kibbutz; number of Jewish camp residents 18 December 1945: 150, 19 November 1946: 119, 31 May 1947: 90, 30 July 1947: 88.

EGG (10 KILOMETERS [6.2 MILES] FROM KONSTANZ)

Southern District; Dror kibbutz; barracks camp; residents arrived at the end of October from the U.S. Zone; number of Jewish camp residents 19 November 1946: 75, 28 February 1947: 80; as of 31 May 1947 no more residents, since they had left the camp in March 1947 without the permission of the French Military Government.

GAILINGEN DROR KIBBUTZ

Southern District; agricultural school; number of Jewish camp residents 19 November 1946: 102, 28 February 1947: 71; as of 31 May 1947 no more residents, since they had left the camp in March 1947 without the permission of the French Military Government.

GAILINGEN FRIEDRICHSHEIM

Southern District; community center; number of Jewish camp residents 19 November 1946: 98, 28 February 1947: 88, 31 May 1947: 104, 30 July 1947: 100.

GAILINGEN HAGANAH KIBBUTZ

Southern District; number of Jewish camp residents 19 November 1946: 48; shortly thereafter the camp was empty.

GAILINGEN MOLEDETH KIBBUTZ

Southern District; number of Jewish camp residents 19 November 1946: 36, 28 February 1947: 36, 31 May 1947: 20, 30 July 1947: 20.

KIßLEGG

Southern District; small camp; opened in September 1948 to evacuate Jews from the French sector of Berlin (see Wittenau).

LINDAU

Southern District; small camp; opened in September 1948 to evacuate Jews from the French sector of Berlin.

NIEDERLAHNSTEIN

Northern District; kibbutz; number of Jewish camp residents 28 February 1947: 35, 31 May 1947: 8; as of 30 July 1947 no more residents.

WITTENAU (BERLIN)

Opened on 1 December 1945; block of apartment houses; school (director: Leo Warshawsky) March 1946: 24 students; synagogue; number of Jewish camp residents December 1946: 175, 30 July 1947: 220, December 1947: 182, April 1948: 179; closed: 12 September 1948; the last 220 DPs were evacuated to other camps in the French Zone, for example Kißlegg.

❀

Notes

The following abbreviations are used in the notes:

IfZ Instiut für Zeitgeschichte (Institute for Contemporary History [Munich])

OMGUS Office of Military Government of the United States for Germany

YIVO Yidisher Visnshaftlekher Institut (Yiddish Scientific Institute)

Translator's Note

1. Steven A. Jacobson, *A Guide to the More Common Hebraic Words in Yiddish,* 3d ed. (Fairbanks, Alaska, 1994), p. 2.

Introduction

1. IfZ Fi 01.76: J. J. Schwartz, DP-Report, 19 August 1945, p. 1.
2. Leonard Dinnerstein, *America and the Survivors of the Holocaust* (New York, 1982), p. 1.
3. American Jewish Committee—Blaustein Library, *The Problem of the Displaced Persons: Report of the Survey Committee on Displaced Persons of the American Council of Voluntary Agencies for Foreign Service Inc.,* June 1946.
4. YIVO LWSP fol. 135: Protokoll Nr. 13 der Sitzung des Rates beim Zentral-Komitee der befreiten Juden in Bayern (Minutes No. 13 of the Meeting of the Council of the Central Committee of Liberated Jews in Bavaria) (Deutsches Museum [Munich], 14 October 1945).

5. Peter Jacob Kock, "Das Lager Föhrenwald: 'Eldorado' oder 'Wartesaal der Unglücklichen'?" *Maximilianeum* 4 (1993).

6. "Assembly center" was the name originally applied to one of the basic installations immediately required for the control, maintenance, processing, and repatriation of displaced persons. —Trans.

LIBERATION

1. Leslie H. Hardman as told to Cecily Goodman, *The Survivors: The Story of the Belsen Remnant* (London, 1958), pp. 2–3.

2. See Eberhard Kolb, *Bergen-Belsen, 1943–1945* (Göttingen, 1985), passim; see also *Unruhige Zeiten: Erlebnisberichte aus dem Landkreis Celle, 1945–1949*, ed. Rainer Schulze (München, 1990), pp. 19–21.

3. See Kolb, *Bergen-Belsen*, passim.

4. Yehuda Bauer, *Out of the Ashes: The Impact of American Jews on Post-Holocaust European Jewry* (Oxford, 1989), p. 36.

5. Wolfgang Jacobmeyer "Jüdische Überlebende als 'Displaced Persons': Untersuchungen zur Besatzungspolitik in den deutschen Westzonen und zur Zuwanderung osteuropäischer Juden, 1945–1947," *Geschichte und Gesellschaft* 9 (1983): 452; IfZ Fi 01.76: J. J. Schwartz, DP-Report, 19 August 1945; *Displaced Persons in Europe: Report of the Committee on the Judiciary Pursuant to Senate Resolution 137, March 1948*, p. 16.

6. Percy Knauth, *Germany in Defeat* (New York, 1946), pp. 38–39; cited by Robert H. Abzug, *Inside the Vicious Heart: Americans and the Liberation of Nazi Concentration Camps* (New York and Oxford, 1985), p. 56.

7. Interview with George E. King, witness to the Holocaust; cited by Abzug, *Inside the Vicious Heart*, pp. 111–12.

8. YIVO LWSP fol. 103: Ernest Landau, So wurden wir frei: zum Gedenken an den 29. April 1945 (This is how we were liberated: in memory of 29 April 1945), pp. 6–7.

9. Anton Gill, *The Journey Back from Hell: Conversations with Concentration Camp Survivors* (London, 1988), p. 199.

CONDITIONS IN THE SUMMER OF 1945

1. IfZ Fi 01.76: J. J. Schwartz, DP-Report, 19 August 1945, p. 1.
2. Leonard Dinnerstein, *America and the Survivors of the Holocaust* (New York, 1982), p. 9.
3. Koppel S. Pinson, "Jewish Life in Liberated Germany: A Study of the Jewish DP's," *Jewish Social Studies* 9, no. 2 (April 1947): 101–2.
4. "Homecoming in Israel," in *The Root and the Bough: The Epic of an Enduring People,* ed. Leo W. Schwarz (New York, 1949), p. 310.
5. Pinson, "Jewish Life in Liberated Germany," p. 105.
6. Jacob Biber, *Risen from the Ashes: A Story of the Jewish Displaced Persons in the Aftermath of World War II* (San Bernardino, Calif., 1990), pp. 11–13.
7. Yehuda Bauer, *Flight and Rescue: Brichah* (New York, 1970), p. 50.
8. Dinnerstein, *America and the Survivors of the Holocaust,* pp. 28–30.
9. Ibid., p. 13; YIVO DPG fol. 1501: Memorandum from Displaced Persons Division, Office of Military Government (U.S. Zone) to Joint Anglo-American Committee of Inquiry.
10. Dinnerstein, *America and the Survivors of the Holocaust,* p. 13.
11. *Belsen* (Tel Aviv, 1957), pp. 25–26.
12. See Yehuda Bauer, "The Death Marches: January–May 1945," in *Yahadut Zémanenu,* vol. 1 (Jerusalem: Magnes Press, Hebrew University, 1983), pp. 199–221. Other title listed on title page is *Contemporary Jewry: A Research Annual I.* Article in Hebrew.
13. Bauer, *Flight and Rescue,* pp. 57–59.
14. Yehuda Bauer, "The Initial Organization of the Holocaust Survivors in Bavaria," *Yad Vashem Studies* 8 (1970): 146–48.
15. *Diary of Haim Dan: From the Egyptian Desert to Munich* (Tel Aviv, 1958), cited in *She'erit Hapletah, 1944–1948: Rehabilitation and Political Struggle,* ed. Israel Gutman and Avital Saf (Jerusalem, 1990), p. 70.
16. Irving Heymont, *Among the Survivors of the Holocaust, 1945: The Landsberg DP Camp Letters of Major Irving Heymont, United States Army* (Cincinnati, 1982), p. 6.
17. YIVO LWSP fol. 69: Rabbi Bernstein's Report, p. 11.

18. Dinnerstein, *America and the Survivors of the Holocaust,* p. 16.

19. YIVO LWSP fol. 194: Henry Cohen, Director, UNRRA Team 106, to Sam Zisman, Director, UNRRA District No. 5, 14 May 1946.

20. Cited by Dinnerstein, *America and the Survivors of the Holocaust,* p. 14.

21. YIVO LWSP fol. 69: Rabbi Bernstein's Report, p. 11.

22. Anton Gill, *The Journey Back from Hell: Conversations with Concentration Camp Survivors* (London, 1989), p. 41.

23. Cited by Robert H. Abzug, *Inside the Vicious Heart: Americans and the Liberation of Nazi Concentration Camps* (New York, 1985), p. 42.

24. Abzug, *Inside the Vicious Heart,* p. 152.

25. See, for example, Simon Schochet, *Feldafing* (Vancouver, 1983), pp. 81–83, and Biber, *Risen from the Ashes,* p. 10.

26. Gill, *The Journey Back from Hell,* p. 41; Abzug, *Inside the Vicious Heart,* p. 152.

27. Julius Posner, *In Deutschland 1945–1946* (Jerusalem, 1947), p. 13.

28. Cited by Leonard Dinnerstein, "German Attitudes toward the Jewish Displaced Persons (1945–50)," in *Germany and America: Essays on Problems of International Relations and Immigration,* ed. Hans L. Trefousse (New York, 1980), p. 243.

29. Wolfgang Benz, "Postwar Society and National Socialism: Remembrance, Amnesia, Rejection," *Tel Aviver Jahrbuch für Deutsche Geschichte* 19 (1990): 1.

30. Abzug, *Inside the Vicious Heart,* pp. 154–55.

31. Cited by Abraham S. Hyman, *The Undefeated* (Jerusalem and Hewlett, N.Y., 1993), p. 61.

32. Ibid., p. 62.

33. Ibid., p. 61.

34. Dinnerstein, *America and the Survivors of the Holocaust,* p. 16.

35. Bauer, "The Initial Organization of the Holocaust Survivors in Bavaria," p. 130.

36. YIVO DPG fol. 1041: Miriam Warburg, "Personal Experiences of Camp Inmates at DP Center of Foehrenwald, Bavaria," February 1946, p. 4.

37. Dinnerstein, *America and the Survivors of the Holocaust,* p. 12.

38. YIVO DPG fol. 1041: Warburg, "Personal Experiences," p. 4.

39. Biber, *Risen from the Ashes,* p. 80.

40. IfZ Fi 01.97: L. K. Truscott, Lieutenant General, U.S. Army Commanding, to General Joseph T. McNarney, Commanding General, USFET, U.S. Army, 27 December 1945.

41. Dinnerstein, *America and the Survivors,* pp. 10–11; OMGUS AG 1945–46-25/1: Agreements as to the Relationship of UNRRA to the Commanding General, USFET in the U.S. Zone of Germany, 19 February 1946.

42. Hyman, *The Undefeated,* p. 31.

43. Malcolm J. Proudfoot, *European Refugees, 1939–1952: A Study in Forced Population Movement* (Evanston, Ill., 1956; London, 1957), pp. 500–1; see also Bauer, *Flight and Rescue,* pp. 194–96.

44. OMGUS 3/163–1/9: UNRRA Field Organization Chart. D.P. Operations: Germany, Appendix D.

THE HARRISON REPORT AND ITS REPERCUSSIONS

1. On the Harrison Report, see Leonard Dinnerstein, *America and the Survivors of the Holocaust* (New York, 1982), pp. 34–36, and Yehuda Bauer, *Flight and Rescue: Brichah* (New York, 1970), pp. 76–78.

2. The Harrison Report is reprinted in Dinnerstein, *America and the Survivors of the Holocaust,* pp. 291–93.

3. Ibid.

4. YIVO DPG fol. 324: By Command of General Eisenhower: H. H. Newman, Acting Adjutant General. Subject: Special Camps for Stateless and Non-Repatriables, 22 August 1945.

5. Dinnerstein, *America and the Survivors of the Holocaust,* pp. 44–45.

6. For details, see Yehuda Bauer, *Out of the Ashes: The Impact of American Jews on Post-Holocaust European Jewry* (Oxford, 1989), pp. 40–42, and Dinnerstein, *America and the Survivors of the Holocaust,* p. 44.

7. See Abraham S. Hyman, *The Undefeated* (Jerusalem and Hewlett, N.Y., 1993), pp. 307–9; Dinnerstein, *America and the Survivors of the Holocaust,* pp. 45–46; Bauer, *Out of the Ashes,* p. 60.

8. Bauer, *Out of the Ashes,* pp. 40 and 60.

9. On Bernstein, see Thomas Philip Liebschutz, "Rabbi Philip S. Bernstein and the Jewish Displaced Persons" (diss., Cincinnati, 1965).

10. Hyman, *The Undefeated*, p. 307.

11. Leo W. Schwarz, *The Redeemers: A Saga of the Years 1945–1952* (New York, 1953), p. 44.

12. Hyman, *The Undefeated*, p. 308.

13. Ibid., p. 310; *Belsen* (Tel Aviv, 1957), p. 30.

14. Ursula Büttner, *Not nach der Befreiung. Die Situation der deutschen Juden in der britishcen Besatzungszone 1945 bis 1948* (Hamburg, 1986), pp. 20–21.

15. Hyman, *The Undefeated*, p. 64.

16. Samuel Gringauz, "Our New German Policy and the DP's: Why Immediate Resettlement Is Imperative," *Commentary* 5 (1948): 509.

17. Ibid.

18. Cited by Dinnerstein, *America and the Survivors of the Holocaust*, pp. 295–97.

19. Bauer, *Out of the Ashes*, pp. 48–49.

20. For details, see Thomas Albrich, *Exodus durch Österreich. Die jüdischen Flüchtlinge, 1945–1948* (Innsbruck, 1987), pp. 31–33.

21. Memorandum addressed to the Undersecretary of State for War and signed by Maj. Gen. R. H. Dewing, cited by Bauer, *Flight and Rescue*, p. 71. See also Frank Stern, *Im Anfang war Auschwitz: Antisemitismus und Philosemitismus im deutschen Nachkrieg* (Gerlingen, 1991), pp. 96–97; Büttner, *Not nach der Befreiung*, pp. 15–17.

22. Albrich, *Exodus durch Österreich*, pp. 80–81.

23. OMGUS POLAD 736/25: Final Report by General Eisenhower on Jewish Displaced Persons in Germany, 5 November 1945.

24. Malcolm J. Proudfoot, *European Refugees, 1939–1952: A Study in Forced Population Movement* (Evanston, Ill., 1956; London, 1957), pp. 252–53; YIVO LWSP fol. 497: Report of the Activities of the American Joint Distribution Committee in the British Zone, 8 December 1945–20 September 1946, p. 6.

THE MASS EXODUS OF JEWS FROM EASTERN EUROPE

1. YIVO DPG fol. 1501: AJDC, Summary Report on Infiltree Movement of Jews to U.S. Zone of Occupation in Germany, June 1946–15 November 1946.

2. IfZ Fi 01.83: Report on Jewish Displaced Persons in the Area Celle-Belsen, January 1946; IfZ Fi 01.90: Report on an Investigation Held at Hohne, 11 September 1946; YIVO LWSP fol. 128: Letter from Dr. J. Schwartz to Moses A. Leavitt (Report No. 379) of 9 November 1946; YIVO DPG fol. 36: AJDC Report (No. 352) on Supply and Transportation, September 1945–July 1946, p. 5; YIVO DPG fol. 1530: AJDC Jewish Population Effective 30 November 1946; Zvi Asaria, *Wir sind Zeugen* (Hanover, 1975), p. 166.

3. YIVO DPG fol. 1501: AJDC, Summary Report on Infiltree Movement.

4. OMGUS POLAD 756/7: Analysis of Jewish Situation in Poland, 18 October 1946.

5. Lipman Sznajder, *Wladek war ein falscher Name. Die wahre Geschichte eines dreizehnjährigen Jungen* (München, 1991), pp. 5–7.

6. OMGUS 3/176–2/17: Headquarters OSS Austria, Situation of Jews in Poland, 20 September 1945.

7. YIVO LWSP fol. 22: AJDC Frankfurt. Report on a Kibbutz, Gordonia, en route to U.S. Zone, Related by a Survivor, Mr. Galer, no date.

8. Yehuda Bauer, *Flight and Rescue: Brichah* (New York, 1970), p. 115.

9. Ibid., pp. 124–25.

10. OMGUS 3/176–2/17: Headquarters Austria, Situation of Jews in Poland.

11. *Encyclopaedia Judaica* (Jerusalem, 1972), vol. 10, p. 990.

12. Abraham S. Hyman, *The Undefeated* (Jerusalem and Hewlett, N.Y., 1993), pp. 181–82; Bauer, *Flight and Rescue,* pp. 206–8; Thomas Albrich, *Exodus durch Österreich. Die jüdischen Flüchtlinge, 1945–1948* (Innsbruck, 1987), pp. 100–1.

13. On the history of Brichah, see Bauer, *Flight and Rescue.* The remarks below are based on Bauer's study.

14. Ibid., pp. 119 and 212.

15. Yehuda Bauer, *Out of the Ashes: The Impact of American Jews on Post-Holocaust European Jewry* (Oxford, 1989), pp. 87–88.
16. Bauer, *Flight and Rescue*, p. 81.
17. IfZ Fi 01.82: History—UNRRA—U.S. Zone. Report No. 31—Jewish Infiltrees, July 1947, p. 3.
18. IfZ Fi 01.95: G-5 Division, USFET, 1 October 1946.
19. Bauer, *Flight and Rescue*, p. 270.
20. YIVO DPG fol. 1501: AJDC, Summary Report on Infiltree Movement. The report contains a list of all the newly built camps.
21. Albrich, *Exodus durch Österreich*, pp. 121–22.
22. YIVO DPG fol. 1501: David Wodlinger, Report on the Activities of the AJDC in the British Zone, Germany, 29 October 1946, pp. 1 and 10.
23. IfZ Fi 01.90: Report on an Investigation Held at Hohne, 11 September 1946.
24. IfZ Fi 01.86: UNRRA Monthly Narrative Report, June 1946, p. 14, and UNRRA Monthly Narrative Report, November 1946, p. 7.
25. YIVO LWSP fol. 497: Wodlinger, Report, 8 December 1945–20 September 1946, pp. 1–2.
26. YIVO DPG fol. 1532: AJDC, Jewish Population in the U.S. Zone of Germany in 1946, p. 3.
27. Ibid., p. 5.
28. Koppel S. Pinson, "Jewish Life in Liberated Germany: A Study of the Jewish DP's," *Jewish Social Studies* 9, no. 2 (April 1947): 103–5.
29. YIVO DPG fol. 1532: AJDC, Jewish Population in the U.S. Zone of Germany in 1946, p. 7.

THE JOINT

1. Judith Tydor Baumel, "Kibbutz Buchenwald," in *She'erit Hapletah, 1944–1948: Rehabilitation and Political Struggle*, ed. Israel Gutman and Avital Saf (Jerusalem, 1990), pp. 437–49; YIVO LWSP fol. 64: Protokoll der Geschäftssitzung der Konferenz der befreiten jüdischen politischen Häftlinge in Deutschland (Min-

utes of the Business Meeting of the Conference of Liberated Jewish Political Prisoners in Germany), 25 July 1945, pp. 3–4; see also Alex Grobman, *Rekindling the Flame: American Jewish Chaplains and the Survivors of European Jewry, 1944–1948* (Detroit, 1993), pp. 48–53.

2. YIVO LWSP fol. 52: H. Viteles, Report on Visit to Germany, 6 January–8 April 1946, p. 32.

3. Yehuda Bauer, "The Initial Organization of the Holocaust Survivors in Bavaria," *Yad Vashem Studies* 8 (1970): 137.

4. YIVO LWSP fol. 129: Appell an den Jüdischen Weltkongreß von Dr. Zalman Grinberg vom 31. Mai 1945 (Appeal to the World Jewish Congress by Dr. Zalman Grinberg, 31 May 1945).

5. Malcolm J. Proudfoot, *European Refugees, 1939–1952: A Study in Forced Population Movement* (Evanston, Ill., 1956; London, 1957), pp. 230–32.

6. Ibid., pp. 234–35.

7. Juliane Wetzel, *Jüdisches Leben in München, 1945–1951. Durchgangsstation oder Wiederaufbau* (München, 1987), pp. 70–76.

8. Yehuda Bauer, *Out of the Ashes: The Impact of American Jews on Post-Holocaust European Jewry* (Oxford, 1989), pp. xv–xvi and 27.

9. YIVO LWSP fol. 2: Address of Dr. Joseph J. Schwartz, Country Director's Conference, Covering Meeting of 3 February 1947; YIVO LWSP fol. 2: *Country Director's Conference Bulletin* no. 5, "Remarks of Dr. Joseph J. Schwartz," 4 February 1947; Wetzel, *Jüdisches Leben in München*, p. 76.

10. Bauer, *Out of the Ashes*, p. xviii.

11. YIVO LWSP fol. 7: Description and Definition of American Joint Distribution Committee Operations, U.S. Zone of Germany, 10 June 1947, p. 2.

12. Wetzel, *Jüdisches Leben in München*, pp. 76–77.

13. YIVO LWSP fol. 3: Country Director's Conference AJDC, 5–10 April 1948, p. 48.

14. YIVO LWSP fol. 54: AJDC Report on the Situation of the Jews in the French Zone, 28 April 1947.

15. Bauer, *Out of the Ashes*, p. 87.

16. OMGUS 47/155/1–5: Summary Analysis of AJDC Program in the U.S. Zone of Occupied Germany, Leo W. Schwarz, 13 January 1947, pp. 2–3.

17. Wetzel, *Jüdisches Leben in München,* pp. 126–27.

18. YIVO LWSP fol. 3: Country Director's Conference AJDC, 5–10 April 1948, p. 48.

19. YIVO LWSP fol. 6: AJDC Organizational Structure, 1 November 1947; YIVO LWSP fol. 8: Organizational Structure of the AJDC U.S. Zone Germany, Samuel L. Haber, 15 September 1947, pp. 3–9.

20. YIVO LWSP fol. 2: American Joint Distribution Committee, *Emigration Bulletin* no. 4, 1 July 1946.

21. Ibid.

22. Yehuda Bauer, "The Brichah," in *She'erit Hapletah, 1944–1948,* p. 55.

23. YIVO LWSP fol. 2: Address of Dr. Joseph J. Schwartz, Country Director's Conference, 3 February 1947, p. 3; YIVO LWSP fol. 3: Country Director's Conference AJDC, 5–10 April 1948, p. 123. AJDC Archives Germany localities Munich 1945ff. Letter from Jacob M. Joslow to Rabbi Max Nussbaum, 2 March 1948; ibid. Germany General Report and Statistics, 15 February 1946.

24. YIVO LWSP fol. 3: Country Director's Conference AJDC, 5–10 April 1948, p. 32.

25. Leonard Dinnerstein, *America and the Survivors of the Holocaust* (New York, 1982), pp. 166–67.

26. IfZ Fi 01.24: U.S. Displaced Persons Act of 1948, 1 July 1948; Bauer, *Out of the Ashes,* pp. 284–85.

27. Cited by Jacqueline D. Giere, "'Wir sind unterwegs, aber nicht in der Wüste.' Erziehung und Kultur in den jüdischen Displaced Persons-Lagern der amerikanischen Zone im Nachkriegsdeutschland, 1945–1948" (diss., Frankfurt a.M., 1993), p. 94.

28. YIVO LWSP fol. 22: AJDC Report on Activities, M. J. Joslow, Education Consultant, July 1946.

29. Koppel S. Pinson, "Jewish Life in Liberated Germany: A Study of the Jewish DP's," *Jewish Social Studies* 9, no. 2 (April 1947): 121.

30. YIVO LWSP fol. 3: Country Director's Conference AJDC, 5–10 April 1948, p. 35.

31. *Süddeutsche Zeitung,* 12 November 1946.

32. Wetzel, *Jüdisches Leben in München,* pp. 315–36.

33. YIVO LWSP fol. 2: Address of Dr. Joseph J. Schwartz, Country Director's Conference, 3 February 1947.

34. YIVO LWSP fol. 2: *Country Director's Conference Bulletin* no. 5.

35. Wetzel, *Jüdisches Leben in München*, pp. 106–9.

36. YIVO LWSP fol. 3: Country Director's Conference AJDC, 5–10 April 1948, p. 34.

37. YIVO LWSP fol. 121: Letter from Charles S. Passman, Zone Director AJDC, to Dr. Blumowicz, Central Committee, 16 November 1947; see also YIVO LWSP fol. 149: Correspondence between Representatives of the German Jews and both the AJDC and UNRRA, March 1947.

38. Wetzel, *Jüdisches Leben in München*, pp. 13–15.

THE DPs LEARN TO HELP THEMSELVES

1. YIVO LWSP fol. 53: Summary of Recent Reports from JDC Representatives in Germany, 18 December 1945, p. 6; YIVO LWSP fol. 54: AJDC Report on the Situation of the Jews in the French Zone, 28 April 1947.

2. *Jidisze Cajtung* (*Yidishe Tsaytung* [*Jewish Newspaper*]), 19 August 1947.

3. Leo W. Schwarz, *The Redeemers: A Saga of the Years 1945–1952* (New York, 1953), p. 8.

4. Juliane Wetzel, "'Mir szeinen doh': München und Umgebung als Zuflucht von Überlebenden des Holocaust 1945–1948," in *Von Stalingrad zur Währungsreform: zur Sozialgeschichte des Umbruchs in Deutschland*, ed. Martin Broszat, Klaus-Dietmar Henke, and Hans Woller (München, 1988), pp. 338–39 and 344.

5. YIVO LWSP fol. 135: Protokoll der Konferenz der Juden in Bayern, Feldafing, 1 July 1945 (Minutes of the Conference of Jews in Bavaria, Feldafing, 1 July 1945).

6. Juliane Wetzel, *Jüdisches Leben in München, 1945–1951. Durchgangsstation oder Wiederaufbau* (München, 1987), pp. 149–50.

7. YIVO LWSP fol. 64: Protokoll der Konferenz der befreiten jüdischen politischen Häftlinge in Deutschland, 25 July 1945 (Minutes of the Conference of Liberated Jewish Political Prisoners in Germany).

8. YIVO LWSP fol. 135: Protokoll Nr. 5 der Sitzung des zeitweiligen Zentral-Komitees der befreiten Juden in Deutschland, 3 August 1945 (Minutes No. 5 of the Meeting of the Temporary Central Committee of Liberated Jews in Germany).

9. YIVO LWSP fol. 135: Protokoll Nr. 12 der Sitzung des ZK der befreiten Juden in Bayern, Feldafing, 7 October 1945, pp. 5–6 (Minutes No. 12 of the Meeting of the Central Committee of Liberated Jews in Bavaria, Feldafing).

10. YIVO LWSP fol. 136: Protokoll Nr. 31 der befreiten Juden in der amerikanischen Besatzungszone, München, 29 January 1946 (Minutes No. 31 of the Liberated Jews in the American Occupation Zone).

11. Schwarz, *The Redeemers,* pp. 32–33, and interviews with Samuel L. Haber on 27 June 1984 and 17 July 1984.

12. Chronologically, the committees at Belsen were as follows: First Temporary Committee, April–September 1945; First Central Committee, September 1945–July 1947; Belsen Committee, March 1947; Second Central Committee, July 1947. The Belsen members of the Central Committee served simultaneously as the Belsen Committee. The chairmanship of the Central Committee and the Belsen Committee were held by the same person.—Trans.

13. YIVO LWSP fol. 52: H. Viteles, Report on Visit to Germany, 6 January–8 April 1946, pp. 39–40.

14. *Belsen* (Tel Aviv, 1957), p. 196.

15. Wetzel, *Jüdisches Leben in München,* p. 36.

16. YIVO LWSP fol. 64: Satzung des Verbandes der befreiten Juden in der amerikanischen Besatzungszone Deutschlands (erster Satzungsentwurf) (Charter of the Federation of Liberated Jews in the American Occupation Zone in Germany [first draft]).

17. Wetzel, *Jüdisches Leben in München,* pp. 160–62.

18. YIVO LWSP fol. 8: Organizational Structure of the AJDC U.S. Zone in Germany, Samuel L. Haber, 15 September 1947.

19. Wetzel, *Jüdisches Leben in München,* p. 163.

20. YIVO LWSP fol. 52: Viteles, Report on Visit to Germany, p. 38.

21. *Belsen,* p. 196.

22. See Wetzel, *Jüdisches Leben in München,* pp. 177–97.

23. YIVO LWSP fol. 133: B. Sapir, Memorandum No. 339, 25 May 1948, Third Congress of Liberated Jews in the U.S. Zone of Germany, 30 March–2 April 1948, pp. 2–4.

24. Leo W. Schwarz, *The Root and the Bough: The Epic of an Enduring People* (New York, 1949).

25. Wetzel, *Jüdisches Leben in München,* pp. 181–83.

26. YIVO LWSP fol. 104: Noe Heitlinger, Di Liquidatcje fun C. K. (The Liquidation of the ZK).

27. Gerd Korman, "Survivors' Talmud and the U.S. Army," *American Jewish History* 73 (1984): 252–54. As early as 1946, the U.S. Third Army published, with the help of Chaplain Abraham J. Klausner in Munich, *A Survivor's Haggadah,* a self-styled supplement to the Passover Haggadah by Yosef Dov Sheinson. It is now republished in facsimile with translation and commentary by Saul Touster and the American Jewish Historical Society (Waltham, Mass., 1999).

FÖHRENWALD

1. IfZ Fi 01.76: Henry Cohen to World Jewish Congress, 7 November 1946.

2. YIVO DPG fol. 584: Belegung des Lagers Föhrenwald am 18. Juli 1944 (Population of Camp Föhrenwald).

3. YIVO DPG fol. 585: Tagesbericht, Föhrenwald, 13 June 1945 (Daily Report, Föhrenwald); YIVO LWSP fol. 164:Vocational, Cultural and Educational Program. Camps Landsberg, Fahrenwald [*sic*] and Feldafing, October 1945.

4. Jacob Biber, *Risen from the Ashes: A Story of the Jewish Displaced Persons in the Aftermath of World War II* (San Bernardino, Calif., 1990), p. 53; YIVO LWSP fol. 164: Vocational, Cultural and Educational Program.

5. STA München Polizeipräsidium Oberbayern 290. Landpolizei Oberbayern, Bez.-Inspektion Wolfratshausen an Präsidium der Landpolizei von Bayern, 24 September 1948 (Staatsarchiv, Munich. Police Headquarters Upper Bavaria 290. State Police Upper Bavaria, District Inspector Wolfratshausen to Bavarian State Police).

6. YIVO LWSP fol. 135: Protokoll Nr. 15 der Sitzung des Zentralkomitees der befreiten Juden in Bayern vom 4. November 1945, p. 4 (Minutes No. 15 of the Meeting of the Central Committee of Liberated Jews in Bavaria of 4 November 1945).

7. Biber, *Risen from the Ashes*, p. 21.

8. Ibid., p. 53.

9. YIVO LWSP fol. 57: AJDC, Jewish Population in the U.S. Zone of Occupation in Germany, 3rd Army Area, 27 January 1946.

10. YIVO DPG fol. 585: Wahl, Lager Föhrenwald, den 27.11.1945 (Election, Camp Föhrenwald, 27 November 1945); *Bamidbar. Wochncajtung fun di befrajte Jidn*, 12 December 1945 (*Bamidbar: Vokhentsaytung fun die bafraytn Yidn* [*Bamidbar: Weekly Newspaper for the Liberated Jews*]).

11. *Bamidbar. Wochncajtung fun di bafrajte Jidn*, 19 December 1945.

12. YIVO LWSP fol. 194: Letter from Henry Cohen, Director, UNRRA Team 106 Wolfratshausen, to Sam Zisman, Director, UNRRA District No. 5, 14 May 1946.

13. YIVO DPG fol. 584: Bekanntmachung, Protokoll Nr. 1, 5 February 1947 (Announcement, Minutes No. 1).

14. IfZ Fi 01.61: René Ristelhueber, The International Refugee Organization, April 1951, p. 193.

15. YIVO DPG fol. 585: Statistik, 3 October 1945 (Statistics).

16. YIVO LWSP fol. 135: Protokoll Nr. 13 der Sitzung des Rates, p. 14 (Minutes No. 13 of the Council Meeting).

17. YIVO DPG fol. 584: Josef Richter, Registrationsbüro, an Gesundheitsamt Camp Föhrenwald, 13 October 1946 (Josef Richter, Registration Office, to Public Health Office, Camp Föhrenwald).

18. Biber, *Risen from the Ashes*, pp. 43–45.

19. IfZ Fi 01.81: Miriam Warburg, Conditions of Jewish Children in a Bavarian Rehabilitation Camp, November 1945.

20. YIVO LWSP fol. 164: Report on Camp Föhrenwald, 10 November 1945, p. 2.

21. IfZ Fi 01.81: Warburg, Conditions of Jewish Children.

22. Biber, *Risen from the Ashes*, p. 51.

23. IfZ Fi 01.81: Warburg, Conditions of Jewish Children.

24. Marie Syrkin, *The State of the Jews* (Washington, D.C., 1980), pp. 21–22.

25. Ibid., p. 22.

26. YIVO DPG fol. 1044: Marion von Binsbergen to Helen Matovskova, 11 February 1946.

27. YIVO DPG fol. 99: Bescheinigung im Zusammenhang mit der Eröffnung der Gymnasialkurse im Lager "Föhrenwald," 10 March 1946 (Certification in Connection with the Establishment of High School Programs at Camp Föhrenwald).

28. YIVO DPG fol. 1044: Marion von Binsbergen to Helen Matkovskova, 11 February 1946.

29. YIVO DPG fol. 584: Memorandum von Bet Jakow Föhrenwald, 21 July 1946 (Memorandum from Beth Jacob Föhrenwald).

30. YIVO DPG fol. 1044: Marion von Binsbergen to Helen Matovskova, 11 February 1946.

31. Biber, *Risen from the Ashes,* p. 43.

32. YIVO LWSP fol. 255: Brief der Central Administration of Jeshivah-Shearith-Hapletah School of Rabbis in Germany (Letter from Central Administration of Yeshiva She'erit Hapletah School of Rabbis in Germany).

33. YIVO DPG fol. 136: AJDC, Education Department. Monthly Report of Activities for July 1947 and October 1947.

34. YIVO LWSP fol. 417: Report of Activities for March 1948.

35. YIVO LWSP fol. 417: AJDC, Dr. Philipp Friedman to Samuel L. Haber, Monthly Report of Activities for March and April 1948, 3 May 1948.

36. Jacqueline D. Giere, "'Wir sind unterwegs, aber nicht in der Wüste.' Erziehung und Kultur in den jüdischen Displaced Persons-Lagern der amerikanischen Zone im Nachkriegsdeutschland 1945–1949" (diss., Frankfurt a.M., 1993), p. 382.

37. Biber, *Risen from the Ashes,* p. 72; Yehuda Bauer, *Out of the Ashes: The Impact of American Jews on Post-Holocaust European Jewry* (Oxford, 1989), p. 274.

38. YIVO DPG fol. 1041: Miriam Warburg, Personal Experiences of Camp Inmates at D.P. Center of Foehrenwald, Bavaria, February 1946.

39. YIVO DPG fol. 1044: Marion von Binsbergen to Helen Matovskova, 11 February 1946.

40. YIVO DPG fol. 136: AJDC, Education Department. Monthly Report of Activities for October 1947.

41. Abraham S. Hyman, *The Undefeated* (Jerusalem and Hewlett, N.Y., 1993), p. 396.

42. YIVO DPG fol. 1553: Jacob Oleiski, Schöpferische Arbeit der Sinn des Lebens. Rede, gehalten beim Festabend anläßlich der Eröffnung der Schulen im Lager am 1. Oktober 1945 im Kinosaal der Kaserne Landsberg/Lech (Creative Work—the Meaning of Life. An Address Delivered in the Barracks Cinema on the Evening of 1 October 1945 to Celebrate the Opening of School at the Landsberg Camp).

43. Samuel Gringauz, "ORT: Geschichte, Programm, Leistung," *Jüdische Rundschau* 14/15 (June 1947): 3–4.

44. YIVO DPG fol. 1391: Rundschreiben Nr. 111 von Jacob Oleiski an alle Distriktleiter, 3 December 1947 (Circular No. 111 from Jacob Oleiski to All District Directors).

45. Yad Vashem RA 0–70/17, 64/27: World ORT Union, Headquarters British Zone, Letter from Dr. Oswald Dutch to Sam Dallob, AJDC, 29 April 1948; Leon Shapiro, *The History of ORT: A Jewish Movement for Social Change* (New York, 1980), p. 243.

46. YIVO DPG fol. 1423: Verzeichnis sämtlicher Diplome, die für die Zeit vom 1. Januar 1947 bis 1. Dezember 1947 ausgestellt wurden (List of Diplomas Awarded for the Period from 1 January 1947 to 1 December 1947).

47. YIVO DPG fol. 1390: Rundschreiben Nr. 13. Regulamin wegen Ausgabe von Ort-Diplomen (Circular No. 13. Regulations for Awarding ORT Diplomas).

48. YIVO DPG fol. 1482: Vortrag über World ORT Union im Radio München (Talk about World ORT Union on Radio Munich).

49. YIVO DPG fol. 1392: Rundschreiben Nr. 164. Betrifft: Die von der IRO anerkannten bzw. nicht-anerkannten Schulen, Fächer bzw. Kurse (Circular No. 164. Re: Schools, Courses or Classes Recognized or Not Recognized by IRO).

50. YIVO DPG fol. 1390: Rundschreiben Nr. 3. Regulamin der ORT-Fachschulen (Circular No. 3. Regulations for ORT Trade Schools).

51. YIVO DPG fol. 1390: Rundschreiben Nr. 40. Betreff: Unterrichtsfächer der Damen-, Kinderschneiderei, Herrenwäsche, Korsetterei und Modisterei (Circular No. 40. Re: Courses in

Tailoring for Women and Children, Men's Underwear, Corsetry, and the Milliner's Art).

52. YIVO DPG fol. 1407: Report of the Progress of ORT Schools in the U.S. Zone for the Months of August–September 1947.

53. YIVO DPG fol. 1494: *Wochnleche "ORT" Jedijes fun der U.S. Zone*, 14 January 1948 (*Vokhenlikhe "ORT" Yedies fun der U.S. Zone* [*Weekly ORT News in the U.S. Zone*]).

54. YIVO DPG fol. 585: Bescheinigung, 26 November 1945 (Certification).

55. YIVO LWSP fol. 164: Report on Camp Foehrenwald.

56. YIVO DPG fol. 1044: Marion von Binsbergen to Helen Matovskova, 11 February 1946.

57. YIVO DPG fol. 562: Programm eines sechsmonatigen Schneiderkurses (A Six-Month Tailoring Program).

58. Biber, *Risen from the Ashes*, p. 82.

59. YIVO DPG fol. 1432: ORT-Fachschule Föhrenwald. Stundenplan und Arbeitsplan des Uhrmacher-Kurses (ORT Vocational School. Föhrenwald. Time Table and Curriculum of the Watchmakers' Course).

60. YIVO DPG fol. 585: Regulation about System of Working in Camp Foehrenwald, 20 October 1945.

61. YIVO LWSP fol. 164: Report on Camp Föhrenwald.

62. OMGUS 47/155/1–5: Leo W. Schwarz to Joseph Schwartz. Summary Analysis of AJDC Program in the U.S. Zone of Occupation, Germany, 13 January 1947, p. 8.

63. YIVO DPG fol. 1044: UNRRA Monthly Team Reports, 29 August 1946.

64. YIVO LWSP fol. 192: Projekt zur Sozialen Arbeiterversicherung, gez. Ing. Schuster (Industrial Insurance Project, signed by Schuster, Engineer).

65. A *Landkreis* is a rural administrative area similar to a U.S. county.—Trans.

66. Simon Schochet, *Feldafing* (Vancouver, 1983), p. 79.

67. IfZ Fi 01.75: Henry Cohen to World Jewish Congress.

68. YIVO DPG fol. 15: Programm vom "Bunten Abend." Ausgeführt durch den jüdischen Dramatischen Kreis Föhrenwald am 28.10.1945 (Program of the "Evening Variety Show" Put

On by the Jewish Theater Group of Föhrenwald on 28 October 1945).

69. Biber, *Risen from the Ashes*, p. 27.

70. Ibid., pp. 27–28.

71. Ibid., p. 31.

72. YIVO LWSP fol. 427: M. Ben-Yitzchok, Theatre.

73. *Bamidbar. Perjodisze Cajtung fun di bafrajte Jidn* (*Bamidbar: Peryodishe Tsaytung fun die bafrayte Yidn* [*Bamidbar: Periodic Newspaper of the Liberated Jews*]), 4 June 1946; YIVO DPG fol. 104: Poster Announcing the Performance in January 1947.

74. YIVO DPG fol. 1334: Agreement between the Föhrenwald Theater Group and Landsberg Cultural Department regarding Performances.

75. YIVO LWSP fol. 427: M. Ben-Yitzchok, Theatre.

76. YIVO LWSP fol. 1303: Invitation to the Performance on 27 January 1948.

77. YIVO LWSP fol. 1302: Invitation to the Performances on 9 and 10 August 1947.

78. *Ibergang*, 19 October 1947.

79. YIVO DPG fol. 1301: Bestätigung des Kulturamtes Föhrenwald über die Aufführung am 22. Juni 1947 (Confirmation by the Föhrenwald Cultural Department of the Performance of 22 June 1947).

80. YIVO DPG fol. 1319: Report to the Managing Director of the Cultural Department S. Lewis Gaber, 28 June 1948.

81. Biber, *Risen from the Ashes*, p. 31; *Jidisze Cajtung* (*Yidishe Tsaytung* [*Jewish Newspaper*]), 3 June 1947.

82. Biber, *Risen from the Ashes*, p. 51.

83. YIVO DPG fol. 643: Transcript of a Court Hearing, 12 November 1946.

84. Biber, *Risen from the Ashes*, p. 49; *Münchener Jüdische Nachrichten* (*Munich Jewish News*), 30 June 1952.

85. AJDC Archives, German Education, Religious and Vocational Activities 1948–1963: Letter from Judah J. Shapiro to M. W. Beckelman, 24 October 1951.

86. IfZ Fi 01.81: Gerhard Jacoby, *The Story of the Jewish "DP,"* p. 9.

87. Juliane Wetzel, *Jüdisches Leben in München, 1945–1951. Durchgangsstation oder Wiederaufbau* (München, 1987), pp. 291–93.

88. Koppel S. Pinson, "Jewish Life in Liberated Germany: A Study of the Jewish DP's," *Jewish Social Studies* 9, no. 2 (April 1947): 124.

89. Abraham S. Hyman, *The Undefeated: The Story of the Jewish Displaced Persons,* unpublished manuscript, p. 221.

90. Pinson, "Jewish Life in Liberated Germany," p. 126.

91. YIVO LWSP fol. 423: Letter from S. Lewis Gaber to Sam Haber, 10 May 1948.

92. Pinson, "Jewish Life in Liberated Germany," p. 125; Hyman, *The Undefeated,* p. 253.

93. YIVO DPG fol. 562: Appeal to Jewish Youth, 22 November 1945.

94. Biber, *Risen from the Ashes,* p. 30.

95. YIVO DPG fol. 43: Center far fiziszer Dercijung bajm Central Komitet in US-Zone Daj. Tetikajts-Baricht fun 2. Oktober biz dem 12. Now. 1947 (Tsenter far Fizisher Dertsiung baym Tsentral Komitet in U.S.-Zone Day. Tetikeits-Baricht fun 2. Oktober biz dem 12. Nov. 1947 [Center for Physical Education under the Central Committee in the U.S. Zone of Germany. Activity Report from 2 October–12 November 1947]).

96. YIVO DPG fol. 43: Tetikajts-Baricht fun Center far fiziszer Dercijung, 1. April–1. August 1948 (Tetikeits-Baricht fun Tsenter far fizisher Dertsiung [Activity Report of the Center for Physical Education, 1 April–1 August 1948]).

97. *Bamidbar. Wochncajtung fun di bafrajte Jidn,* 12 December 1945.

98. IfZ Fi 01.07: Judah Nadich to Chief of Staff, Headquarters USFET, 22 October 1945.

99. YIVO DPG fol. 1044: Marion von Binsbergen to Helen Matovskova, 11 February 1946.

100. YIVO DPG fol. 281: Meeting of Representatives of the Camp Administrations and Representatives of the Labor Committees on 10 March 1947 in the Gauting Warehouse.

101. *Bamidbar. Wochncajtung fun di bafrajte Jidn,* 12 December 1945.

102. YIVO DPG fol. 845: Majsterszafts tabele fun der Dorem-Liga farn jor 1947 (1. un 2. runde) (Maystershafts tabele fun der Dorem-Liga farn jor 1947 [1. un 2. runde] [Standings of the Dorem (Southern) League for 1947 (1st and 2d Rounds)]).

103. YIVO DPG fol. 1339: Disciplinar Komisje Bajm Farband fun

Jidisze Turn un Sportfarejnen der Szeejrit Hapleta in der Amerikaner Zone. Circular Nr. 17 (Komisye Baym Farband fun
Yidishe Turn un Sportfareynen der Sheerit Hapleta in der Amerikaner Zone. Tsirkular Nr. 17 [Rules Committee of the Association of Jewish Gymnastic and Sport Clubs of the She'erit
Hapletah in the U.S. Zone. Circular No. 17]).

104. *Bamidbar. Perjodisze Cajtung fun di bafrajte Jidn,* 15 April 1946.

105. YIVO DPG fol. 43: Tetikejts-Baricht fun Center far Fiziszer
Dercijung bajm C. K. Barichts-period fun 1. IV. bizn 1. VIII.
1948 (Tetikeits-Baricht fun Tsenter far Fizisher Dertsiung baym
Z. K. Barichts-period von 1.IV. bizn 1.VIII. 1948 [Activity Report of the Center for Physical Education of the Central Committee Reporting Period, 1 April–1 August 1948]).

106. YIVO DPG fol. 427: PCIRO, Area Team 1065. Re: Area Sports
Competitions, 26 August 1947; *Bamidbar. Periodisze Cajtung fun
di bafrajte Jidn,* 4 June 1946.

107. YIVO LWSP fol. 69: Rabbi Bernstein's Report, 26 October
1947, p. 7.

108. Pinson, "Jewish Life in Liberated Germany," pp. 110–11.

109. Anton Gill, *The Journey Back from Hell: Conversations with Concentration Camp Survivors* (London, 1989), p. 184.

110. Leonard Dinnerstein, *America and the Survivors of the Holocaust*
(New York, 1982), p. 64.

111. Bauer, *Out of the Ashes,* pp. 212–13.

112. Pinson, "Jewish Life in Liberated Germany," p. 111.

113. YIVO DPG fol. 566: Weekly Report, 20 December 1945.

114. OMGUS 5/324–1/27: USFET (McNarney) to Eastern and Western Military District, 24 December 1945.

115. Pinson, "Jewish Life in Liberated Germany," p. 111.

116. YIVO DPG fol. 567: Letterhead, 13 January 1947.

117. AJDC Archives, German Education, Religious and Vocational
Activities 1948–1963: Judah J. Shapiro, AJDC Paris, 23 January 1953, p. 27.

118. YIVO LWSP fol. 51: Rabbi Rosenberg to AJDC. Subject: The
Religious Problems in Germany and the Approach to their Solution in Germany, 27 February 1946, p. 14.

119. YIVO LWSP fol 164: Report on Camp Föhrenwald, 10 November 1945.

120. YIVO LWSP fol. 194: S. Abramowicz, Camp Föhrenwald. Review, 4 May 1946, p. 5.

121. YIVO DPG fol. 584: Menu for 14 February 1946.

122. YIVO LWSP fol. 69: Rabbi Bernstein's Report, p. 10.

123. A *Landrat* is the chief administrative officer of a *Landkreis,* or county.—Trans.

124. A *Regierungspräsident* is the head of a *Regierungsbezirk,* that is, the primary division of a *Land,* or German state, such as Bavaria.—Trans.

125. STA München LRA Wolfratshausen 144808 (Staatsarchiv, Munich. *Landratsamt* Wolfratshausen 144808).

126. YIVO LWSP fol. 69: Rabbi Bernstein's Report, p. 9

127. See Bauer, *Out of the Ashes,* p. 268.

128. Biber, *Risen from the Ashes,* p 112.

129. Bauer, *Out of the Ashes,* pp. 83, 205, and 268.

130. OMGUS AG 47/156/1: Walter J. Muller (Brigadier General) to Inspector General. Subject: Investigation of Certain Members of Central Jewish Committee Involved in Illegal Export Activities, 4 October 1947.

131. Biber, *Risen from the Ashes,* pp. 21–22.

132. Dinnerstein, *America and the Survivors,* pp. 49–50; IfZ Fi 01.82: History—UNRRA—U.S. Zone, Report No. 31, July 1947, p. 10.

133. IfZ Fi 01.81: Gerhard Jacoby, *The Story of the Jewish "DP,"* p. 7.

134. YIVO DPG fol. 732: Policej Regulamin (Politsey Regulamin [Police Regulations]).

135. YIVO DPG fol. 280: Protokoll über die am 18. November 1946 in Starnberg stattgefundene Sitzung der Polizeichefs der Lager Föhrenwald, Landsberg, Neu-Freimann und Feldafing (Minutes of the Meeting of the Police Chiefs of the Föhrenwald, Landsberg, Neu-Freimann and Feldafing Camps That Took Place on 18 November 1946 at Starnberg).

136. YIVO DPG fol. 359: Sitzung des Rates der 4 Lager am 29. November 1946, 10 Uhr vormittags in Starnberg (Meeting of the Council of the 4 Camps on 29 November 1946 at 10 A.M. in Starnberg).

137. IfZ Fi 01.92: S. B. Zisman to Major General H. L. McBride, 27 November 1946.

138. A *Landratsamt* is the office of the chief administrative officer of a *Landkreis.*—Trans.

139. STA München LRA Wolfratshausen 144809: LRA Wolfratshausen an Regierung von Oberbayern, 2 November 1949 (Staatsarchiv, Munich. *Landratsamt* Wolfratshausen 144809 to the Government of Upper Bavaria).

140. YIVO DPG fol. 240: Henry Cohen to Sam Zisman, 14 May 1946, p. 5.

141. OMGUS 17/261–3/7: Subject: Difficulties Encountered in Law Enforcement in the Near Vicinity of DP Camps, 15 January 1948.

142. IfZ Fi 01.52: Displaced Persons and the International Refugee Organization, Report of a Special Subcommittee on Foreign Affairs, Washington, 1947, pp. 36–37.

143. Hyman, *The Undefeated,* pp. 160–61.

144. YIVO DPG fol. 585: Announcement, 1 November 1945.

145. YIVO DPG fol. 281: Meeting of Representatives of the Camp Administrators, 10 March 1947.

146. *Bamidbar. Perjodisze Cajtung fun di bafrajte Jidn,* 4 June 1946.

147. IfZ Fi 01.93: Benjamin L. Weakley, Confidential Report of Informal Investigation Föhrenwald DP Camp Internal Court System.

148. For example, YIVO DPG fol. 639: Depositions taken in January and February 1948.

149. YIVO DPG fol. 732: Reply by Dr. Zygmunt Herzig to a letter from Landsberg, 2 January 1947.

150. See YIVO DPG fol. 667.

151. See, for example, YIVO DPG fol. 562: Record of the Camp Court for 25 January 1946. Re: Birth Date.

152. YIVO DPG fol. 613: Record for 16 April 1947.

153. YIVO DPG fol. 622: Record of a Court Proceeding, 4 September 1947.

154. YIVO DPG fol. 602: Indictment, 4 September 1947.

155. YIVO DPG fol. 608: Application for Justice to the Jewish Camp Court, 13 August 1946.

156. YIVO DPG fol. 643: Verdict and Court Record 18/46.

157. YIVO DPG fol. 689: Verdict of the Camp Court, 29 July 1947.

158. YIVO DPG fol. 646: Camp Court to the D.P. Police, 20 September 1946.

159. OMGUS POLAD 756/7: Political Report (Illegal Courts in Jewish Displaced Persons Camps), 6 December 1946.

160. YIVO DPG fol. 183: Complaint by Josef Schawinski (Yosef Shavinski) and Verdict of the Central Court of Honor in Munich.

161. YIVO DPG fol. 364: PCIRO, Gauting Area VI. Subject: Camp Courts and Camp Disciplinary Commissions, 21 May 1948; YIVO DPG fol. 714: Legal Counselor of Camp Föhrenwald on Behalf of Field Supervisor Mr. Sorin to the Camp Leader in Camp Föhrenwald, 25 July 1948.

162. YIVO DPG fol. 716: Report Bearing upon the Lawfulness of the Activity of the Court in Camp Föhrenwald, 4 November 1946.

163. *Encyclopaedia Judaica* (Jerusalem, 1972), vol. 8, pp. 1466–68.

164. IfZ Fi 01.73: Political Adviser to Secretary of State, 3 March 1948, pp. 3–4.

165. Biber, *Risen from the Ashes,* p. 88.

166. OMGUS 7/22–1/23: Investigation of Illegal Jewish Activity, 26 March 1947.

167. OMGBY 10/78–3/3: Monthly Historical Report, April 1946.

168. Bauer, *Out of the Ashes,* p. 264.

169. Irving Heymont, *Among the Survivors of the Holocaust, 1945: The Landsberg DP Camp Letters of Major Irving Heymont, United States Army* (Cincinnati, 1982), pp. 65–66.

170. *Süddeutsche Zeitung,* 25 January 1946.

171. Pinson, "Jewish Life in Liberated Germany," p. 116.

172. Yoav Gelber, "The Meeting between the Jewish Soldiers from Palestine Serving in the British Army and *She'erit Hapletah,*" in *She'erit Hapletah, 1944–48: Rehabilitation and Political Struggle,* ed. Israel Gutman and Avital Saf (Jerusalem, 1990), p. 72.

173. Giere, "'Wir sing unterwegs,'" p. 125.

174. YIVO DPG fol. 1501: I. Dijour to Robert Murphy, 28 November 1945.

175. YIVO LWSP fol. 69: Rabbi Bernstein's Report, 26 October 1947, p. 13.

176. IfZ Fi 01.80: Dr. Leo Srole, Report to Anglo-American Commission [*sic*] for Palestine, p. 4.

177. YIVO DPG fol. 1041: Miriam Warburg, Personal Experiences, February 1946.

178. George Vida, *From Doom to Dawn: A Jewish Chaplain's Story of Displaced Persons* (New York, 1967), pp. 53 and 55.

179. Bartley C. Crum, *Behind the Silken Curtain: A Personal Account of Anglo-American Diplomacy in Palestine and the Middle East* (New York, 1947), p. 91.

180. Bauer, *Out of the Ashes,* pp. 279–80.

181. Ibid., p. 43.

182. YIVO LWSP fol. 75: William Haber to Abram Rothfeld, American Jewish Conference, 31 August 1948, p. 4; Bauer, *Out of the Ashes,* p. 280.

183. Bauer, *Out of the Ashes,* p. 291.

184. Hyman, *The Undefeated,* p. 435.

185. Bauer, *Out of the Ashes,* p. 289.

186. YIVO LWSP fol. 224: Letter from Theodore D. Feder to M. W. Beckelman, Paris, Consolidation, Liquidation and Hard Core Group, 13 June 1949, Breakdown Showing Estimated Composition of Present Camps as of June 1, 1949—U.S. Zone Germany.

187. *Isar-Loisachbote,* 21 December 1949.

188. Hyman, *The Undefeated,* pp. 438–39.

189. AJDC Archives, Germany, Education, Religious and Vocational Activities 1948–1963: Letter from Judah J. Shapiro, ADJC, to M. W. Beckelman, 24 October 1951, p. 5.

190. YIVO DPG fol. 581: Lager-Verwaltung Föhrenwald (Camp Administration Föhrenwald), 28 October 1951.

191. AJDC Archives, Germany DP's Camp Föhrenwald 1945–1953: Jerry Kolieb, AJDC Representative, to Miss Gandal, AJDC Welfare Director Munich, 3 December 1951.

192. STA München, Polizipräsidium Oberbayern 298. Kriminalabteilung des Präsidiums der Landpolizei von Bayern (Staatsarchiv, Munich. Police Headquarters Upper Bavaria 298. Criminal Investigation Division of the Headquarters of the Bavarian State Police), 29 October 1951.

193. YIVO DPG fol. 591: Letter, 16 December 1952.

194. Bay HSTA Marb 879: Stellungnahme zur Anfrage des Bayer. Landesentschädigungsamtes vom 2. Dezember 1953, 9. April

1954 (Bayerisches Hauptstaatsarchiv Munich. Statement re: Request by the Bavarian State Office of Compensation of 2 December 1953, 9 April 1954).

195. STA München. Polizeipräsidium Oberbayern 298. Regierung von Bayern an Lager Föhrenwald, 19 February 1952 (Staatsarchiv, Munich. Police Headquarters Upper Bavaria 298. Government of Bavaria to Camp Föhrenwald).

196. AJDC Archives, Germany DP's Camp Föhrenwald 1945–1953: Sam Haber to C. Jordan, AJDC Paris, 29 May 1952.

Einsatzgruppen literally means "operational groups," that is, mobile killing units that operated behind the front lines and disposed of large numbers of Jews and other selected enemies of the Third Reich.—Trans.

197. *Manchester Guardian,* 9 September 1952.

198. STA München. LRA Wolfratshausen 144809. Monatsbericht an die Regierung von Oberbayern, 29 May 1952 (Staatsarchiv, Munich. *Landratsamt* Wolfratshausen 144809. Monthly Report to the Government of Upper Bavaria).

199. STA München. LRA Wolfratshausen an Regierung von Oberbayern 30 June 1952 (*Landratsamt* Wolfratshausen to the Government of Upper Bavaria).

200. Bay HSTA Marb 879. Bayerisches Hauptstaatsarchiv, Munich: Dr. Wilhelm Hoegner to the Government of Upper Bavaria, 15 December 1951, pp. 5f.

201. Bay HSTA Marb 879. Bayerisches Hauptstaatsarchiv, Munich: The Bavarian State Ministry of the Interior to the Government of Upper Bavaria, 2 April 1952.

202. Bay HSTA Marb 879. Bayerisches Hauptstaatsarchiv, Munich: The Federal Minister of the Interior to the Bavarian State Ministry of the Interior, 24 July 1952, and a note signed Zuodar, 20 August 1952.

203. Bay HSTA Marb 879. Bayerisches Hauptstaatsarchiv, Munich: *Ministerialrat* [assistant head of a government department] Dr. Seemeier to the Government of Upper Bavaria, 27 August 1952.

204. Bay HSTA Marb 879. Bayerisches Hauptstaatsarchiv, Munich: The Government of Bavaria to the Bavarian State Ministry of the Interior, 5 September 1953; Bay HSTA Marb 879. Bayerisches Hauptstaatsarchiv, Munich: Open Door House, the Gov-

ernment Camp at Föhrenwald to the Government of Upper Bavaria, 12 August 1953; Bay HSTA Marb 879. Bayerisches Hauptstaatsarchiv, Munich: *Ministerialrat* Dr. Seemeier re: Meeting at the Föhrenwald Camp, 27 March 1952.

205. Bay HSTA Marb 879. Bayerisches Hauptstaatsarchiv, Munich: The Government of Upper Bavaria to the Bavarian State Ministry of the Interior, 23 March 1954.

206. Bay HSTA Marb 879. Bayerisches Hauptstaatsarchiv, Munich: Letter from *Regierungsdirektor* [senior government official] Ziegler to the Bavarian State Ministry of the Interior, 1 September 1954.

207. Bay HSTA Marb 879. Bayerisches Hauptstaatsarchiv, Munich: Föhrenwald Government Camp to the Government of Upper Bavaria, 22 August 1955, and *Ministerialrat* Dr. Seemeier re: A Meeting at Camp Föhrenwald, 27 March 1952.

208. *Münchener Jüdische Nachrichten,* 15 March 1956.

209. Ibid., 27 April 1952.

210. Ibid., 14 March 1954.

211. *Amerikahäuser* are information centers and libraries funded by the U.S. government as part of a cultural exchange program.— Trans.

212. *Münchener Jüdische Nachrichten,* 31 March 1954.

213. Ibid., 30 June 1952.

214. Ibid., 9 March 1952.

215. STA München Polizeipräsidium Oberbayern 298. Landpolizeidirektion Föhrenwald an Landpolizeiinspektion Wolfratshausen, 4 September 1953 (Staatsarchiv, Munich. Police Headquarters Upper Bavaria 298. Föhrenwald Police Headquarters to Wolfratshausen Police Headquarters).

216. YIVO LWSP fol. 135: Minutes No. 20 of the Meeting of the Central Committee of Liberated Jews in Bavaria, 2 December 1945, p. 2.

217. YIVO LWSP fol. 135: Report on Camp Föhrenwald, 10 November 1945.

218. Johannes Menke, *Die soziale Integration jüdischer Flüchtlinge des ehemaligen Regierungslagers Föhrenwald in den drei westdeutschen Großstädten Düsseldorf, Frankfurt und München* (Hamburg, 1960), pp. 48–49.

219. Bay HSTA Marb 879. Bayerisches Hauptstaatsarchiv, Munich: Auflösung des Krankenhauses und der Apotheke im Regierungslager Föhrenwald, 9 December 1953, pp. 1–2 (Closing the Hospital and Pharmacy in the Government Camp at Föhrenwald).

220. Wetzel, *Jüdisches Leben in München,* pp. 252–54.

221. STA München, LRA Wolfratshausen 144857. Regierungslager Föhrenwald, betr. Erholungsfürsorge für Kinder 1952–55 (Staatsarchiv, Munich, *Landratsamt* Wolfratshausen 144857. Government Camp at Föhrenwald, re: Child Care 1952–55).

222. AJDC Archives, Germany DP's Camp Föhrenwald 1945–1953: Minutes of Meeting Camp Föhrenwald, 7 December 1951.

223. Angelika Schardt, "'Der Rest der Geretteten': jüdische Überlebende im DP-Lager Föhrenwald 1945–1957," *Dachauer Hefte* 8 (1992): 65–66; cited by Vida, *From Doom to Dawn,* p. 112.

224. *Münchener Jüdische Nachrichten,* 20 May 1955.

225. YIVO DPG fol. 581: Orientierung über die Lage der Flüchtlinge in Norwegen, 12 May 1955 (Orientation to the Situation of Refugees in Norway).

226. *Münchener Jüdische Nachrichten,* 28 June 1953.

227. Ibid., 21 January 1955.

228. YIVO DPG fol. 589: AJDC cu ale alt-ajnwojner in lager Foehrenwald, 18 June 1954 (tsu ale alt-aynvoyner in lager Foehrenvald [To all former residents of the Föhrenwald camp]).

229. Abraham S. Hyman, "Displaced Persons," *American Jewish Yearbook* 52 (1951): 308.

230. Schardt, "'Der Rest der Geretteten,'" p. 66; cited by Vida, *From Doom to Dawn,* p. 91.

231. Vida, *From Doom to Dawn,* p. 94.

232. IfZ Fi 01.64: "Sonderbericht aus Deutschland: Rückkehrer aus Israel," in *Yedioth Hayom* (Tel Aviv). Appendix in Gabriele Wülker, *Probleme der soziologischen Eingliederung fremder ethnischer Gruppen in die deutsche Bundesrepublik* (Ms., Cologne, 1953).

233. Hyman, *The Undefeated,* p. 443.

234. AJDC Archives, Germany DP's Camp Föhrenwald 1954: The Föhrenwald Story, February 1954, p. 3.

235. YIVO DPG fol. 580: Bekanntmachung Nr. 4/54 von Lagerleiter Weigand, 13. Januar 1954. Betr.: Neuwahl des Lagerausschus-

ses (Announcement No. 4/54 from Camp Director Weigand, 13 January 1954. Re: New Elections to the Camp Committee).

236. YIVO DPG fol. 580: Dienstanweisung Nr. 14 von Lagerleiter Weigand, 4. September 1953. Betr. Registrierte Illegale (Regulation No. 14 from Camp Director Weigand, 4 September 1953. Re: Registered Illegals).

237. *Allgemeine Wochenzeitung der Juden in Deutschland,* 5 March 1954.

238. YIVO LWSP fol. 4: Report on Germany to 1953 Country Director's Conference, p. 5.

239. STA München Polizeipräsidium Oberbayern 298, 15 October 1953 (Staatsarchiv, Munich. Police Headquarters Upper Bavaria 298).

240. *Süddeutsche Zeitung,* 28 December 1955.

241. STA München LRA Wolfratshausen 144809. LRA Wolfratshausen an Regierung von Oberbayern, 1 July 1953 (Staatsarchiv, Munich. *Landratsamt* Wolfratshausen to the Government of Upper Bavaria).

242. *Münchener Jüdische Nachrichten,* 21 March 1954.

243. Bay HSTA Marb 879. Bayerisches Hauptstaatsarchiv, Munich: Aktenvermerk (Memorandum), 18 July 1953, p. 6.

244. *Isar-Loisachbote,* 16–17 March 1957.

245. Menke, *Die soziale Integration,* p. 10.

246. *Münchener Jüdische Nachrichten,* 27 April 1954.

247. Wetzel, *Jüdisches Leben in München,* p. 261.

248. Menke, *Die soziale Integration,* p. 75.

249. Ibid., p. 9.

250. STA München LRA Wolfratshausen 144861 (Staatsarchiv, Munich. *Landratsamt* Wolfratshausen 144861).

251. STA München Polizeipräsidium Oberbayern 298 (Police Headquarters Upper Bavaria 298).

252. STA München LRA Wolfratshausen 144861. Antrag auf einstweilige Aussetzung der Vollziehung der Verfügung des Beklagten vom 15. Februar 1956, 1. März 1956 (Motion to Reconsider Vacating the Order Issued on 15 February 1956, 1 March 1956).

253. STA München Beschwerdebescheid der Regierung von Oberbayern, 15 March 1956 (Decision by the Government of Upper Bavaria on Defendant's Appeal).

254. Menke, *Die soziale Integration,* p. 6.

255. Ibid., p. 38.
256. Ibid., p. 103, table 26.
257. Ibid., pp. 66 and 104, table 27.
258. Ibid., p. 10.
259. *Isar-Loisachbote,* 31 July/1 August 1976.

BELSEN

1. Eberhard Kolb, *Bergen-Belsen, 1943–1945* (Göttingen, 1985), pp. 48–49.
2. Cited in ibid., p. 49.
3. Cited in *Unruhige Zeiten: Erlebnisberichte aus dem Landkreis Celle, 1945–1945,* ed. Rainer Schulze (Munich, 1990), p. 28. [The English-language original can be found in Report on Belsen Concentration Camp, Appendix to Military Government 8 Corps Weekly Survey (12 April to 20 April 1945), PRO: WO 171, No. 4041.]
4. Eberhard Kolb, *Bergen-Belsen: Geschichte des "Aufenthaltslager,"* *1943–1945* (Hannover, 1982), p. 315.
5. YIVO DPG fol. 1501: I. Dijour, HIAS, to Robert Murphy, Ambassador United States, 28 November 1945, p. 3.
6. Report on the Situation of the Jews in Germany, October/December 1945, ed. Union Oeuvre de secours aux enfants (Geneva, 1946), passim.
7. Hadassa Bimko-Rosensaft, "The Children of Belsen," in *Belsen* (Tel Aviv, 1957), pp. 106–7.
8. YIVO LWSP fol. 500: W. R. F. Collins, "Belsen Camp: A Preliminary Report," *British Medical Journal,* 9 June 1945, p. 815.
9. Ibid.
10. Josef Rosensaft, "Our Belsen," in *Belsen,* p. 27.
11. YIVO LWSP fol. 52: H. Viteles, Report on Visit to Germany, 6 January–8 April 1946, pp. 54–55.
12. Ibid., p. 54.
13. See Leslie H. Hardman as told to Cecily Goodman, *The Survivors: The Story of the Belsen Remnant* (London, 1958).
14. Yehuda Bauer, *Out of the Ashes: The Impact of American Jews on Post-Holocaust European Jewry* (Oxford, 1989), p. 99.

15. Abraham S. Hyman, *The Undefeated: The Story of the Jewish Displaced Persons,* unpublished manuscript, p. 262.

16. Report, O. S. E., p. 40.

17. Hagit Lavsky, *British Jewry and the Jews in Post-Holocaust Germany: The Jewish Relief Unit, 1945–1950* (ms., London, 1993), pp. 5–7 (kindly made available to us by the CBF World Jewish Relief, Drayton House, London).

18. On the JRU, see Norman Bentwich, *They Found Refuge: An Account of British Jewry's Work for Victims of Nazi Oppression* (London, 1956).

19. Report by Jane E. Leverson on Braunschweig [Brunswick], 30 November 1945, p. 8, Henriques Collection/Diepholz Reports, Braunschweig; cited in Lavsky, *British Jewry and the Jews in Post-Holocaust Germany,* pp. 8–9.

20. Zvi Asaria, *Wir sind Zeugen* (Hannover, 1975), p. 119.

21. YIVO LWSP fol. 13: AJDC Personnel in Germany, 14 October 1945.

22. Bauer, *Out of the Ashes,* p. 99.

23. YIVO LWSP fol. 500: Maurice Eigen, Report on Belsen Camp, 31 August 1945; Report, O. S. E., p. 75.

24. YIVO LWSP fol. 500: Eigen, Report on Belsen; Report, O. S. E., p. 89.

25. YIVO LWSP fol. 53: Telegram from Warburg to Moses Leavitt, AJDC New York, 15 November 1945; YIVO DPG fol. 1501: I. Dijour to Robert Murphy, p. 3.

26. YIVO LWSP fol. 497: Letter from David B. Wodlinger to AJDC New York, 2 May 1946.

27. YIVO LWSP fol. 497: David Wodlinger, Report on the Activities of the AJDC in the British Zone, Germany, 8 December 1945–20 September 1946, p. 3.

28. IfZ Fi 01.82: A. H. Robertson, Agreements for DP Operations in Germany, p. 16.

29. YIVO LWSP fol. 497: Report on Bergen Belsen by Shlomo Michael Gelber, Director-J.D.C. Activities in Paris, 28 June 1946, pp. 5–6.

30. YIVO LWSP fol. 497: Report of Activities of AJDC in British Zone of Germany, 1 January–30 June 1947, p. 18.

31. YIVO LWSP fol. 497: Report on Bergen Belsen, 28 June 1946, p. 6.

32. IfZ Fi 01.86: UNRRA Monthly Narrative Report, June 1945, p. 14.

33. Ibid. Fi 01.90: Report on an Investigation Held at Hohne by Major K. H. Barany and Major A. S. Farrar, 11 September 1946.

34. Yad Vashem RA 0–70/6, 3/17: Report submitted by Central Jewish Committee, British Zone (signed Josef Rosensaft), 23 August 1946, pp. 3–4.

35. Bentwich, *They Found Refuge,* p. 151.

36. YIVO LWSP fol. 500: Collins, "Belsen Camp," p. 815.

37. Report, O. S. E., p. 57.

38. YIVO LWSP fol. 497: Report of Activities of American Joint Distribution Committee in British Zone of Germany, 1 January–30 June 1947, pp. 30–31.

39. YIVO LWSP fol. 271: Report of Conference of Country Medical Directors in Europe of the American Joint Distribution Committee in Paris, 14–17 May 1947, p. 14.

40. YIVO LWSP fol. 272: Report on Visits to Berlin 28 January–4 February and to Belsen 4 February–8 February, 17 March 1947, p. 4.

41. Report, O S. E., p. 56.

42. YIVO LWSP fol. 449: Letter from Dr. A. Kurzke to Leo W. Schwarz, 12 October 1949.

43. YIVO LWSP fol. 271: Report of Conference of Country Medical Directors, 14–17 May 1947, p. 14.

44. Bentwich, *They Found Refuge,* p. 149.

45. YIVO LWSP fol. 502: The Belsen-Merano TB Transport.

46. YIVO LWSP fol. 497: Report of Activities of American Joint Distribution Committee, 1 January–30 June 1947, pp. 31–32.

47. YIVO LWSP fol. 271: Report of Conference of Country Medical Directors, 14–17 May 1947, p. 15; YIVO LWSP fol. 3: Country Director's Conference American Joint Distribution Committee, Paris, 5–10 April 1948, p. 47.

48. YIVO LWSP fol. 271: Report of Conference of Country Medical Directors, 14–17 May 1947, p. 15.

49. The title Elder of the Jews (*Judenältester*) was conferred by the Nazis on the head of the ghetto's Council of Elders.—Trans.

50. *Unruhige Zeiten,* p. 287.

51. On the school system as a whole, see YIVO LWSP fol. 497: Report of Activities of American Joint Distribution Committee, 1 January–30 June 1947, pp. 24–26; YIVO LWSP fol. 510: Letter from Samuel Dallob, AJDC British Zone of Germany, to M. Beckelman, AJDC Paris, 6 December 1948; YIVO DPG fol. 1627: *Jüdisches Gemeindeblatt,* 20 July 1947; Yad Vashem RA 0–70/4, z/5–1: Jidiszer Central Komitet Bergen-Belsen, Baricht 25 September 1945, p. 4 (Yidisher Tsentral Komitet Bergn Belzn, Barikht [Jewish Central Committee Bergen Belsen, Report]).

52. YIVO LWSP fol. 244: Annual Report of Vaad Hatzala Activities in Operations, 15 June 1946–15 June 1947.

53. YIVO LWSP fol. 497: Report of Activities of American Joint Distribution Committee, 1 January–30 June 1947, pp. 25–27.

54. Ibid., pp. 21–22.

55. Ibid., p. 23.

56. *Jüdisches Gemeindeblatt für die britische Zone,* 23 June 1948.

57. YIVO LWSP fol. 497: Report of Activities of American Joint Distribution Committee, 1 January–30 June 1947, pp. 15–17.

58. IfZ Fi 01.83: British O.R.T., Work of O.R.T. in the Displaced Persons Camps in Germany and Austria, 5 May 1947, p. 3.

59. YIVO DPG fol. 1578: Survey of Educational Work in Bergen-Belsen, 30 July–10 September 1946, p. 2.

60. *Jüdisches Gemeindeblatt für die britische Zone,* 20 July 1947.

61. In January 1948 there were 2,610 apprentices being taught by 98 instructors in the ORT schools in the British Zone. Yad Vashem RA 0–70/17, 64/27: Letter from O. Dutch, Director British Zone World ORT Union, to Sam Dallob, AJDC, Teachers and Students in ORT Schools, *hakhsharot,* etc., 29 April 1948. *Hakhsharot (Hakhsharah* [Hebrew, "preparation"]): training or preparation, both intellectual and physical, for settlement in Israel, in pioneering movements, applied particularly to training in physical labor, especially farming, in the Diaspora. The training farms these movements established were called *hakhsharot.*—Trans.

62. YIVO DPG fol. 1443: World ORT Union Training Center, Bi-Monthly Statistical Report, July–August 1948; YIVO LWSP fol. 510: Letter from Samuel Dallob, AJDC British Zone of Germany, to M. Beckelman, AJDC Paris, Hard Currency Payments to ORT Instructors, 6 December 1948.

63. YIVO DPG fol. 1443: World ORT Union, British Zone Headquarters, Monthly Report, 15 January–15 February 1949; YIVO DPG fol. 1443: Graduation Party at Belsen ORT School, 5 January 1949.

64. YIVO LWSP fol. 497: Report of Activities of American Joint Distribution Committee, 1 January–30 June 1947, p. 29; YIVO DPG fol. 1578: Survey of Educational Work in Bergen-Belsen, 30 July–10 September 1946, p. 4.

65. The term *Kazet* derives from the German letters "K," or *Ka*, and "Z," or *Zet*. Together they formed a popular abbreviation for *Kazetlager* or *Konzentrationslager*, that is, concentration camp. When transliterated from Yiddish, the term sometimes appears as *katset*, *katzet*, or *kotset*. A *katzetnik*, for example, is a former concentration camp internee.—Trans.

66. Yad Vashem RA 0–70/4, z/5–1: Baricht (Report), 25 September 1945, p. 3.

67. Samy Feder, "The Yiddish Theatre of Belsen," in *Belsen*, pp. 138–39.

68. For the Kazet-Theater's other productions, see *Jüdisches Gemeindeblatt für die britische Zone*, 6 May 1946 and 30 April 1947.

69. YIVO DPG fol. 1606: Jid. dram. Studio "Kazet-Theater" beim Central Comitet fun di bafrajte jidn in der brit. Zone, Bergn-Belzn, Ajnladung (Yid. Dram. Studio "Kazet-Theater" baym Tsentral Komitet fun di bafrayte Yidn in der brit. Zone, Bergn-Belzn, Aynladung [The Yiddish Dramatic Studio's "Kazet-Theater" Attached to the Central Committee in the British Zone, Bergen-Belsen, Invitation]).

70. Yad Vashem RA 0–70/37, 49/26: Daily News Bulletin, Jewish Telegraphic Agency, No. 148, 29 June 1947.

71. Sam E. Bloch, ed., *Holocaust and Rebirth: Bergen-Belsen, 1945–1965* (New York, 1965), p. liii.

72. YIVO DPG fol. 1334: Kontrakt geszlosen cwiszn di "Jidisze Arbeter-Bine" fun Bergen Belzen un Kultur Amt in Landsberg,

15 October 1947 (Kontrakt geshlosen tsvishen die "Yidishe Arbeter-Bine" fun Bergn Belzn un Kultur Amt in Landsberg [Contract between the "Yidishe Arbeter-Bine" of Bergen-Belsen and the Cultural Office at Landsberg]).

73. YIVO DPG fol. 1323: Jewish Committee, Bergen-Belsen, Cultural Department, 5 December 1948.

74. YIVO DPG fol.122: Letter from the Presidium of the Central Committee of Liberated Jews in the American Occupied Zone to the Cultural Office, 16 May 1947.

75. Josef Butterman, *Jewish Displaced Persons in Germany and in the United States of America, 1945 to 1960* (n.p., 1960), p. 40.

76. YIVO LWSP fol. 502: Letter from Sam Dallob, Director British Zone, to M. W. Beckelman, AJDC Paris, Program of Herman Yablokoff in British Zone of 11 August 1947; *Jidisze Cajtung* (*Yidishe Tsaytung* [*Jewish Newspaper*]), 10 June 1947.

77. Juliane Wetzel, *Jüdisches Leben in München, 1945–1951: Durchgangsstation oder Wiederaufbau* (München, 1987), pp. 288–89.

78. B. Kosowski, *Bibliographie der jüdischen Ausgaben in der Britischen Zone Deutschlands, 1945–1950* (Bergen-Belsen, Mai 1950), pp. 7–8 (Yad Vashem).

79. Yad Vashem RA o–70/5, 7/8: Brief Notes of Interview with Mr. Friedenberg of PW & DP Division, 28 May 1947 (Rosensaft), p. 7.

80. Kosowski, *Bibliographie,* pp. 7–8.

81. Ibid., p. 25.

82. YIVO *Jewish Displaced Persons Periodicals* (New York, 1990).

83. Kosowski, *Bibliographie,* pp. 14 and 26.

84. YIVO *Jewish Displaced Persons Periodicals;* Kosowski, *Bibliographie,* pp. 12, 15, and 28.

85. Kosowski, *Bibliographie,* passim; Josef Fraenkel, "The Cultural Liberation of Belsen," in *Belsen,* pp. 166–67.

86. Wetzel, *Jüdisches Leben in München,* p. 145.

87. YIVO LWSP fol. 52: Viteles, Report on Visit to Germany, p. 96.

88. Yad Vashem RA o–70/13, 72/5: Central Committee of Liberated Jews in the British Zone, Bergen-Belsen, Circular No. 13, 17 September 1946.

89. YIVO LWSP fol. 497: Report on Activities of American Joint Distribution Committee, 1 January–30 June 1947, p. 28.

90. Ibid., pp. 20 and 28.

91. *Jüdisches Gemeindeblatt*, 20 July 1947; YIVO LWSP fol. 111: Zentral-Komitee der befreiten Juden in der britischen Zone, Kulturamt, Bericht über das Treffen der Kulturschaffenden in der britischen Zone, 19 May 1948 (Central Committee of Liberated Jews in the British Zone, Cultural Department, Report on the Meeting of Creative Artists in the British Zone).

92. *Jüdisches Gemeindeblatt*, 20 July 1947.

93. Butterman, *Jewish Displaced Persons*, p. 53.

94. This word is usually transcribed as *ekhad*.—Trans.

95. YIVO DPG fol. 845: Poster: Croise Futboll-Sensacije, Mittwoch, dem 19. Juni (1946) Bergen-Belsen "Hatikwa" un Landsberg "Ichud"; *Landsberger Lager Cajtung*, 19 July 1946 (Poster: Groyse Futbol-Sensatsye, Mitvokh, 19 Yuli [1946] Bergn-Belzn "Hatikva" un Landzberg "Ikhud"; *Landzberger Lager Tsaytung* [Major Soccer Sensation, Wednesday, 19 June [1946] Bergen-Belsen's "Hatikva" vs Landsberg's "Ikhud"]).

96. YIVO DPG fol. 845: Plakat: Boks-Match czwiszen Hagibor un Ichud; *Landsberger Lager Cajtung*, 19 April 1946, Sport-Bajlage (Plakat: Boks-Matsh tsvishen Hagibor un Ikhud; *Landzberger Lager Tsaytung*, 19 April 1946, Sport-Baylage [Poster: Boxing Match between Hagibor and Ikhud; *Landzberger Lager Tsaytung*, 19 April 1946, Sports Supplement]).

97. *Jidisze Sport Cajtung*, April 1948 (*Yidishe Sport Tsaytung* [*Jewish Sports Newspaper*]).

98. *Landsberger Lager Cajtung*, 25 September 1946 (*Landzberger Lager Tsaytung*); YIVO DPG fol. 834: Program fun die erszte Jidisze Szach-Olimpiade in Landsberg 1946 (Program fun die ershte Yidishe Shakh Olimpyade at Landsberg 1946 [Program for the First Jewish Chess Olympiad at Landsberg, 1946]).

99. Bloch, ed., *Holocaust and Rebirth*, unpaginated illustrated section.

100. Asaria, *Wir sind Zeugen*, pp. 154–55.

101. Ibid., p. 120.

102. Butterman, *Jewish Displaced Persons*, p. 14.

103. See YIVO LWSP fol. 266: Report No. 6 from Rabbi J. Asher, Cologne, 22 June 1947.

104. YIVO DPG fol. 1626: Rabbinical Council to the Central Committee of Liberated Jews in the British Zone, 10 August 1948.

105. Butterman, *Jewish Displaced Persons,* p. 11.

106. *Belsen,* p. 36.

107. See YIVO DPG fols. 1596–1600.

108. Yad Vashem RA 0–70/6, 3/5: Memorandum re: Crime among Jewish DPs, 16 December 1945.

109. *Unruhige Zeiten,* p. 291.

110. Ibid., pp. 299–300.

111. YIVO LWSP fol. 508: E. M. Tobis, PW/DP Branch HQ Land Niedersachsen [State of Lower Saxony]. Subject: Allegations of Black Market Belsen-Bergen [*sic*], 15 July 1948.

112. Yad Vashem 0–70/17, 64/24: Samuel Dallob to Herbert Katzki, Raid on Belsen—18 February 1948, 3 March 1948.

113. The Haganah, or Irgun Haganah Ha'ivrit Be'Erets Yisrael (Hebrew Defense Organization in Palestine), was the underground military organization of the majority of the Jewish population in Palestine, controlled by the Jewish Agency for Palestine.—Trans.

114. See Bauer, *Out of the Ashes,* pp. 220–21; Leo W. Schwarz, *The Redeemers: A Saga of the Years 1945–1952* (New York, 1953), pp. 245–63; Horst Siebecke, *Die Schicksalsfahrt der "Exodus 47." Eine historische Dokumentation* (Frankfurt a. M., 1987), passim.

115. IfZ Fi 01.101: Displaced Persons 1 July 1947–30 June 1948, p. 134.

116. YIVO LWSP fol. 481: ZK radio service in the U.S. Zone, 9 October 1947.

117. See YIVO LWSP fols. 504 and 505.

118. Bauer, *Out of the Ashes,* pp. 229–30.

119. YIVO LWSP fol. 3: Country Directors' Conference AJDC, Paris, 5–10 April 1948, p. 47.

120. Asaria, *Wir sind Zeugen,* pp. 169–71.

121. YIVO DPG fol. 1626; Jidiszer Central Komitet Bergen-Belsen, Baricht, 25 September 1945 (Yidisher Tsentral Komitet Bergn-Belzn, Baricht [Jewish Central Committee Bergen-Belsen, Report]).

122. S. Adler Rudell, "The Surviving Children," in *Belsen,* p. 125.

123. YIVO LWSP fol. 135: Protokoll Nr. 13 der Sitzung des Rates beim ZK der befreiten Juden in Bayern, 14 October 1945, p. 15

(Minutes No. 13 of the Meeting of the Council of the Central Committee of Liberated Jews in Bavaria).

124. Asaria, *Wir sind Zeugen,* p. 121.

125. Ibid., pp. 131–33.

126. Yad Vashem RA 0–70/13, 72/30: Central Jewish Committee, Mitteilung an das Präsidium des ZK, 1 February 1949 (Memorandum to the Presidium of the Central Committee).

127. Yad Vashem RA 0–70/13, 72/31: Central Jewish Committee, Mitteilung an das Präsidium des ZK, 31 January 1949 (Memorandum to the Presidium of the Central Committee); YIVO LWSP fol. 18: Memorandum from Jacob Joslow, 1 December 1948.

128. YIVO LWSP fol. 495: *Jüdisches Gemeindeblatt Düsseldorf,* 25 March 1949.

129. YIVO LWSP fol. 497: Report on the Activities of AJDC, British Zone, 8 December 1945–20 September 1946, pp. 7–8.

130. Ibid., p. 8.

131. YIVO LWSP fol. 377: Jointfund Emigration, Paris, Memorandum of 28 September 1946; YIVO LWSP fol. 497: Report on Activities of the AJDC, 8 December 1945–20 September 1946, p. 8.

132. YIVO LWSP fol. 504: AJDC, British Zone, Monthly Report 15 October–15 November 1947.

133. *Allgemeine Wochenzeitung der Juden in Deutschland,* 14 July 1950; YIVO LWSP fol. 224: Associated Press report, 10 July 1950: Belsen Camp Is Closed.

134. Yad Vashem RA 0–70/11, 61/4–61/6: Letter from Josef Rosensaft to *Land* Commissioner Niedersachsen, 28 February 1950.

135. Yad Vashem RA 0–70/11, 61/39: Telegram from the Central Committee for the British Zone, 7 March 1950.

136. Yad Vashem RA 0–70/11, 92/53–92/56: IRO Jever, Nominal Roll of DPs Transferred, 13 August 1951.

137. Yad Vashem RA 0–70/11, 92/59: Josef Rosensaft to *Land* Commissioner Niedersachsen, 15 August 1951.

138. *Belsen,* pp. 186–88.

139. *Unruhige Zeiten,* p. 3; Yad Vashem RA 0–70/13, 72/27: Central

Jewish Committee, Informationsübersicht No. 1/49, 19 October 1949 (Information Survey).

140. Ulrike Puvogel, *Gedenkstätten für die Opfer des Nationalsozialismus. Eine Dokumentation* (Bonn, 1987), pp. 395–97.

FINAL REFLECTIONS

1. YIVO DPG fol. 68: Letter from the representative of the Landsberg a. Lech city council's housing office to Commissioner Aumer, 28 November 1945.

2. German and ethnic German refugees in Germany west of the Oder-Neisse line.—Trans.

3. YIVO DPG fol. 49: Protestschreiben der Jüdischen Gemeinde Bamberg, 16 July 1950 (Letter of Protest from the Bamberg Jewish Community).

4. Werner Bergmann and Rainer Erb, eds., *Antisemitismus in der politischen Kultur nach 1945* (Opladen, 1990), p. 113.

5. Werner Bergmann, "Antisemitismus in der öffentlichen Meinung Ost- und Westdeutschlands," in *Forschung Aktuell* (Technische Universität Berlin), 39/41 (1993): 11–15.

6. Ino Arndt and Angelika Schardt, "Zur Chronologie des Rechtsextremismus," in *Rechtsextremismus in der Bundesrepublik: Voraussetzungen, Zusammenhänge, Wirkungen,* ed. Wolfgang Benz (Frankfurt a. M., 1989), p. 281.

APPENDIX: LIST OF CAMPS

1. *Dror* (Hebrew, literally "freedom"): Zionist youth movement affiliated with the left-wing Kibbutz Meuchad federation of kibbutzim in Palestine (and today in Israel).—Trans.

2. Hashomer Hatzair (Hebrew, literally "young guardsmen"): Oldest Zionist youth movement; left-wing socialist and Marxist; affiliated with the Kibbutz Artzi federation of kibbutzim in Israel.—Trans.

3. Bnei Akiva (Hebrew, literally "sons of Akiva"): Zionist religious youth movement of Mizrachi with a moderately left-wing hue,

allied to the Palestinian religious kibbutz movement. Named after Joseph ben Akiva, founder of rabbinic Judaism and systematizer of Jewish law (born circa C.E. 40 or 50; died circa C.E. 135). Founded in Jerusalem in 1927.—Trans.

4. *Cheder* (Hebrew, literally "room"): Common name for the old-fashioned elementary school for teaching Judaism.—Trans.

5. *Hafets Hayim* (Hebrew, literally "desirer of life"; known in Yiddish as *Chofetz Chaim*). The name derives from Israel Meir ha-Kohen (1838–1933), a rabbi, writer on ethics, and talmudist, one of the most saintly figures in modern Judaism; he became known as *Hafets Hayim* after the title of his first work.—Trans.

6. On Berlin, see Angelika Königseder, *Flucht nach Berlin. Jüdische Displaced Persons 1945–1948* (Berlin, 1998).

7. *Mosad hinukhi* (Hebrew, literally "educational institution").—Trans.

8. Yiddish spelling of the Hebrew *Amkha,* literally "your people."—Trans.

9. Israel's national theater company, created in Moscow in 1918, moved to Tel Aviv, Palestine, in 1925.—Trans.

10. Rabbi Avraham Yitzhak Kook, the chief rabbi of Palestine, served as the spiritual leader of the Bnei Akiva movement.—Trans.

11. Dror kibbutz named after Hanna Szenes (romanization of the Yiddish transcription of the Hungarian is "Senesh"), 1921–44, poet and Haganah fighter, who parachuted into Nazi-occupied Europe to rescue Allied prisoners of war and organize Jewish resistance. She was executed by Hungarian fascists in Budapest.—Trans.

12. *Der kibbutz auf dem Streidner-Hof: Die vergessene Geschichte der jüdaischen?* 1945–48 [Text: Jim G. Tobias] variant title: *Kibbuz auf dem Streicher-Hof* (Nürnberg: Dahlinger und Fuchs, 1997. *Guide to the Exhibition* "The Kibbutz at Streicher-Hof: The Forgotten Story of the Jewish Collective Farms, 1945–48."

13. *Nokham* (Hebrew, literally "redemption"): A nonparty Halutzim movement. *Halutzim,* or "pioneers," was the name for those who chose to serve the Zionist cause primarily through agricultural settlement of a collectivist nature.—Trans.

14. Noar Zioni (Hebrew, literally "Zionist youth"): Zionist youth movement of a nonsocialist liberal tendency.—Trans.

❖

Selected Bibliography

Abzug, Robert H. *Inside the Vicious Heart: Americans and the Liberation of Nazi Concentration Camps.* New York and Oxford: Oxford University Press, 1985.

Agar, Herbert. *The Saving Remnant: An Account of Jewish Survival since 1914.* London: Hart-David, 1960.

Albrich, Thomas. *Exodus durch Österreich. Die jüdischen Flüchtlinge, 1945–1948.* Innsbruck: Haymon, 1987.

Asaria, Zvi. *Wir sind Zeugen.* Hannover: Niedersächsische Landeszentrale für politische Bildung and Institut für Sozialgeschichte [Federal Institute for Political Education of Lower Saxony and Institute for Social Research], 1975.

Barish, Louis. *Rabbis in Uniform: The Story of the American Jewish Military Chaplain.* New York: Jonathan David, 1962.

Bauer, Yehuda. *Flight and Rescue: Brichah.* New York: Random House, 1970.

———. "The Initial Organization of the Holocaust Survivors in Bavaria," *Yad Vashem Studies* 8 (1970): 127–57.

———. *Out of the Ashes: The Impact of American Jews on Post-Holocaust European Jewry.* Oxford: Pergamon Press, 1989.

Belsen. Published by Irgun Sheerit Hapleita Me'Haezor Habriti, Tel Aviv (London: Narod Press, 1957).

Bernstein, Philip S. "Displaced Persons." In *American Jewish Yearbook 1947–1948.* Vol. 49. Philadelphia, 1948.

Biber, Jacob. *Risen from the Ashes: A Story of the Jewish Displaced Persons in the Aftermath of World War II.* San Bernardino, Calif.: Borgo Press, 1990.

Bloch, Sam E., ed. *Holocaust and Rebirth: Bergen-Belsen, 1945–1965.* New York: Bergen-Belsen Memorial Press, 1965.

Brenner, Michael. *After the Holocaust: Rebuilding Jewish Lives in Postwar Germany*. Princeton, N.J.: Princeton University Press, 1997.

Büttner, Ursula. *Not nach der Befreiung. Die Situation der deutschen Juden in der britischen Besatzungszone 1945 bis 1948*. Hamburg: Christians Verlag, 1986.

Crum, Bartley C. *Behind the Silken Curtain: A Personal Account of Anglo-American Diplomacy in Palestine and the Middle East*. New York: Gollancz, 1947.

Dinnerstein, Leonard. *America and the Survivors of the Holocaust*. New York: Columbia University Press, 1982.

"Displaced Persons." In *American Jewish Yearbook 1946–1947*. Vol. 48. Philadelphia, 1947.

Gringauz, Samuel. "ORT: Geschichte, Programm, Leistung," *Jüdische Rundschau* 14/15 (June 1947).

Grossmann, Kurt Richard. *The Jewish DP Problem: Its Origin, Scope, and Liquidation*. New York: Institute of Jewish Affairs, World Jewish Congress, 1951.

Gutman, Israel, and Avital Saf. *She'erit Hapletah 1944–1948: Rehabilitation and Political Struggle*. Jerusalem: Yad Vashem, 1990.

Hardman, Leslie H., as told to Cecily Goodman. *The Survivors: The Story of the Belsen Remnant*. London: Vallentine Mitchell, 1958.

Heymont, Irving. *Among the Survivors of the Holocaust, 1945: The Landsberg DP Camp Letters of Major Irving Heymont, United States Army*. Cincinnati: American Jewish Archives, 1982. German edition published as *Bei den Überlebenden des Holocaust, 1945. Landsberger Briefe des Majors Irving Heymont, United States Army*. Cincinnati: American Jewish Archives, 1989.

Hyman, Abraham S. "Displaced Persons." In *American Jewish Yearbook 1948–1949*. Vol. 50. Philadelphia, 1949.

———. *The Undefeated*. Jerusalem and Hewlett, N.Y.: Gefen Publishing House, 1993.

Jacobmeyer, Wolfgang. "Jüdische Überlebende als 'Displaced Persons.' Untersuchungen zur Besatzungpolitik in den deutschen Westzonen und zur Zuwanderung osteuropäischer Juden 1945–1947." *Geschichte und Gesellschaft. Zeitschrift für Historische Sozialwissenschaft* 9 (1983): 421–52.

———. "Polnische Juden in der amerikanischen Besatzungsone

Deutchlands 1946/47." *Vierteljahrshefte für Zeitgeschichte* 25, no. 1 (January 1977): 120–35.

―――. *Vom Zwangsarbeiter zum heimatlosen Ausländer. Die Displaced Persons in Westdeutschland 1945–1951.* Göttingen: Vandenhoek & Ruprecht, 1985.

Königseder, Angelika. *Flucht nach Berlin. Jüdische Displaced Persons 1945–1948.* Berlin: Metropol Verlag, 1998.

Liebschutz, Thomas Philip. "Rabbi Philip S. Bernstein and the Jewish Displaced Persons." Diss., Cincinnati, 1965.

Menke, Johannes. *Die soziale Integration jüdischer Flüchtlinge des ehemaligen Regierungslagers "Föhrenwald" in den drei westdeutschen Großstädten Düsseldorf, Frankfurt und München.* Hamburg: Bertelsmann, 1960.

Oberhaus, Herbert, ed. *Im Schatten des Holocaust. Jüdisches Leben in Niedersachsen nach 1945.* Hannover: Hahnsche Buchhandlung, 1997.

Pinson, Koppel S. "Jewish Life in Liberated Germany: A Study of the Jewish DP's." *Jewish Social Studies* 9, no. 2 (April 1947).

Proudfoot, Malcolm J. *European Refugees, 1939–1952: A Study in Forced Population Movement.* Evanston, Ill.: Northwestern University Press, 1956; London: Faber and Faber, 1957.

Schochet, Simon. *Feldafing.* Vancouver: November House, 1983.

Schwarz, Leo W. *The Redeemers: A Saga of the Years 1945–1952.* New York: Farrar, Straus and Young, 1953.

―――, ed. *The Root and the Bough: The Epic of an Enduring People.* New York: Rinehart, 1949.

Stern, Frank. *The Whitewashing of the Yellow Badge: Anti-Semitism and Philosemitism in Postwar Germany.* Oxford: Pergamon Press, 1992. German edition: *Im Anfang war Auschwitz. Antisemitismus und Philosemitismus im deutschen Nachkrieg.* Gerlingen: Bleicher Verlag, 1991.

Syrkin, Marie. *The State of the Jews.* Washington, D.C.: New Republic Books/Herzl Press, 1980.

Vida, George. *From Doom to Dawn: A Jewish Chaplain's Story of Displaced Persons.* New York: Yonathan David Publishers, 1967.

Wetzel, Juliane. *Jüdisches Leben in München 1945–1951. Durchgangsstation oder Wiederaufbau.* Munich: Miscellanea Bavarica Monacensia, 1987.

Wischnitzer, Mark. *Visas to Freedom: The History of HIAS.* Cleveland and New York: World Publishing Co., 1956.

❀

Jewish Lives

INGEBORG HECHT
Invisible Walls *and* To Remember Is to Heal

DAN JACOBSON
Heshel's Kingdom

ANGELIKA KÖNIGSEDER AND JULIANE WETZEL
Waiting for Hope: Jewish Displaced Persons
in Post–World War II Germany

SZYMON LAKS
Music of Another World

ERICH LEYENS AND LOTTE ANDOR
Years of Estrangement

RUTH LIEPMAN
Maybe Luck Isn't Just Chance

ERIC LUCAS
The Sovereigns: A Jewish Family in the German Countryside

ARNOŠT LUSTIG
The Bitter Smell of Almonds
Children of the Holocaust
The House of Returned Echoes
The Unloved (From the Diary of Perla S.)

LIANNA MILLU
Smoke over Birkenau

ZOFIA NAŁKOWSKA
Medallions

BERNHARD PRESS
The Murder of the Jews in Latvia, 1941–1945

ARMIN SCHMID AND RENATE SCHMID
Lost in a Labyrinth of Red Tape

WIKTORIA ŚLIWOWSKA, ED.
The Last Eyewitnesses: Children of the Holocaust Speak